PILGRIMS OF CHRIST
ON THE MUSLIM ROAD

D0613395

PILGRIMS OF CHRIST ON THE MUSLIM ROAD

Exploring a New Path
between Two Faiths

PAUL-GORDON CHANDLER

A Cowley Publications Book
ROWMAN & LITTLEFIELD PUBLISHERS, INC.
Lanham • Chicago • New York • Toronto • Plymouth, UK

A Cowley Publications Book

ROWMAN & LITTLEFIELD PUBLISHERS, INC.

Published in the United States of America
by Rowman & Littlefield Publishers, Inc.
A wholly owned subsidiary of The Rowman & Littlefield Publishing Group, Inc.
4501 Forbes Boulevard, Suite 200, Lanham, Maryland 20706
www.rowmanlittlefield.com

Estover Road
Plymouth PL6 7PY
United Kingdom

Copyright © 2007 by Paul-Gordon Chandler

All rights reserved. No part of this publication may be reproduced, stored in a retrieval system,
or transmitted in any form or by any means, electronic, mechanical, photocopying,
recording, or otherwise, without the prior permission of the publisher.

Library of Congress Cataloging-in-Publication Data

Chandler, Paul-Gordon
  Pilgrims of Christ on the Muslim Road L exploring a new path between two faiths .
Paul-Gordon Chandler.
    p. cm.
  Includes bibliographical references.
  ISBN-13: 978-1-56101-317-3 (cl. : alk. paper)
  ISBN-10: 1-56101-317-X (cl. : alk. paper)
  ISBN-13: 0-7425-6603-3 (alk. paper)
  ISBN-10: 0-7425-6603-X (alk. paper)
  eISBN-13: 978-0-7425-6604-0
  eISBN-10: 0-7425-6604-8
  1. Islam—Relations—Christianity. 2. Christianity and other religions—Islam. 3. Jesus
Christ—Islamic interpretations. 4. Malluhi, Mazhar. I. Title.
  BP172.C416 2007
  261.2'7—dc22   2007010372

To

CHRISTINE "AMAL" MALLOUHI

whose deep love for Mazhar, passion for the Arab Muslim world,
and commitment to following in the way of Christ, together with her
exceptional talents, has enabled Mazhar to become the unique person he is,
living out his extraordinary calling.

Without her loving devotion to him and her organizational and literary
skills, I would not have been able to even consider writing this book.

CONTENTS

Acknowledgments   xi

Introduction   1

Part I. Pilgrim of Allah: Devotion to Christ within the Line of Muhammad

CHAPTER 1
Pilgrimage to Faith   13

CHAPTER 2
Journeying among Muslims   25

CHAPTER 3
Discovering Home   49

Part II. Bridging Two Worlds

CHAPTER 4
Salaam on Islam   73

CHAPTER 5
A Muslim Disciple of Christ   101

Part III. New Directions for the Journey

CHAPTER 6

Resurrecting the Eastern Christ: Embracing the Semitic Face
of Jesus   127

CHAPTER 7

Opening a Middle Eastern Book: Returning the Christian Scriptures
to their Middle Eastern Origin   147

CHAPTER 8

Once upon a Time: Telling Eastern Stories of Faith to
Muslim Audiences   161

CHAPTER 9

Questions to a Muslim Christian Pilgrim: An Interview with
Mazhar Mallouhi   175

Appendix: Mazhar Mallouhi's Primary Works to Date   207

Notes   209

About the Author   217

Acknowledgments

"I write this book for love of your love"

I AM INDEBTED TO MANY PEOPLE in the writing of this book. My deepest gratitude:

To *Mazhar* and *Christine Mallouhi*, whose intimate friendship I consider among the greatest joys in my life, for the generous hospitality at their home in Beirut during the course of writing this book, and for the many days they spent with me patiently and humbly answering question after question that resulted in the pages of this book.

To the *hundreds of individuals, Muslims and Christians,* many whom have now become close friends, who assisted me in the research I undertook for this book by graciously taking time out of their busy schedules to allow me to interview them at length.

To *my family—Lynne, Britelle* and *Treston*—for their endless support throughout this writing adventure, including even moving to the Middle East.

To *Michael Wilt,* the former editorial director of the late Cowley Publications, who first caught the vision for this manuscript and with great professionalism laid the foundation for its publishing. I also wish to thank my first editor, *Ulrike Guthrie,* as well as *Sarah Stanton* and *Lynn Weber* of Rowman & Littlefield, for the extraordinarily skilled editorial and production assistance they have provided.

Of course there are many more individuals I could name from whose assistance I have tremendously benefited, but they would number too many to list here. Suffice it to say that I am the beneficiary of many articulate and thoughtful friends, insightful authors, and even loving critics.

Introduction

I am the son of the road, my country is the caravan, my life the
most unexpected of voyages.

—AMIN MAALOUF (TAKEN FROM *LEO THE AFRICAN*)

I HAVE SPENT MOST OF MY LIFE within an Islamic context and it is the
environment with which I am most familiar and comfortable. Growing up
in Senegal, West Africa, a Muslim-majority country, my closest friends
were often Muslims. As an adult, I have had the privilege of working in various roles with the Anglican/Episcopal Church and other Christian non-
governmental organizations, which have taken me extensively throughout the
Arab Islamic world, North Africa, and the Middle East, and the Muslim
countries within Asia and sub-Saharan Africa. I have also lived in Tunisia,
North Africa, serving as the rector of St. George's Anglican Church in
Tunis/Carthage, and I wrote this book while based in Cairo with the Episcopal Diocese of Egypt & North Africa. All of these experiences have led me
to respect Islam as a religion and to highly regard and admire the rich, varied,
and fascinating culture of Islamic societies. At a deeper level, I have a tremendous love and respect for Muslims, who number among my closest friends.

As a Christian, I am also passionate about the person and revelation of Jesus Christ, whose way I am attempting to follow as I seek to journey closer
to God. And as my Muslim friends, in truly caring about me, wish me to follow the teachings of Muhammad, my strongest desire for them is to clearly
see Christ and examine his life and message without all the sociological, religious, cultural, political and historical barriers that often exist.

Usually at the encouragement of Christians, Muslims who decide to follow Christ and his teachings all too often end up leaving their own culture

and joining a "foreign" one, a "Christian culture." Consequently, they find themselves dislocated from their own communities and families, and not only lose their own sense of identity, but are unable to influence the circle from which they originated, let alone serve as a bridge between the two cultures. I distinctly remember observing this actuality as a young teenager in Senegal, and as an adult this continual observation throughout the Muslim world has developed into a passion for discovering the possibility of another way, a "third way." Addressing this issue has played a significant role in my own spiritual pilgrimage.

It is as if it were a "divine tension," with the consuming question being: Is it possible for someone from a Muslim background to follow Christ uniquely and remain an insider, staying within their Islamic culture? Another way of asking this same question is: "How can Christ be 'naturalized' in the Islamic context?" or "How is Christ walking the Muslim Road?"

The first significant inspiration for me in this regard came in 1991 in India. Having two free days in Bangalore, due to my flight schedule, I went over to the library of the historic United Theological Seminary (UTS). Thanks to a generous librarian, I obtained an extra copy of E. Stanley Jones's *The Christ of the Indian Road*,[1] a book for which I had long been searching. During the next two days, in the colonial-style garden of an Indian hotel, I read the book thoroughly twice, hanging on every sentence. While the language is somewhat dated, having first been published in 1925, it remains one of the books that have most significantly influenced my own faith—a book full of spiritual life, originality, creativity, and fresh perspectives, albeit unorthodox, on communicating and demonstrating Christ among those of other faiths. E. Stanley Jones was a well-known American Methodist minister who spent most of his life serving in India. Nominated for the Nobel Peace Prize several times, and a close friend of Mahatma Gandhi, he greatly influenced the face of the religious world at that time. Clearly very much "ahead of his time," in this book, the first of his nearly thirty titles, he addresses "how Christ is naturalized upon the Indian Road." Central to his thought is the necessity of separating Jesus from "Christianity" and "Western civilization" (in which, of course, Indians had no interest) in order for them to see Christ as "their own." As Jones repeatedly emphasizes, "Christianity and Jesus are not the same."[2] As a result, the book, apart from everything else, stirs one devotionally to look deeply at Jesus, to love him, and to desire all the more to follow in his steps.

Jones's main thrust in the book is that one can fully follow Christ without being a "Christian." He writes, "Just as a stream takes on the coloring of the soil over which it flows, so Christianity in its flowing through the soils of the different racial and national outlooks took on coloring from them. . . . Jesus is universal. He can stand the shock of transplantation."[3] "The Indian should remain Indian [when following Jesus]—he must stand in the stream of India's culture and life and let the force of that stream go through his soul so that the expression of his Christianity will be essentially Eastern."[4] This perspective even led Hindu Brahmins to say to Jones, "I could love and follow the Christ of the Indian Road."[5] There is a beautiful section in his book that describes South Asians finally being able to visualize this reality. Jones writes, "[The Christ of the Indian Road] has caught their imagination. He seemed so intimately theirs. He seemed to have come in from the Indian Road and sat upon the floor with us in the quietness of that Indian twilight."[6]

The freshness and unorthodoxy of Jones's message is his focus on the "irregular channels" that demonstrate Christ. "Christianity is actually breaking out beyond the borders of the Christian Church," wrote Jones, "and is being seen in the most unexpected places . . . those who have the spirit of Jesus are his, no matter what outward symbols they may lack. In a spiritual movement like that of Jesus it is . . . impossible to mark its frontiers."[7] And Jones illustrates this by focusing on his close friend, Mahatma Gandhi. A self-proclaimed Hindu, Gandhi was captivated by the person and message of Christ, resulting in even being called by some one of the most Christ-like men in history. Even missionaries in India would sit at his feet, seeking to learn what it meant to live like Christ within the Indian context. As Jones points out, Gandhi's life, outlook, and methods, which he attributed to Jesus's Sermon on the Mount in the Gospels, provoked great interest—indeed fascination—with Christ.[8] Because of Gandhi, an unorganized "Christ following" arose in India. Perhaps unknown to himself, Gandhi presented an Eastern face of Christ to India. By his life, Gandhi helped Indians visualize Christ on an Eastern road. And many Hindus began to see the meaning of Christ because they had seen it in one of *their* own.[9]

As I read Jones's revolutionary book there in a Bangalore hotel, I embarked on a journey of discovery—of what it might look like for Jesus to be naturalized upon the Arab Muslim road, and of where and how this is taking place. This is the origin of the title of this book, *Pilgrims of Christ on the Muslim Road*.

The second significant inspiration to me in this exploration came in 1992, through a rediscovery of the renowned Sadhu Sundar Singh. Sundar Singh, who lived in the early 1900s, was a follower of Christ from a prominent Sikh heritage. And yet, in his following of Christ, he kept his Sikh culture, becoming a wandering Indian "holy man." A true Indian mystic and devoted disciple of Christ, as he journeyed throughout India, into Tibet and around the world, he offered and demonstrated an authentic Eastern presentation of Christ, full of spiritual depth and freshness. His teachings, which largely took the form of Eastern short stories or parables, captivated and fed many thousands in India and throughout the world. A recent publication of his various writings, titled *Wisdom of the Sadhu: Teachings of Sundar Singh*,[10] in which the sadhu profoundly, yet with great simplicity, brings to life a faith in Christ that fills our inner souls, has been one of the most original presentations I have come across of following Christ. However, more than anything else, studying his life and reading his writings helped me see similar followers of Christ surface in the Arab Muslim world, for Sundar Singh was a beautiful and powerful example of how someone who comes from a non-Christian faith can follow Christ and remain within his own religious culture, thereby bridging the two.

It was in 1993 that I began to see the realization of this journey of discovery. I had just moved to Tunis/Carthage, Tunisia, where I was working with the Anglican Church. There in Tunis I was introduced to a writer and novelist, living there at the time, by the name of Mazhar Mallouhi. That introduction quickly developed into a close friendship that has changed my life. Mazhar Mallouhi, who calls himself a "Muslim follower of Christ," is a celebrated Arab author whose novels and scholarly works have been a powerful demonstration of Christ within the Arab Muslim world, and a significant force for peace and healing between Muslims and Christians. Mallouhi, a Syrian of Muslim background, whose family traces its lineage directly back to the Prophet Muhammad, has written seven novels and numerous other publications, thereby becoming one of the most effective and authentic voices about Christ among Arab Muslims. His novels were the first indigenous Arabic fiction published that presented Christ to a Muslim audience, becoming best sellers in the mainstream markets throughout the Middle East and North Africa. It is estimated that some of his books have been read by more than 1.5 million people.[11] And his life's calling has been to bridge the chasm of misunderstanding between Muslims and Christians by writing and publishing books that explain faith in Christ in culturally acceptable terms and distributing them through Muslim or secular channels.

Over the last thirty-five years, Mallouhi has gained great respect among Muslim leaders and popularity with Muslim readers. His sound scholarship and literary giftedness has earned him unique acceptance in the artistic and intellectual communities of the Middle East. And his approach to communicating Christ has helped thousands of Muslims understand who Jesus is. Mallouhi's uniqueness is that he provides a "voice from the other side," an insider's voice, as he not only comes from a Muslim background, but also, in his following of Christ, has found a way to keep his Islamic and Arab culture. Consequently, he has become an authority in the area of following Christ within Islam, and deserves to be listened to by the West.

In the spirit of E. Stanley Jones and Sadhu Sundar Singh, Mazhar Mallouhi, who follows Christ within Islam, is someone whose life is naturally filled with paradox, often resulting in unconventionality. Mahatma Gandhi's fascination with Christ (which also greatly influenced Jones) played a critical role in Mallouhi deciding to follow Christ. His conversion to the way of love was a direct result of Gandhi's admiration for Christ—not the conquering Christ of "crusading" Western Christendom, but the loving, self-giving, reconciling Christ of the Gospels.

Mallouhi's unorthodox way of following Christ can provide Western Christians a great freshness for their own faith. Every time I am with him I am influenced far more deeply than I anticipated, learning more than I could ever share in this book. He has inspired me, encouraged me, challenged and shaped my views on politics, theology, religion and culture, and taught me so much about Jesus. My warmest memories are of sitting around the Arab water fountain in Mazhar's Beirut courtyard, as he puffs on his *shisha* (a Middle Eastern water-pipe) and fingers his Muslim prayer beads, talking so naturally, beautifully, profoundly, and irresistibly about the sweetness of Christ. The love he exudes for God is contagious. I feel that God has loved me through this Arab writer who has an infectious faith in Christ. And I consider his friendship something that comes along once in a lifetime.

In regard to understanding Islam and demonstrating Christ among his own people, Muslims, he has served as my teacher. What a privilege it has been to spend time with him, in various cities of North Africa and the Middle East, as he shares with other Muslims about this Jesus whom he follows and serves—people from each end of the social spectrum, from Bedouins and Berbers in their simple desert tents, to Islamic sheiks in beautiful mosques and Arab world leaders in their halls of political power. He is someone who is truly free to give his life out of love for his people, and this kind of freedom and love is rare indeed. As someone who truly lives within the clash of cultures and beliefs, he has much to teach us.

As a result of the tragic events of September 11, 2001, an unprecedented interest developed in the West in general, and more specifically in the Western Christian community, to sincerely and open-mindedly seek to learn about Islam and understand Muslims. This is a most encouraging development. At the same time, disturbingly, there is also a quickly growing discord between Christians and Muslims. This has often led to an "Islamaphobia" that results in Westerners being fearful of Muslims, or even seeing Islam as an enemy. Some Christians go so far as actually "demonizing" Islam, and even portray it as the last great enemy to be conquered. All too often the picture given of Islam, vis-à-vis its relations with Christians, is unbalanced, one-sided, and at times mythical. For example, the oft-held idea that Muslim conversions took place primarily by the sword from the Middle Ages on is a myth much propagated in anti-Islamic literature. Rarely is there a positive description of a Muslim. The same trends can be observed among Muslims' perceptions of

Christians, especially in the Arab Islamic world. The result of this developing mentality is that Muslims and Christians continue to be further alienated from each other. This of course all the more hinders Muslims from ever seriously examining the claims of Christ, the great bridge builder.

This growing divide between these two large monotheistic faiths calls for a fresh approach in this area. One positive sign is that many Western Christians have begun to ask hard questions about the negative views so many in the West have of Islam, and have shown an openness to thinking differently about their Muslim brothers and sisters. It is in this light and context that we are able to learn a tremendous amount from Mazhar Mallouhi on how Christ can actually serve to bridge what almost seems an unbridgeable religious and cultural divide. Mazhar's familiarity with Christianity, his love for and service to Christ, and his totally authentic Arab identity, as an insider in Islam, enables him to serve as a mentor to us all.

The purpose of this book is to examine and learn from Mazhar's attitude and approach to Islam as a follower of Christ within the context of his life and today's religious climate. I will give particular attention to the evolution of his thought in regard to Islam and how he models the communication and demonstration of Christ among other Muslims. Writing this book has literally been a global adventure, the research for it having taken me throughout the Gulf States, North Africa, and numerous countries within the Middle East, places where Mazhar has lived or worked, to meet individuals who have been influenced by him. I have had the privilege of interviewing hundreds of people who either know Mazhar or have been affected by his writings—Arab Muslims, Western Christians, Arab Christians, and of course, other followers of Christ from a Muslim background. Numerous people have assisted me in analyzing his many publications for Muslim audiences. Beyond his novels and other publications, with the assistance of his wife, Christine, I have had access to many other primary sources, such as speeches he has given, and the vast correspondence between Mazhar and his wife. During the course of writing this book, I have benefited from the personal insight of some outstanding Islamic scholars, both Christian and Muslim, such as Rev. Colin Chapman, Bishop Kenneth Cragg, and the late Dr. Ahmed Mechraqi. However, the most satisfying part of the research for this book was the many, many hours I spent with Mazhar himself, and Christine, in their lovely home in Beirut, Lebanon, "sitting at his feet."

In the ever-developing religious conflict between East and West, I believe there are major practical and theoretical benefits to gain by looking at Mazhar's life and approach to Islam. To my knowledge, there has not been a similar study done on someone who calls himself a "Muslim follower of Christ" and whose life mission is introducing Muslims to the person of Christ.

I believe that Mazhar's experience, insights, and approach can significantly influence the Christian Church on how it approaches Islam as a religion and Muslims as a people, changing many current practices and behaviors. I hope that this book will help Christians who live among Muslims understand how to be authentic, sensitive, and effective when living out and sharing of their faith in Christ. My personal wish is that this book will help to shatter a great deal of prejudice that exists, advocating for alternative thinking about Islam. Of course, one book alone cannot do everything, but my prayer is that it will be part of a developing stream of information from Christian and Muslim sources that can make a difference in Western Christian postures.

As a by-product, I trust that in looking at Mazhar's life and spiritual pilgrimage, a life in which he was once dislocated from his own Muslim family and community but later became an insider once again, other Muslims who desire to follow Christ may be encouraged to do so while finding ways to stay inside their own culture and communities. Mazhar's example can help Muslims understand that they can become followers of Christ without having to join the "Christian" West.

Three important caveats about this book: First, while the book focuses on Mazhar Mallouhi's lifelong interaction with Islam as a follower of Christ, it is not meant to be a biography. I will leave to someone else the exciting task of writing up in greater detail the fascinating life story of this striking individual. I am reminded, however, as I cover Mazhar's life story in considerable depth, of Anglican Bishop Kenneth Cragg's comment in the preface to his thought-provoking book, *Troubled by Truth—Life Studies in Inter-Faith Concern,* that "biography has always been the first clue to theology, and in Christian tradition the reality of God is believed to have been biographized in Jesus as the Christ."[12] However, instead of biography, Mazhar's extraordinary life and ministry is meant to serve as a teaching vehicle to assist Muslims in seeing Christ as clearly as possible by working to remove all the cultural baggage and trappings associated with Christ in their minds, and thereby stretching current thinking on Christian approaches to Islam. In a larger sense, looking at Mazhar's journey enables us to probe more deeply into how Christ can bridge the gap between Christians and Muslims. In attempting to employ the biographical information as a pedagogical instrument, I have greatly benefited from the narrative history approach used in Fouad Ajami's excellent book *The Vanished Imam.*[13] In his book, Ajami, a professor of Middle Eastern Studies at Johns Hopkins University, tells the recent history of the Lebanese Shia Muslims by using the vivid story of Sayyid Musa al Sadr, who was their religious leader until his mysterious disappearance in 1978.[14] It is a book of unusual artistry and in my view has the literary power of a masterpiece. Another book of Ajami's that I have found to be of great assistance is *The Dream Palace of the*

Arabs.[15] Focusing on the lives of the greatest Arab writers of the twentieth century, Ajami brilliantly weaves together the history, political thought, and Arab literature of that tumultuous era in the Middle East in a most informative, imaginative, and moving way.

Second, Mazhar's life and ministry, and therefore this book, does not offer a methodology. As Mazhar has observed over the years, the nature of Western Christianity is often to look for models, methods, and strategies that can be duplicated. In the realm of faith and spirituality, however, this is not the way things work, as God works differently in each local context. This is certainly true of Mazhar. What is most unique about Mazhar's approach is Mazhar himself. There is a sense that even he does not have a methodology. Rather, his approach has been instinctive, as opposed to being fully thought through. Because he is "one-of-kind," we could never be completely like him and accomplish what he does. And he would not encourage anyone to model himself or herself after him. Rather, instead of sharing any new methodology, by looking at Mazhar's life story and work this book highlights some principles, ideas, and lessons about the interaction between Christians and Muslims from which we can learn and which we can apply to our own life contexts. In this sense, the book is more descriptive than prescriptive.

Third, I will not be addressing Islamic theology, doctrine, or the tenets of Muslim belief and practice. There are many excellent books already written and readily available which effectively cover these topics.[16] Therefore, I am assuming the reader has at least an elementary knowledge of Islamic belief and Muslim religious practice.

As this book is essentially about Mazhar's spiritual pilgrimage with Christ within the Islamic world, and as the concept of pilgrimage is so prevalent in Islam, I have chosen to structure this book around Psalm 84 (verses 2, 5-7), which is known as a "Pilgrim Psalm."

My soul yearns, even faints, for the courts of the Lord; my heart and my flesh cry out for the living God . . . Blessed are those whose strength is in you, who have set their hearts on pilgrimage. As they pass through the Valley of Baca, they make it a place of springs; the autumn rains also cover it with pools. They go from strength to strength, till they appear before God in Zion. (Psalm 84:2, 5-7—NIV)

It is a psalm that most biblical scholars believe describes the journey a Hebrew would have taken through the desert in ancient Judah to the Temple in Jerusalem for one of the High Festivals. However, there are a number of Muslim scholars who believe this psalm actually references the Islamic holy city of Mecca. The Psalmist refers to the pilgrim passing through the "Valley of Baca," which some Muslims claim is the Valley of Mecca ("Bakkah" being the older name that the Qur'an uses for Mecca). Other Muslims go so far as to say that the pilgrimage the psalm is describing is really the Islamic *haj* ("pilgrimage" in Arabic) to Mecca. There have been various interpretations for "Baca." It has been translated as either "weeping" or "balsam trees" (which grow in dry areas).

It is not the place of this book to address whether the Valley of Baca was an actual historical place, in which case it was a valley through which the pilgrims passed during their journey, or whether it was a figurative expression of passing through deep sorrow (hence the translation "weeping") or difficulty (the "balsam tree" interpretation, indicating extreme dryness). Instead I have selected to shape the book around these verses in this "Pilgrim Psalm," which is accepted by Christians and admired by some Muslims, as the theme of this book is very much one of pilgrimage—from Mazhar's faith pilgrimage to our own spiritual pilgrimages as we seek to better understand how to best love the other, Christian to Muslim and vice versa, in the name and manner of Christ.

Section 1, *Pilgrim of Allah: Devotion to Christ within the Line of Muhammad*, is largely biographical in nature, with the objective of providing the readers with an introductory foundation to Mazhar's life, faith pilgrimage, and work, building on the phrase in Psalm 84:5, "Blessed are those . . . who have set their hearts on pilgrimage." The focus of section 2, *Bridging Two Worlds*, is to address the issue of approaching and dealing with Islam as Christians by learning from the life experience of Mazhar—who has passed through the "Valley of Baca" (Psalm 84:6)—symbolically representing both Islam and great difficulty. And section 3, *New Directions for the Journey*, highlights the fresh thinking, unique approaches, and original contribution Mazhar has made and continues to make in his presentation of Christ in the Muslim Arab context. *"As they pass through the Valley of Baca, they make it a place of springs; the autumn rains also cover it with pools. They go from strength to strength"* (Psalm 84:6, 7).

As we learn about how Christ may "walk the Muslim Road" once Jesus is respectfully and properly introduced to Muslims, it is of supreme importance that we adopt the posture of allowing Muslims to walk their own road with Christ, leaving them complete freedom to work out their relationship with Jesus in ways that are right for them, and discovering what it means for them to follow him in their respective communities. This ultimately requires from Christians great humility and profound trust. Christians need to trust the Muslim world with Christ, and trust Christ with the Muslim world. For Christ and Muslims must journey the rest of the way together.

Allow me to introduce you to Mazhar Mallouhi, an extraordinary man of profound spiritual depth and a heart of love who has influenced countless people, as he seeks to win a home for Christ in the hearts of Muslims, enabling them to meet the Middle Eastern Prince of Peace.

PILGRIM OF ALLAH: DEVOTION TO CHRIST WITHIN THE LINE OF MUHAMMAD

I

My soul yearns, even faints, for the courts of the Lord; my heart and my flesh cry out for the living God. . . . Blessed are those whose strength is in you, who have set their hearts on pilgrimage.

—PSALM 84:2, 5

Pilgrimage to Faith

1

The veil that clouds your eyes shall be lifted
by the hands that wove it,
And the clay that fills your ears shall be pierced
by those fingers that kneaded it.
And you shall see
And you shall hear.

—KHALIL GIBRAN (TAKEN FROM *THE PROPHET*)

A Foundation Is Laid

ON AN UNBEARABLY HOT SUMMER Delhi afternoon, I found myself standing barefoot in pilgrim reverence at the memorial to Mahatma Gandhi, the man who pointed Mazhar Mallouhi, the celebrated Arab novelist and disciple of Jesus, to Christ. Mazhar, a Syrian of Muslim background, whose family traces its lineage directly back to the Prophet Muhammad, has become one of the most effective and authentic voices for Christ among Muslims in the Arab world, by maintaining his Islamic and Arab culture while being a fully committed follower of Jesus.

A common thread in spiritual journeys is that God works through paradox and irregular channels. Such is the case with Mazhar, an example of "Christian fruit" from Mahatma Gandhi's life. The great paradox is that it was Gandhi, a self-proclaimed Hindu, who through his life and writings, having been deeply influenced by the Jesus of the Gospels, led Mazhar from a Muslim background to faith in Christ. Within the various religious faiths, there are those in love with God who devoutly seek that deeper spiritual dimension. These individuals recognize each other across their faith traditions, as heart speaks to heart. And the spiritual link between Mahatma Gandhi, a Hindu, and Mazhar Mallouhi, a Muslim, was Christ. It could well be that, due to his family heritage and the Islamic context in which he grew up, the only way Mazhar would have ever taken a serious look at Christ in his own spiritual quest was through such an irregular channel as that of a Hindu who loved Jesus and his teachings.

Mazhar was born around 1935 into a large Muslim family, the fourth of seven children, in the small Syrian city of Salimiyyeh. It is a place with a special reputation in the country, for it is known as a city of diversity, where various sects and branches of Islam are represented. Most of the population of Salimiyyeh is Sunni, with a large minority Ismailiyya and smaller Alouite groups both originating out of the Shia branch of Islam. Salimiyyeh also had a substantial Sufi element in its Islamic expression of faith. Sufis, the mystics of Islam, though generally but nonetheless cautiously accepted by the more orthodox segments of Islam, tend to be viewed with some suspicion, as they focus in their religious lives much more on personal spiritual experience than doctrine and religious laws.

Mazhar's family was proudly from the Sunni branch of Islam, which constituted the majority of Muslims in Syria, and the Sunnis in Salimiyyeh tended to be religiously conservative. However, while religiously conservative, Salimiyyeh was intellectually liberal and radical.

In a city whose people were passionate about their Islamic diversity and heritage, Mazhar's family was no exception. Today, on the wall of Mazhar's oldest brother's house hangs the family's most prized possession: the family tree in a gold embossed frame declaring the Mallouhi family's descent from the Prophet Muhammad. His siblings are quick to point out that this genealogical tree is from a "reputable firm." With this family heritage, the Mallouhi family is considered *shorafa*, "a noble family." It is known to have produced some venerable Muslim leaders, such as Mazhar's uncle, Hajj Anis Mallouhi, an imam who was a famous religious judge (Cadi Isharia) in Syria.

While the whole Mallouhi clan is Sunni, Mazhar's mother comes from an Ismailiyya background, which probably had some influence toward broadening his immediate family's tolerance of those from other religious traditions. Syria itself was known as a religiously tolerant society in the Middle East at that time. For example, in the 1950s, the speaker of the Syrian Parliament was a Protestant Christian by the name of Faris Khouri. In fact, Mazhar and Christine Mallouhi named their first son after this man, whose name means "knight."

The city of Salimiyyeh is also known in Syria as having given birth to many progressive Arab thinkers and writers. In the 1950s various well-known Syrian existentialists, Communists, and political leaders came out of this small city. Mazhar's extended family contributed to this literary and political reputation, having produced a number of well-known writers and politicians. For example, a relative of Mazhar's, Abdul Muwayn Mallouhi, a well-known Syrian Communist, was known as one of the first to translate Chairman Mao's works into Arabic. Another relative of his, Adnan Mallouhi, a famous journalist and writer, published the first Arabic language Communist newspaper. Even the head of the Ministry of Culture at that time, Abdul El Moein, a poet as well, was part of the Mallouhi clan.

The Islamic diversity, literary focus, and political activism of his hometown environment undoubtedly played a significant role in Mazhar's early formation. As Syrian political thinker, Abdullah Turkmani, political science researcher with the Palestinian Liberation Organization (PLO) and assistant to the Arab Institute for Human Rights, says, "Mazhar is unique, not just because he follows Christ, but because of having grown up in Salimiyyeh."[1] At the same time, though part of a well-known and respected family clan, Mazhar came from the poorest of the family branches, the one thought of as "country people." His father was a sheep trader with close Bedouin connections, who raised and traded sheep for a living. His father's brother, Mustapha Mallouhi, had a guesthouse for strangers (*menzuul*) in need of shelter, demonstrating the family's generous Middle Eastern trait of hospitality. Regardless of where they came from or of their religious affiliation, these guests were allowed to stay in the guesthouse for free for three days before they were asked their names and their business in the town. His uncle's compassionate example greatly influenced an impressionable young Mazhar, and served as a model to him of how one should treat others, even strangers. Some of his fondest memories are of his uncle taking him to the market at the age of eight or nine, watching his all-embracing spirit in action. So despite their poor economic status, the Mallouhi family had a strong tradition of helping people in need, both inside and outside of the local community. Mazhar recalls his uncle telling him that he himself didn't need to travel and see the world, because through the visitors he housed he already had the whole world in his own home.

Mazhar remembers his father and mother as loving and kind, doing their best to provide for the family. He has fond memories of the various enjoyable activities in which the whole family participated, from sitting down and eating together—a communal event in the Middle East—to traditional dancing at parties. The harvest and sheep-shearing festivals were particularly enjoyable for a child, with their horse dancing, swordsmanship events, and Bedouin music using the flute and the *rubaba*, a Bedouin stringed instrument.

Yet despite this richness of family life, from a very young age Mazhar powerfully experienced the economic poverty in which they lived, and remembers not being able to buy his first brand-new shirt until the age of eighteen. He also found terribly frustrating his parents' apparent disinterest in actively improving their status in life. Attributing this to their lack of education, already as a boy Mazhar became determined to find a way out of that small world.

As a means of escape, Mazhar turned to books. Somewhat of a loner as a young boy, he spent much time alone reading obsessively. Not able to purchase all the books he desired to read, he and his friends would share the books they owned. Whenever Mazhar was given the opportunity to receive gifts, he would always choose books. A respected cousin who had obtained his engineering degree in Germany told how his parents held up Mazhar as an example for all the children of how they should approach their studies and take advantage of every opportunity they were given to educate themselves.

Yet such commendation was double-edged: all the attention Mazhar received created a deep jealousy in his oldest brother, Ali, who was illiterate and sought to forbid Mazhar from reading. Ali would actually tie Mazhar to a chair and beat him in order to punish him for reading books. This only created a yet deeper hunger for learning in Mazhar, and frequently he would sneak outside of the home and read at night under the streetlights. He was determined to "not stay there, remaining poor and ignorant."

From the outset, in his family and local community, Mazhar was considered a very special child. The family's women perpetuate the myth that he spoke while still in his cradle, an event which in Arab culture symbolizes uniqueness. In a similar vein, when she went to cover his head as a baby, his older sister, Nedra, insists he spoke out the words, "Miracle Mazhar," leading his family to call him that to this day. This perspective of his "specialness" is also what caused him to be named "Mazhar," a very unusual name which means "appearance." Incidentally, his family name, Mallouhi, means "salty." Putting the two together, his name "salty appearance" has certainly proven to be prophetic.

As a very young boy, Mazhar had a deep spiritual orientation. At an early age, he began to have religious questions, but he was strongly discouraged from asking them, for according to the Islamic culture in which he grew up, it was considered blasphemous to question God. In addition to reading fiction, he began to enjoy classical philosophical literature. Observing Mazhar's passion for education and his natural spiritual orientation, his family expected him to follow in his well-known uncle's footsteps and pursue a religious vocation as a Muslim cleric. At the age of six he began attending a Qur'anic school that was under the influence of the Muslim Brotherhood, a fundamentalist Islamic movement founded by an Egyptian schoolteacher named Hasan al-Banna. For the next seven years he was taught a conservative view of Islamic doctrine and practice, which included having to memorize most of the Qur'an, as is the typical method of religious education in Islam. From the beginning he found himself having a very negative view of Islam as a religion. Mazhar recalls, "When I read the Qur'an, I pictured God up in the sky smoking his water pipe. He had given me his book but had no involvement in my daily life or in the suffering of humanity below."

At the age of sixteen Mazhar finished his primary education (the educational level of a thirteen-year-old in the West, as he began school late), and as his family was too poor to afford secondary school, his formal education ended at this point. Instead, he worked the family farm, helping with the little produce they grew and the sheep-trading business. From this point on, all of Mazhar's remarkable education would be attributed to self-study.

During this period, Mazhar entered into a profound depression. Internally miserable, he hated himself and others, and continued to escape from the world by retreating to books. It was during this time he began to find that writing was a natural and healthy outlet. Even as early as age thirteen, he began writing poetry. But, by and large, these poems reflected the hell he was experiencing inside. Turning to alcohol, he began to drink excessively, often returning home drunk. He describes his state of mind at that time as, "afraid of life, and afraid of God."

A deep spiritual restlessness led Mazhar to first read extensively in philosophy—Voltaire, Jean-Jacques Rousseau, Albert Camus. He developed a particular appreciation for the French existentialist Jean-Paul Sartre. After having saturated himself in philosophical thought, he concluded, "I found it very interesting, but saw it as being like water; nice, but having no taste." He then began to read the greatest and the most profound of the Arab writers, such as Egyptian novelist and Nobel Prize laureate Naguib Mahfouz.

Having been so negatively affected in his view of Islam during his Qur'anic training, by the age of eighteen Mazhar was at first hesitant to read anything religious again. However, his spiritual hunger won out and he began to study the Eastern religions, such as Buddhism. However, the Buddhist goal of non-existence was not what he was looking for to fill the emptiness he was experiencing. He began to look at Hinduism through the teachings of Rama, a guru with a substantial following in New York City in the 1930s. Rama had concluded that the best way to see God was through other human beings, which was not far from an incarnational view of God. This approach impressed Mazhar, who, while at the time not yet fully conscious of the goal of his spiritual journey, was ultimately on a search for God (or *Allah*—the Arabic word for God, used by both Arab Muslims and Christians).

He also immersed himself in ancient Greek, Roman, and Egyptian religious beliefs. His intense search led him to conclude that "because humanity had created a hell on earth, 'God' also had been created as an escape and for their peace of mind." Furthermore, he observed that all these religious and philosophical leaders preached something they could not live themselves, and strove for something they never actually experienced or realized. This conclusion led him to reject his family's plan for him of a religious vocation. And at the age of fifteen, Mazhar stopped participating in prayers at their local mosque.

While Muslims highly respect Christ, Mazhar refused to study the Christian faith. Muslims believe Christ was a great prophet of God born of the Virgin Mary, and see him as a word and spirit of God. When the Jewish people rejected him and tried to crucify him, Muslims believe God rescued Jesus from death and translated him bodily into heaven, from which he will descend at the end of time to judge the world. While Jesus is greatly admired by Muslims, Mazhar understandably saw Christianity as a tool of oppressive colonialists, a Western religion that was continuing the medieval Crusades against the Arab people as Western "Christian" nations gave blind support to the injustices caused by the State of Israel to the Palestinian people. Local Western Christians were viewed as complicit in what was considered the grievous wrongdoing of uprooting the Palestinians in order to establish a Jewish homeland. Mazhar observed how, "Christians calling Christ 'the Prince of Peace,' supported and waged war." This continued feeling is illustrated by Muslim writer Muhammad al-Sayyid al-Julaynd. In his book, published in Cairo in 1999, he suggests that the religion of Western Christians should be called *salibiyya,* "Crusaderism," as opposed to *masihiyya,* "Christianity."[2]

During Mazhar's growing up years, Western Christianity was viewed as a form of "cultural imperialism" as missionaries to the Middle East had for centuries benefited from Western intervention in the affairs of Muslim states. This was especially true in the nineteenth and early twentieth centuries, during which Britain and France imposed forms of colonial control in the Arab world, and in the second half of the twentieth century, when the United States repeatedly intervened in the region. Consequently, Western missionary activities were viewed by many as a kind of religious wedge used to break apart the culture of Islamic societies in order to make them more vulnerable to what was seen as the Western imperial crusade against Islam. American and British missionaries arrived in the Middle East as early as the 1820s, and as Westerners in Ottoman Empire domains they had access to special legal rights and exemptions, similar to diplomatic immunity. These privileges were used to assist them in their attempts to convert Muslims to Christianity, and therefore these missionaries under the umbrella of Western imperialism were able to do what would have been impossible under normal Islamic state conditions. In this sense, Western missionary activity was a vivid reminder to Muslims of their political and military weakness due to Western imperialism.[3]

In the 1920s, various Islamic movements were founded. One of the most prominent was the Muslim Brotherhood, mentioned already as the group that influenced Mazhar's Qur'anic schooling. One of its fundamental concerns was to stop Christian missionary activities in Egypt and beyond. The Muslim Brotherhood was formed during a period in Egypt when the Arab media was falsely sensationalizing activities of Western Christian missionaries, saying they kidnapped, brainwashed, or abused Muslim children with the objective of religious conversion. Therefore, many Muslims saw Western Christian influence in the region as a kind of disease to be eradicated.[4]

The reaction of the Arab Muslims to Western Christianity was powerfully illustrated in the leading Arabic Muslim periodical of that time, *Al Manar Journal* (1898-1935), under the direction of Muhammad Rashid Rida, who died in 1935, the year Mazhar was born. This popular journal became the major source for the Arab Muslim public response to the evangelizing efforts of Western Christians, and focused on the perceived threats by foreign missionaries of westernization, imperialism, and Orientalist visions of Arabs as backward and of Islam as "a religion of darkness." The journal clearly shows that the Muslim viewpoint of the time was that it seemed the imperialistic West was out to destroy the only power standing in its way—Islam, represented by the Ottoman Empire. As a Muslim journal, it closely associated the political goals of England, France, and the United States with the religious ones of missionaries from those countries, as there is no separation of religion and state in Islam.[5] The journal's response was to promote Islamic unity as the best way to counteract Western influence, "painting the political situation as a confrontation between Christian and Islamic civilizations."[6]

Perhaps the most vivid example of Arab Muslim views of Western Christian activities in the Middle East is the path-breaking book by Mustafa Khalidi and Umar Farrukh titled *Evangelism and Imperialism in the Arab World*. First published in 1953, it has been so popular that it has gone through at least six subsequent editions, with the most recent as late as 1991. Khalidi was a professor at the American University of Beirut (AUB), and Farrukh was a specialist in early Islamic history, classical Arabic poetry, and Sufism. Their main argument is that Western Christian activities were "the most powerful and dangerous agents of Western imperialism and that missionary institutions (schools, hospitals, bookstores, etc.) were tools for the Western assertion of political and economic hegemony (*saytara*) over the Middle East."[7] They portray Western missionaries as modern crusaders, "distinguished by their intense animosity toward Arab Muslims . . . "[8] The authors apply these views to American, British, French, and Italian Christian missionaries, both Protestant and Catholic. This book continues to be very highly regarded in the Middle East and has inspired the thinking of a number of other more recent and contemporary key Muslim Arab writers on the continued Western Christian influence in the region, such as Ibrahim Ahmad (an Egyptian Christian turned Muslim who used to work for an American Christian mission agency), Emad Sharaf, Abdul al Midani, Karam Shalabi, Qasim al Samara'i, and Muhammad al Talibi. These writers illustrate Arab Muslims' continued deep and abiding mistrust of Western Christianity.

Growing up, Mazhar's own experience of direct contact with Christians had been minimal. In his town of Salimiyyeh, there was only one Christian, an Armenian, who ran the local bar. As alcohol is forbidden in Islam, Mazhar didn't regard this person highly. Another Christian he was aware of in Syria ran a prostitution house, which further solidified his unfavorable impression of Christians. As Mazhar says, "I was poisoned by the milk of my mother against Christianity." From the outset, through his family, his study of history, and the influence of the Arab media, he came to the conclusion that Christians were the enemy. Reflecting on what he had been taught about Christians as a young boy, Mazhar says, "Christianity was seen as the enemy. And you need your enemy to be ugly. You don't want to discover anything good in your enemy, or you will find yourself in the wrong." He was, however, impressed with the Syrian Orthodox Church's Easter celebration, which he found very beautiful. Having no contact whatsoever with Christians, this Easter festival was literally "another world" to him, one of whose significance he had no understanding.

The Golan Heights

Coming to the conclusion that the key to a better future was through changing the political scene in the Middle East, during the early 1950s, Mazhar, like many moderate Syrian intellectuals, joined a popular secular political party, the Baath Party. This was a political party founded in Syria by Michel Aflaq, a Syrian Christian intellectual, which focused on separating religion and government and sought to unite the Arab world in a movement called "Arab Nationalism." The slogan of the Baath Party in Syria was "Religion is for God and the country is for everyone." In 1955, Mazhar, at the age of 20, was required to serve one year in the Syrian Army, as were all young men. Mazhar's first assignment was on Mt. Herman (Jebel Sheikh), where he was involved in a civil war in Lebanon at that time. It was a miserable experience. During one forty-day period he was not even able to take off his shoes, as the soldiers slept in the snow high up on that mountain. However, after it was discovered he was a writer, he was eventually transferred to office work. Having no idea what he would do with his life, he extended his military service for another five years.

His second military assignment positioned him on the disputed Golan Heights, considered the territory of Syria at that time (now occupied by Israel); it was the Russians, from the former Soviet Union, who came to train them. During this time, Mazhar began to write for newspapers and publish his poetry. His writings were largely reflections on life, suffering, and God. It was during this period that he started reading Mahatma Gandhi's works to learn about Gandhi's nonviolent movement, and soon discovered Gandhi's great respect for Christ. Through Gandhi's eyes, Mazhar began to see a different Christ than he had encountered previously. He was fascinated to see how "Gandhi took Christian principles without Christ against a Christian nation [England] without Christian principles and won the battle. Gandhi stands out to me as the one person who most dramatically demonstrated Christ's teaching." Mazhar saw Gandhi as one of the few spiritual leaders who lived what he preached. In this way Gandhi's life and writings opened Mazhar's heart to consider Christ.

Gandhi had indeed been captivated by the person and message of Christ. "It was the New Testament that fixed it in my heart," he said. More specifically he speaks of the Sermon on the Mount going ". . . straight to [his] heart."[9] While Gandhi remained fundamentally a Hindu in outward things, he was more Christ-like than most Christians, with his inner life more and more transformed toward Christ's spirit. His internal character portrayed Christ in the actions of his daily life. In many ways Gandhi, a non-Christian, helped to Christianize unchristian Christianity.

In this sense, one of the most "Christ-like" men in history was not called a Christian. When India, a Hindu-majority nation with a large Muslim population, wanted to pay her highest compliment to her most famous native son following Gandhi's assassination over fifty years ago, she searched for the most honorable term she knew and called Gandhi "a Christ-like man."[10] His influence for Christ on Hindus and Muslims was even greater. By his life, outlook, and methods, he was the medium through which a great interest and fascination in Christ developed.[11] A Hindu opponent of Christianity in India during Gandhi's lifetime said, "I never understood the meaning of Christianity until I saw it in Gandhi."[12] Likewise, among Muslims, Muhammad Ali, a contemporary of Gandhi's and the leader of India's Muslims, in his presidential address to Congress spoke of Mahatma Gandhi as "that Christ-like man."[13]

Gandhi's influence on Mazhar was extensive. Through reading the correspondence between Gandhi and the great Russian novelist Leo Tolstoy,

Mazhar was introduced to Tolstoy's books and novels, including the book that had transformed Gandhi, *The Kingdom of God Is within You*. This led Mazhar further into great Russian literature, where he soaked up Fyodor Dostoevsky's novels, being introduced to the power of grace and forgiveness.

Mazhar's introduction to Christ through the writings of Gandhi came at a time when he was undergoing a deep depression. Often staying in his tent the entire day, he would typically just read and smoke excessively. He had great difficulty sleeping. He felt terribly alone and remained aloof from others. Amazingly, when he did socialize with other soldiers he was known as a great practical joker, but this was a cover-up for the internal misery he was experiencing. Too poor to afford prostitutes like other soldiers, he would instead get "officially engaged" (an allowance in Islam which involves a betrothal ceremony with a ring), in order to be with them. Mazhar also turned to alcohol. In fact, he determined to commit suicide by drinking too much, as did the character of Ivan, of whom he had read in Dostoevsky's *The Brothers Karamazov*. Completely disillusioned about religion, he left Islam feeling that "God had given me a book, but had walked out of my life." He was so turned off by religion that when he once saw a military officer reading the Bible, Mazhar determined that the person must have been mentally ill.

Gandhi's unintentional witness of Christ to Muslims stretched chronologically to 1959 and geographically west from India to the Middle East, to a young man looking for spiritual life as a soldier in the Syrian army on the Golan Heights. In despair, with nothing to do all day, and influenced by Gandhi's love for the teachings of Christ, Mazhar decided to read the Bible himself. Going to that same officer he had seen reading the Bible, who happened to be a Presbyterian Syrian by the name of Nagib Jarjour, he requested a copy for himself. As was typical of Mazhar's personality at that time, he began to obsessively study the Christian Scriptures. In a year he had read the Old Testament thirteen times and the New Testament twenty-seven. Not understanding all he read, he sought guidance from the Christian officer. His reading of the Bible coincided with his lowest moment—emotionally, psychologically, and spiritually. Yet it was during those two years (1957–1959) that he observed the difference between Christ and the other religious leaders he had previously studied. As had impressed him about Gandhi, he saw that Christ matched his teaching with his life. Mazhar says, "I was so terribly empty. I knew what hell was, for I was living in it. Life to me was not worth living and I came to the point of deciding either to commit suicide or somehow find a new beginning. I saw a difference between this Christ that I was reading about in the Gospels and other religious leaders. Christ combined his teaching with his lifestyle. He didn't just give me an ideal, but he showed me how to live by living it for me, and he promised me that I could begin life anew. From the beginning, I came to the conclusion that Christ never intended to establish a new religion, but instead came to simply establish his life in and among us."

Mazhar was particularly moved by the story of Jesus's encounter with the woman taken in adultery, whom the Jewish religious leaders were going to execute. It reminded him of an incident that he liked very much in Dostoevsky's novel *Crime and Punishment*, in which the criminal character meets Sonya, who had become a prostitute in order to feed her family. He bows at her feet, exclaiming that he does so because she represents to him human suffering. Noted Mazhar, "When Christ, in the Gospels met the woman caught in adultery who was condemned by the religious leaders, he also bowed toward the ground, and did not look her in the face as the leering crowd was doing. He did not add to the shame she was already experiencing, but instead he participated in her pain as he bent over and wrote with his fingers in the ground" (The concept of *shame* in Middle Eastern culture is the worst humiliation an individual can experience). Mazhar found this Jesus immeasurably attractive and ultimately irresistible.

In spiritual turmoil, on the verge of committing suicide, having no contact with or knowledge of the Church or Christianity, the words of Christ, "come to me all you who are weary and I will give you rest," lured him. One day, reading from St. John's Gospel, Jesus's promise, "I have come that you may have life, and have it abundantly," was strongly impressed upon him. At the age of twenty-four, standing on the Golan Heights in 1959, his heart responded, crying out, "This Christ that I am reading of is truly my Lord. Please give me this new life you promise."

While dramatic transformations are not necessarily the norm in the spiritual life, this certainly was the case for Mazhar. That very day people in the military office in which he worked began to ask him what had happened to him, as the change in him was so visible. Not only did he begin immediately to experience a new life, but it seemed that the whole world came to life with him. Mazhar reflects, "I was not the only one given new life that moment. The whole world came alive with me. The sky was bluer, the flowers sweeter. I started to dance with joy. And people were different to me now. I discovered they all had beautiful faces. I literally went from hating people to being quite unable to live without being surrounded by them. Even my addictions ceased, as my tastes changed."

Mazhar's Golan Heights transformation experience was just the beginning of what would be an adventurous spiritual pilgrimage far beyond anything he could have ever imagined—all because of God's Spirit working through one humble Indian, Mahatma Gandhi, who did his best to live his life in the shadow of Christ as taught in the Sermon on the Mount.

Shortly after Mazhar's decision to follow Christ, Khalil Brieze, an intelligence officer in the military and member of the Muslim Brotherhood, utterly displeased with Mazhar's new faith, began to share false negative reports about him in order to discredit him. This smear campaign resulted in Mazhar being discharged from the Syrian army in 1961, a year and a half after his Golan Heights transformation. How beneficial it was to Mazhar to have been introduced to a life with Christ through Gandhi, as this greatly influenced Mazhar's approach to living out his new faith among his fellow Muslims.

Several years later, this same intelligence officer led a failed coup d'état in Syria, resulting in the Syrian government offering a reward of $25,000 for any information on his whereabouts. One day, in 1966, walking down Abdel Aziz Street, where he was living in Beirut, Mazhar happened to run into this same officer, who was still hiding from the Syrian government. Khalil was immediately afraid that Mazhar would turn him in to the Syrian authorities for the financial reward, especially after having wronged Mazhar a few years earlier by the smear campaign. However, Mazhar, in the spirit of Christ, hugged him warmly, invited him to his house, and instead of returning the hardship this man had brought upon him, took the approach of love; forgiving him and in grace introducing him to other exiled Syrian political leaders also in Beirut. Khalil, amazed at Mazhar's actions and ever grateful, opened doors for Mazhar with publishing houses of the Muslim Brotherhood, resulting in books about Christ being made officially available through their distribution channels in various conservative Muslim countries, even in Saudi Arabia.[14]

Discharged from the Syrian military, Mazhar headed for his hometown, unaware of the great hardship he would soon face. In reading about Christ's life in the Gospels on the Golan Heights, he had been much impressed with how much suffering Christ had had to undergo. This admiration for Christ's suffering would serve as the inspiration and encouragement he would need to persevere in the times of great difficulty that lay ahead.

Journeying among Muslims

2

No, I would not return. I would not look backwards. I had started as a traveler and as a traveler I would continue on my way. It was both decision and destiny, both vision and action, both beginning and end.

—NAGUIB MAHFOUZ (TAKEN FROM *THE JOURNEY OF IBN FATTOUMA*)

Family Honor Is Shaken

"IF YOU ARE NOT GOING TO CEASE being a Christian, then go and at least be a *good* Christian," Mazhar's uncle exhorted him. Amazingly, this was only three days after that same uncle had attempted to take Mazhar's life by slitting open his throat in public with a large knife.

When Mazhar initially returned to his hometown after having been expelled from the military, his family and his local community were both shocked and wonderfully pleased at the dramatic change in his life. He had left them as an irresponsible drunkard, and returned a completely different person. Instead of being aloof and isolating himself from others, he aggressively sought out ways to help them—even to the point of volunteering to cut the nails and wash the feet of his elderly uncle (something seen in that society as a lowly task, and therefore culturally considered a very honorable thing of someone of Mazhar's status to do). A few years later, Ahmed Swayden, a well-known Muslim writer from his hometown, wrote the introduction to Mazhar's first novel, *The Traveler*, which focuses on the transformation Christ can bring to a person, and in it Swayden described the tremendous difference he observed in Mazhar after his decision to follow Christ.

Though Mazhar's family was overcome with joy at the change they observed in him, it was Mazhar's insistence that it was all because he had become a "Christian" that caused them deep grief. Not understanding anything about his new faith in Christ, they felt as if their son or brother was rejecting them and all they believed in, loved, and stood for—culturally, socially, and spiritually. Also, they had secretly continued to hope that Mazhar would still someday become a Muslim cleric, and that was now an impossible dream. The only followers of Christ that Mazhar had met so far were Arab Protestant Christians, and therefore he naturally assumed, knowing of no other possible identity at the time, that following Christ made him "a Christian." However, the term "Christian" is a term loaded with negative associations in the Muslim context due as we have seen to the atrocities of the medieval Crusades, to the Church's link with Western colonialism, to the values of the "Christian" West, and to perceived lifestyles of many of the historic Arab Christians. Albeit with good intentions, having been influenced by the beliefs of the few Arab Christians he knew, but really with very little understanding of his own new "Christian" faith, Mazhar even went to the local mosque and shared with them his view that they were worshipping the wrong God. Understandably this provoked a strong reaction from both his family and the local Islamic community, and led to his being completely rejected by them. With their long history and rich culture, Syrians are a very proud people. Maintaining one's honor and avoiding shame at any cost, while important all over the Arab world, is especially so in Syria. Consequently, shortly after this, his uncle attempted to murder Mazhar directly in front of the local mosque for having shamed his family. A scar on Mazhar's neck still testifies to this attack. The attempted "honor killing" was a deliberate act to publicly clear his family's name in the community, thereby removing their shame. However, as the murder was not successful, Mazhar today believes that perhaps it was attempted with the intention of only appearing to be a murder. Mazhar was rushed to the hospital, unconscious. Upon his release three days later, he went to see the uncle who had tried to take his life. Mazhar told him how much he still loved him. It was then that the uncle, amazed at Mazhar's response, gave him his blessing and told him in that case to "go and be a *good* Christian," as opposed to the morally, religiously, and socially bad perception his community had of Christians otherwise, particularly those involved in what Muslims considered disreputable occupations—the selling of alcohol and prostitution.

Undeterred in his quest for a "Christian" identity, which is what local Christians were putting pressure on him to undertake, he tried to officially change his religion. However, in Syria, as in most Muslim countries, it is illegal for Muslims to convert to Christianity or otherwise change their religious identity. Even today, having been a follower of Christ for over thirty years, Mazhar is still registered as a Muslim, as are his Christian wife and their two children. When Mazhar submitted an application to the court in his province to change his religious identity, he was promptly called in by the provincial governor. The governor, who was from a traditional Muslim family, was very kind and listened to Mazhar's faith journey. He was so taken by the radical transformation that had resulted in Mazhar that he said to him, "I wish I had more time to listen to you, as I do want to know what really happened in your life. I don't know much about Islam, and I am not trying to make you return to it. Maybe I could walk with you in your journey. I would like to learn more. Do you have something I could read?" Nevertheless, knowing how delicate and sensitive of a situation Mazhar's desire to change his religious identity would be, the local governor advised him that it would not be possible, and strongly encouraged Mazhar to leave Syria, believing "any idiot could now kill you without having to have a reason." Mazhar sent him a New Testament not long after, and a few years later, when his first novel was published, sent him that as well.

Mazhar's decision to follow Christ was a revolutionary event in that small and completely Muslim town. Naturally the talk of the entire community, it still intrigues those living there. Over thirty years later, when Mazhar returned to live in Syria for a short time, an old acquaintance whom he had not seen all those years recognized him, and came over to welcome him. Immediately after the greetings, he asked, "So are you still following Christ?"[1] Another occurrence, albeit a humorous one, illustrates the long-term impact Mazhar's actions had on the entire community. More than thirty-five years after leaving Syria, while at the Tunis Book Fair in Tunisia, North Africa, Mazhar ran into a distant relative who did not recognize him. Immediately this relative began to recount the tragedy the Mallouhi family had suffered many years ago with "this person who brought shame on them all by becoming a Christian." Mazhar led the man on for a while, suggesting they get rid of him once and for all. The relative responded by saying, "He must have 'connections,' as he is one of the most public followers of Christ in the Arab World today and his books are everywhere, and he somehow doesn't seem to be afraid." Eventually Mazhar showed his relative the scar on his neck and with a smile asked him, "My uncle began here, do you want to finish it?" Until fairly recently, Mazhar was the only known person in his hometown of thirty thousand to have become a follower of Christ. However, the number of those in Mazhar's greater family following Christ today is slowly increasing—not officially as Christians, but instead in the manner Mazhar himself chooses: following Christ within their Islamic culture.

Exiled

Beirut, Lebanon

Unsure of where to go next, Mazhar decided to move to Brazil, as many Syrians were doing at the time. Local Arab Protestant Christians had strongly encouraged him to go to the West, as they thought only there could he be fully free to be a "Christian." However, his various emigration attempts to Brazil were not successful. With Lebanon bordering Syria, Mazhar packed up, said his goodbyes, left his hometown, and headed to Beirut, unaware that he would not be able to return for another thirty years.

Beirut had emerged as the new capital of Arabic literature and was considered the city of Arab enlightenment. Previously that position in the Arab world had been Cairo's, but the military rule of Egyptian president Gamal Abdul Nasser had begun to limit progressive thinking, stifle free press and speech, and persecute the intellectual community. Lebanon was considered a country of liberties, with its capital, Beirut, fostering a reputation as an emancipated city that allowed its residents much more freedom than any other Arab environment. This was a "neutral city," wrote Adonis, the pen name of the well-known Syrian writer and poet Ali Ahmad Said, who, in the late 1950s, also immigrated to Beirut.[2] Adonis himself had undergone great hardship in Syria because of his political affiliations. He had been hauled off to prison for a year following his graduation from the University of Damascus.[3]

In the early 1960s, when Mazhar arrived in Beirut, the life of letters was in ferment. This was a time when authoritarian leadership was the norm in many of the surrounding Arab countries. It seemed that whenever a nearby country exiled an aspiring or outspoken writer, he or she would end up in Beirut, a place where they could not only heal their wounds but build a new life in the nourishing literary and artistic context of cultural and political freedom. This "city of refuge" had attracted such great literary figures as the Syrian poets Nizar Qabbani and Adonis, Iraqi poets Buland Haidari and Abdul al-Wahhab al-Bayati, Palestinian poets Fayiz Suyyagh and Tawfiq Sayigh, and many others. Beirut made room for them all.[4] It was to this city, where the Arab literati were in full force, that Mazhar, the young writer and new follower of Christ, journeyed.

Mazhar relished the liberties of Beirut, understanding how treasured these freedoms were. It presented an environment that nurtured him and laid the artistic foundation of his writing life. Beirut also became the place that would shape him spiritually, in positive and negative ways, with many ramifications for years to come. Mazhar arrived in Beirut with a handful of names in his pocket entrusted to him by the Christian Syrian military officer who had given him a Bible when stationed on the Golan Heights. Through these few contacts he was soon able to find work at an American Presbyterian printing press, now known in Lebanon as the Librairie du Liban. From the beginning, however, he did not feel fully welcomed and was treated as an outsider; the local Arab Christians he met had deep reservations about Muslim converts. Exhibiting a continual lack of trust in him, they frequently questioned the genuineness of his decision to follow Christ, wondering if he had come to them instead for financial gain. Always second-guessing his motives, they kept him at a distance, even inferring at times that he might possibly be a spy in their midst on behalf of the Muslim authorities.

Mazhar also found these local Christians very much soured against Islam, and even "Arab culture," often choosing to practice their faith in culturally Western ways instead. They even sought to inspire him to hate Islam, his religious heritage, and his culture. While feeling uncomfortable with all of this, as a young man in a large city who had been ostracized from his family and community (something considered a curse in the Arab world), Mazhar deeply longed to be accepted by local Christians. In order to prove his authenticity, he found himself criticizing Islam, cutting off contact with all his Muslim friends, and attempting to remove from his life any traces of its religious culture. Welcoming this move on his part, local Christians strongly encouraged him to take a "Christian" name. At that time, most Muslim converts changed their names to give them a new Christian identity. However, after wrestling deeply with this for some time, he simply could not take such a step, believing that to do so would be to deny his own family. Nevertheless, he immersed himself completely in their Christian culture. Not only did his actions and his thinking change, so too did his use of the Arabic language; he took on Arabic Christian phraseology as opposed to the standard Arabic greetings and phrases the majority of Arabs use in the Middle East. Feeling the tremendous pressure to be accepted, Mazhar went overboard in his adoption of this new religious culture. He recalls friends from those times in a similar situation to his own who responded similarly and ended up mentally ill, to this day living in a state of paranoia about Islam.

In addition to entering into the local Arab Protestant Christian community, Mazhar had his first direct experience with Western Christians when he began to teach Arabic at an orphanage run by a U.S. church denomination. What struck him more than anything else when working there was how the Western missionaries who ran the orphanage kept the Arab children at a distance and were not really involved in their lives.

In the midst of the challenges of adopting and adapting to a new religious culture, Mazhar's own faith in Christ nevertheless grew. During those early years in Beirut he read the Bible through repeatedly, soaking it up and studying it intensely. It was also during this time that he developed a strong vision to write in order to communicate to other Muslims about this Christ who had so changed his life and whom he was seeking to follow. This would turn out to be his primary mission in life. Interestingly, this vision came to Mazhar when he himself was personally experiencing the great cultural and religious separation between Christians and Muslims. The deliberate isolation Christians felt from Muslims rendered them unable to communicate effectively with them about Christ. It was this desire to write for Muslim audiences about the person of Christ that led him to apply to the Lebanon Bible Institute, believing he needed to learn more about the Christian faith. The institute's enrollment included students from Lebanon, Syria, Egypt, and Iraq. Mazhar, knowing local Christians were still suspicious of his motives, determined to work and pay his own way through school instead of accepting the scholarship funding available, so as to not be dependent on Western Christian institutions like most of the students.

While he gained biblical and theological knowledge through his education there, he found the institute's staff to be extremely narrow in their thinking. "I felt that they were trying to close my mind to every aspect of life except that of the Bible," says Mazhar. Paradoxically, there were similarities with the teaching and worldview that he had experienced as a young boy in the Qur'anic school run by the Muslim Brotherhood. Mazhar was once even reprimanded by the principal of the Christian institute for reading Voltaire, and was forbidden to do so again. Today Mazhar describes the institute's staff as having been "fine people with fundamentalist ideas." He unfortunately found this overall experience to be spiritually and intellectually stifling.

In order to pay the college tuition fees, Mazhar found employment with a Christian publisher called the Arab Christian Literature Mission (formerly based in Cairo and called the Nile Mission Press, it was moved to Beirut after President Nasser's coming to power). The publishing house had recently appointed a new director by the name of Hugh Thomas, a Cambridge University graduate. Hugh was very familiar with the Middle East, having come to Lebanon from a posting in Yemen, studied Arab culture at Cambridge, and spent a couple years in Egypt. Unlike the other Westerners Mazhar had observed, Hugh genuinely loved the Middle East and found Arab culture rich and intellectually stimulating. Through asking Mazhar to help him improve his Arabic, with a special desire to learn the Muslim phrases and terminology, the two struck up a close and what was to become lifelong friendship. Hugh, coming from a cultured segment of society himself, albeit from England, loved the best of Arab music, literature, and the arts. Paradoxically, through their friendship, Mazhar found himself falling in love again with his own Arab culture. He fondly recalls the many evenings they would sit together on the rooftop and read and discuss Arab poets, listen to Arab music, and generally relish the richness of Arab culture. In this sense, Hugh Thomas informally "mentored" Mazhar back into his own culture. "He brought me back to my roots and contacts with Muslims again," recounts Mazhar.

As a publisher, Hugh was also in need of writers, and on learning about Mazhar's gift, encouraged him to begin to write. This was the stimulus Mazhar needed and he began to work earnestly on his first novel. His modern-day Arab prodigal story titled *The Traveler*, was first published in 1963 and was distributed throughout the Middle East, in Jordan, the West Bank, Iraq, Syria, and of course Lebanon. To date, *The Traveler* has sold over 120,000 copies. The success of his first novel confirmed to Mazhar that writing was an effective way in which to share with other Muslims about Christ, this treasure he had discovered. This experience also influenced the shape and style that his future novels would take—a focus on spiritual themes, often related to Jesus's teaching in the Gospels, in the mode of Tolstoy or Dostoevsky, writers that have greatly influenced his own faith and life. While living in Beirut, Mazhar went on to write four more novels in the same genre: *Miriam*, *The Fugitive*, *The Rebel*, and *Lost in the City*.[5]

Wanting their literary efforts to be more effective in communicating to Muslims, together Hugh and Mazhar began to reshape the publishing house, which until then had been particularly associated with the smaller Arab Christian segment of society. They made many strategic changes to help bring about this objective. They moved the publishing house office from a remote location in a Christian suburb of Beirut to the heart of the city, where all the other influential publishers, Muslim and non-religious, were located. In an attempt to broaden their market and be more sensitive to Muslims, they dropped the word "Christian" from their publishing house's name. They attempted to be more relevant to Muslims in the titles they selected, working hard to Arabize their books' design; up to this time books from Christian publishers in the Middle East tended to be quite Western in appearance. They soon began to build close business relationships with some of the most respected publishing enterprises in the Middle East, such as Dar Yaqada. Piggybacking on the distribution networks of these larger publishing operations, their own distribution channels spread throughout the Middle East, enabling many thousands of their books to be made available to the wider Arab Muslim world, even to countries like Saudi Arabia. As part of the book exchange arrangement, they would in return distribute some of the other publishing houses' titles to Christian circles, including a biography of the life of Muhammad.

It was during this period that Mazhar married a young Syrian woman by the name of Selwa, a gifted writer herself. She had originally come from a Catholic background, but was associated with a Protestant church community. Hugh Thomas, the person to whom Mazhar was closest in Beirut, actually traveled to the city of Homs in Syria to meet Selwa's family, representing Mazhar, who himself did not feel comfortable returning to his country. Most Christian Arab families did not allow their daughters to marry men from Muslim backgrounds. So it was often the case that such men would only be given the opportunity to marry Christian women whose families thought, for one reason or another, they would not be able to find a husband otherwise—which was considered shameful for an Arab woman and her respective family. Selwa had numerous problems, including some mental illness, and from the beginning the marriage had great difficulties. Nevertheless, in the four short years they were married, they were blessed with two children, a son, Hassan, and daughter, Miriam (who later died of leukemia at the age of twelve).

As Mazhar faced the challenges of this marriage, his friend Hugh was undergoing a crisis at the publishing house. The Christian owners had decided that their literature company should be very clear doctrinally on what it did and did not believe. A statement of faith was drafted that all senior foreign employees were expected to sign. However, Hugh Thomas disagreed with the document, feeling strongly that it was theologically much too narrow and conservative, and decided that as the director he could not sign it in good conscience. This conflict resulted in his resignation and return to England. A new director was appointed, an American with a very conservative Christian orientation. Soon after the new director took up the position, a local Arab Protestant minister complained to him about the biography of Muhammad which the publishing house was selling. Shocked to see that these titles existed on their shelves, the new director insisted they immediately be returned to the Muslim publisher with whom they had a partnership arrangement. Mazhar protested this decision with all his might, which resulted in a major struggle at the publishing house. Realizing he would lose the battle, he even went so far as to suggest they burn the books rather than return them, as this would not only break the unique partnership agreement that enabled their own books to be distributed throughout the Arab Muslim world, but it would also be considered very offensive and disrespectful culturally. Disregarding Mazhar's pleas, the new director returned the books and the publisher cancelled the partnership arrangement, returning every one of their titles, closing the door on all their distribution channels.

When Hugh Thomas left Beirut, emotionally and spiritually Mazhar began to sink. As Mazhar had been ostracized from his own family, Hugh had effectively become his older brother. With Hugh gone, he felt he had no one who understood or supported him. The family community is the single most important place where Arabs find their sense of identity and security. Without that or its surrogate in Hugh, and with his marriage in crisis and his work environment hostile, Mazhar began to flag.

It was about this time that an article Mazhar had written arguing against Christian Zionism was published, resulting in a strongly negative reaction against him from the Christian evangelical community (many evangelical Christians in Lebanon at that time were behind the establishment of the State of Israel). This article turned the tide of the local Protestant Arab Christians' perception of Mazhar. Having never fully trusted him because he had come from a Muslim background, they now began to pull away from him, treating him as a "black sheep" in their community. In addition, because of the marriage turmoil with his wife and then their eventual separation, the Christian community in Beirut in effect blacklisted him for the next ten years and sided with Selwa, as she was from a Christian family.

Unable to resolve their differences, his wife, Selwa, returned to Syria with their children. Back in Syria, with the purpose of keeping Mazhar away from the children, she sought to stir up political accusations about him in order to prevent him from ever returning to Syria. In the 1960s many Syrian political opposition leaders, out of grace with the authoritarian government in power, fled to Beirut. Mazhar already knew many of them, having been an active member of the Baath Party when he lived in Syria. While his contact with them in Beirut was not political, he maintained his friendships with them, even hosting them in his home from time to time. Among the individuals whom he befriended were the former president of Syria, Amin al Haafaz, as well as the former Syrian vice-president and prime minister. In 1970, Haafaz and his supporters moved to Iraq to be involved with the Iraqi Baath Party's activities against the Syrian regime. Attempting to implicate Mazhar using these opposition leaders, his wife Selwa turned over to the Syrian authorities the names of the political activists she had seen with him in Beirut. Saladin Ben Ohbed, a Tunisian lawyer and university professor active in creating peaceful East/West relationships, describes the political situation at the time: "The movement of Arab Nationalism had taken on an authoritarian form and the first agenda was to remove people like Mazhar Mallouhi from the scene."[6] Even Mazhar's close hometown friend, Muslim writer Ahmed Swayden (who wrote the introduction to Mazhar's first novel), was imprisoned for almost fifteen years due to his political outspokenness. Consequently, not long after this, as a result of the misinformation given to the Syrian security, there was a warrant out for Mazhar's arrest, which resulted in his official exile from Syria, his homeland.

The Kingdom of Morocco

In 1968, having lost his second family, his literary work, and his second home country, Mazhar entered into a period he refers to as his "dark night of the soul." Gratefully, he soon met a young American Christian named Greg, who had recently moved to Lebanon and who was also passionate about serving local Muslims. Greg and his organization, against the advice of local Christians, decided to befriend Mazhar and assist him, forming the beginning of a close friendship that continues to this day. Greg describes Mazhar at that time as being tremendously disappointed with the publishing house's insensitivity to Muslims and very hurt by and even resentful toward the local Christian community because of all the hardships he had experienced because of them. Greg recalls that Mazhar was so disgruntled with Christians that he would from time to time threaten their work in various ways. Completely disillusioned with the local Christian community, Mazhar left Beirut and headed to the farthest country away from Lebanon in the Arab world, the Kingdom of Morocco, in Northwest Africa.

A number of Mazhar's Syrian Muslim friends had moved to Morocco for business purposes; it was a place he felt he could start anew. "I left the Christian world, but kept my faith in Christ," reflects Mazhar. The original idea was for Mazhar to open a bookshop with funding assistance from Greg's organization, which was involved globally in book publishing and distribution. The support and funding did not materialize, so Mazhar began a coffee company in Casablanca that became quite successful. While the time in Morocco served to help Mazhar rebuild his life, including his financial stability, he was at the same time undergoing an intense spiritual crisis. With no indigenous Christian community in Morocco then, Mazhar was once again completely immersed in an Islamic culture, and Muslims supported and assisted him. The only Christian who kept encouraging Mazhar during this time of spiritual disillusionment was Hugh Thomas through his letters, though by now he had returned to England.

America

Gradually Mazhar healed, emotionally and spiritually. He regained his passion and sense of calling in life: to bridge the misunderstanding between Muslims and Christians through his own writing and the publishing of relevant literature explaining who Christ is in a culturally acceptable way. In the midst of this time of spiritual renewal, a Lebanese friend suggested he go to Canada to begin a new life. For some time Mazhar had been corresponding with someone in Canada interested in his life and work, so if he was ever to head to the West, this was a natural time and place to begin. After arriving in Canada and renting a room from a Polish family, Mazhar looked up his friend Greg, who had helped him back in Beirut and who was now living there. In seven months, Greg facilitated Mazhar's move to Southern California, where, as a special student, he entered a branch of Fuller Theological Seminary, the School of World Mission. The institution had a special programmatic focus on the Islamic World, and Mazhar was able to be of assistance to professors in some of the classes. While in California, he continued to develop a close friendship with Greg, a new brother ("new family") in his life. Greg had come to California to do graduate work in psychology. Following the completion of his studies, Greg moved to Aspen, Colorado, to serve as a pastor. Once Mazhar completed his studies at Fuller, he planned to move to Egypt to begin a publishing house.

Living in the U.S., Mazhar came to realize how wide the cultural and religious divide was between both the East and West, and Islam and Christianity. As he contemplated marriage once again, he began to pray for a Western wife, someone who could help him to bridge this gap and enable the West to better understand Islam and the Arab world. Unbeknownst to Mazhar at the time, a young Australian woman, Christine Hutchins, had also been praying for an Arab husband, having planned for many years to serve in the Middle East. Upon the completion of her theological training in Sydney, she agreed to take up a position in a desert hospital in Abu Dhabi, in the Gulf state of the United Arab Emirates. On her way to the Arabian Gulf, she stopped over in Southern California to attend a few lectures on Islam and the Middle East at the seminary where Mazhar was studying. Hearing Dr. Donald McGavaran, a professor, speak about the student on campus who was an Arab writer who followed Christ, she left him a message asking to meet him. Both passionate about living in the Arab world and serving Muslims, they shared an immediate affinity of heart. Discovering they had similar dreams and life visions, Mazhar began to talk about the possibility of her joining him in Egypt, instead of her continuing with her plans to go to the Gulf. Serendipitously, due to various organizational complications related to her working with the hospital in Abu Dhabi, Christine was required to extend her stay in the U.S., giving her a natural opportunity to contemplate a change in destination.

Cairo, Egypt

Mazhar and Christine soon became engaged and Mazhar left for Egypt to begin setting up a publishing operation, returning for their wedding four short months later. Having met only six months earlier, they were married in Aspen on December 31, 1975. "We had the sense that this was somehow a divinely arranged marriage," says Christine today. Now, over thirty years later, having served all over the Arab world as a team, it is clear that it is indeed a very special union.

Beginning married life in Cairo was not without its difficulties. The vision had been to found a publishing house, and yet the lack of funding prevented this from taking place. Instead, Mazhar and Christine lived among the Egyptian people, serving in various ways those primarily from the lower economic segment of society; they too found their own financial situation extremely difficult. There were months, due to all their hosting of local Egyptian Muslims, that they would spend more money on sugar (enjoyed in large quantities when serving tea Middle Eastern–style) than they did on the rent for their apartment. In order to help pay the bills, Mazhar started a small business selling artifacts.

Having recently come out of the Nasser era, Egypt was in an economic depression, with the population increase having overtaken the economic growth. Though President Nasser, the popular leading figure of the Arab Nationalism movement, had focused on establishing social programs to improve the living and working conditions of the peasants and workers, the masses in Egypt were still extremely poor. The new president, Anwar Sadat, attempting to reverse Nasser's socialist programs by opening the doors wide to capitalism and the West, greatly increased the gulf between the rich and the poor. Sadat also began to distance Egypt politically and religiously from the rest of the Arab world. Consequently, Islamic opposition groups began to form in reaction to Sadat's capitalistic and secularist agenda for Egypt, leading to his eventual assassination by Islamic fundamentalists on October 6, 1981.

In Cairo, Mazhar teamed up initially with another Syrian, Abdul Massih Hamra, who also loved Muslims and had a similar passion to introduce them to the person of Jesus in a culturally sensitive manner. Together they worked almost exclusively with Muslims, without any official contact with the Christian churches. The few local Christians they related to were those also interested in the work they were doing among Muslims. Seeking to help the local Egyptian Christians appreciate and love Muslims more, Mazhar would bring Muslim sheiks to speak with them about Islam, who in turn would take him to the mosque. Mazhar became good friends with various Muslim sheiks, including those working at the famous Al Azhar Mosque in Cairo, the intellectual and spiritual heart of Sunni Islam (to which the majority of Muslims in the world ascribed). A particular emphasis for Mazhar at that time was to encourage Egyptian Christians to socialize and develop friendships with their Muslim brothers and sisters, and to actually be involved in their lives. The relational divide between Christians and Muslims was very wide at the time. A Westerner living in Egypt at that time recalls some local Christians once making contact with Mazhar to ask him to help them understand how to better share their Christian faith with Muslims. Yet when Mazhar asked to meet their local Arab Muslim friends, their response was that they didn't have any. Mazhar's work at the time greatly influenced the local Arab Christians toward focusing on serving their Muslim neighbors in the spirit of Christ. A local Egyptian Christian leader reflects on the impact of Mazhar's role at that time: "In those days [late 1970s] not one church was open to work among Muslims, and no one was even thinking about it. It was like hitting a rock. But [Mazhar] showed us it could be done even in those hard times. If [Mazhar] hadn't showed us it was possible, we wouldn't be here today working with Muslims."

During those years literally hundreds of Muslims passed through the Mallouhi apartment every month. Christine and Mazhar opened their home to people in need—whether Mazhar had found them in the street or they were brought to them through friends—attempting through this to demonstrate God's love for each individual. It was not long until a number of Muslims, attracted to the Christ that Mazhar followed, took faith steps similar to his own in their spiritual journeys. Together with a small local group of Christians, they would pray and study the Scriptures together in an informal gathering on a converted rooftop structure with church pews; Coptic Orthodox icons that lined the walls aided their worship. It was an exciting time, as their small group of fifteen grew quickly to eighty. They would sing for hours, pray, study the Bible, and then share a meal afterwards.

During this time, Mazhar's own spiritual nourishment came partially through the writings of Matta Meskin, a Coptic Orthodox monk known for his deep Eastern spirituality—presently based at St. Marcarius monastery in the Wadi Natrun area of Egypt. Mazhar also led weekly study groups of the Christian Scriptures, some gatherings were just with Muslims interested in learning about Jesus, and others were mixed, Christians and Muslims. Frequently visiting with sheiks in mosques, Mazhar had a unique relationship with Rev. Dr. Harold Vogelaar, the pastor of an international church in Cairo, who greatly impressed him with his love and openness toward Muslims. Desiring to learn more about Islam, Vogelaar would go to mosques and dialogue with sheiks and Muslim leaders. However, when they in turn had questions about Christ and even Christianity, he would introduce them to Mazhar. Dr. Vogelaar had some especially good relationships at the renowned Al Azhar Mosque, and he would often take Mazhar with him. It was a unique collaborative relationship, with both Christians and Muslims benefiting.

Life in Cairo was so busy that Mazhar struggled to find time for writing. However, Rev. Labib Mashriki, the head of the Presbyterian church in Egypt (Synod of the Nile), the largest Protestant denomination in the country, took Christine Mallouhi aside and shared with her his belief that Mazhar, her husband, was the only follower of Christ he knew of who could write so as to effectively communicate to the hearts of Muslims. He went on to suggest that one of the most important things she could do in life was to guarantee that Mazhar kept writing. With this encouragement, Mazhar worked on revising an unpublished manuscript he had written earlier. Shortly after, he published his novel *The Long Night*, which examines the human struggle for freedom through the life of a Syrian youth, and his exploration of Christ.

The growth of Mazhar's and his colleagues' various activities eventually attracted the attention of the secret police, and they began to note that they were under surveillance. President Nasser had established a vast secret police force in Egypt, the Muxhabaraat, modeled after the Soviet police system, with which he collaborated closely. Ironically, the local Protestant churches were not supportive of the work Mazhar was doing with Muslims, as they were concerned that it might destabilize their own status quo with the Muslim governmental authorities. One of the key local pastors even began to spread false rumors about their work. Some Christian leaders forbade their staff from having contact with Mazhar, considering him too radical in his thinking to be safe. Eventually, Mazhar was called in for questioning by the local authorities. It became apparent that someone in the Christian community had leaked to the police the names of all the Egyptians meeting with him, both Christian and Muslim. As it was evident that a crackdown was taking place—some individuals already having disappeared—many were concerned that Mazhar himself would be arrested. One night Mazhar and Christine returned home to find a police patrol wagon out front. Knowing the police had come to take Mazhar away, instead of entering the couple walked around the block making plans for what seemed his impending imprisonment. After deciding what Christine would do if Mazhar was taken away, they returned to the house holding hands as they prayed for strength. Christine was nine months pregnant. Thankfully, the police had already gone, but before doing so had interrogated the landlord about Mazhar. One of Mazhar's close Egyptian colleagues, another follower of Christ from a Muslim background, was not so lucky, and disappeared under strange circumstances. His older brother had appeared at his workplace and announced to the employer that his brother would not be returning. From that point on, no one ever heard from him again. The suspicion is that his family may have killed him as a result of his decision to follow Christ.

Living in a polluted, dusty, and overcrowded city like Cairo, which today has a population of over 22 million, is difficult enough. However, experiencing constant police surveillance, two near-death car accidents, the birth of their first child, a son, the strain of living with the tensions between the Muslim and Christian communities in Egypt, the lack of time and space to write, and the lack of support from local churches for their work combined to make life very emotionally draining for Mazhar and Christine during this time.

Morocco Revisited

About this time, Mazhar had a dream about the king of Morocco, who was polishing the entrance door of a house. In the dream, Mazhar asked him why he was polishing the door and the king said, "For you when you come here." Not long after this, the Mallouhis received an invitation from Western friends to move to Morocco, a place with which Mazhar was already well acquainted. After such an intense and exciting time in Egypt, the beautiful North African Arab Kingdom of Morocco sounded very appealing—a country bordering the Atlantic Ocean, with a rich history, ancient cities, and the beautiful snow-capped Atlas mountains. Morocco's religious context was very different from that of Egypt, as there was no indigenous historic Christian community. The only official Christians in the country were Westerners. In the fall of 1979, the Mallouhis headed to Morocco, with Mazhar making the long journey by driving from Cairo, through Europe, to Casablanca.

Unexpectedly, their beginning in Morocco was beset with various complications. The Mallouhis did not receive the warm welcome they expected from the local Western Christian community. They had understood that their American contacts there would host them for a short time while they looked for a place to live, but once in Morocco, no such offer was made, and they were forced to stay in a damp, rundown hotel, with Christine expecting their second son. It transpired that the American Christians, being very theologically conservative, did not approve of Mazhar's divorce and remarriage, and wanted him to prove himself before they associated with him. Upon learning a few weeks later of the lack of hospitality extended to them, the few Moroccan followers of Christ were shocked; had these Christians known the Mallouhis at the time, generous Arab hospitality would have been extended to them. Instead, just as Mazhar had experienced in Beirut years before, the American fundamentalist Christians appeared to live by the letter of their law, not by grace. So it was Mazhar's Muslim Syrian friends, the ones he had known in the 1960s when he ran a coffee company in Morocco, who were thrilled to have Mazhar back and invited the family to meals every day while they were in transition. Ahmed Aisa, a wealthy book distributor and philanthropist, and his family were particularly hospitable. So once again, while the Christians rejected them, the Muslims welcomed the Mallouhis with open hearts and homes.

Not long after their arrival, a country-wide Christian meeting was scheduled for which they signed up. While some of the Western Christians were kind to them, most did not treat them warmly. The Mallouhis quickly observed that many negative things were said about Moroccans and the country itself; a number of the children present had obviously been influenced by this line of thinking. As opposed to finding a home in Casablanca, which had been the original plan, they decided to settle in the ancient city of Fez, distancing themselves from these foreign Christians.

Fez turned out to be the perfect place for their work. Mazhar, needing to produce an income beyond just his writing, began to develop a carpet business. Morocco, the land of the ancient Berber tribes, is known around the world for its beautiful and exotic rugs. Quickly learning the field, Mazhar became known as one of the most successful carpet dealers and earned great respect within the diplomatic and business communities. He assisted foreign groups in various ways, such as a carpet raffle to raise donations for the charity arm of an American expatriate association. At a large gathering, even the U.S. ambassador's wife presented Mazhar with a gift honoring him for his business and charitable efforts.

However, Mazhar's primary passion continued to be sharing about Christ with fellow Muslims. One benefit of the carpet business was that Mazhar naturally had contact with the full scope of Moroccan society, from Berber tribes on the edge of the desert who wove the rugs, to the highest echelons of those in diplomatic circles who purchased them. Increasingly, during this time in Morocco, as Mazhar shared with Muslims about Christ, he found himself doing so in more contextualized ways—as he himself continued his slow, but steady, return journey to the Arab and Islamic culture from which he came, albeit as a follower of Christ. As in Cairo, he and his wife began to host informal meetings in their home with Muslims interested in learning more about Nabi Isa (Jesus's name in the Qur'an). Sometimes up to thirty people would attend these gatherings. However, as individuals chose to follow Christ and his way, very often they were shunned by their families, with the result that many either ran away or ceased pursuing their new faith in Christ. To address this sad plight, Mazhar slowly began to focus on various Islamic ways of following Christ, such as encouraging the use of audiocassettes that chant the Gospels in the Islamic Qur'anic tradition.

Muhammad is a fascinating example of someone who decided to follow Christ during this period. Highly educated, having obtained his doctorate in Sharia (Islamic law), and a key member of the Muslim Brotherhood, he served in a prominent mosque in the country. After learning about Christ, he made a decision to follow his way, yet selected to stay within his own religious community. As a follower of Christ, he found himself desiring to worship God all the more reverently, with "his whole being, body and spirit." So Mazhar encouraged him to continue using the Muslim prayer postures and even chant the Psalms as prayers, similarly to how the Qur'an is chanted by Muslims. Today, many years later, Muhammad continues in his faith in Christ, but does so deep within the heart of a Moroccan mosque, not desiring to have contact with a Christian community.

Always facing the challenge of finding enough time to write in the midst of running a business, Mazhar nevertheless finished another novel while living in Morocco. Titled *Moment of Death*, the novel powerfully explores the reality of human suffering, particularly as experienced by some in the Arab world.

As Mazhar continued to bridge the two faiths through the person of Christ, some individuals on both sides of the divide naturally became uncomfortable. Interestingly, many of the tensions Mazhar has experienced come first from the Christian side, and then are quickly mirrored by the Muslims. This was the situation in Morocco. Some Iraqi followers of Christ living in Morocco who desired to leave the Muslim world and immigrate to the West became very antagonistic toward Mazhar when he chose to not give them the financial support to do so, but instead strongly encouraged them to stay in the Arab World. Once they had succeeded in immigrating to the U.S., they wrote a poisonous letter with false accusations against Mazhar to the Moroccan security. Soon after, the Mallouhis' residence visa application was refused. After eleven years, Fez had become their home. Unclear of where to move next, Mazhar and Christine, together with their two young sons, drew straws with different Arab countries' names on them, and Egypt was the one chosen.

Egypt: Amidst the Rise of Muslim Fundamentalism

Egypt had changed greatly since they left in 1979. Throughout Cairo, billboards announced, "Islam is the solution." During the decade they had been away, a quickly growing Islamic conservatism had taken root. The developing Muslim fundamentalist movement was very visible. During the 1970s, when the Mallouhis had last lived in Egypt, only about 2 percent of the women wore veils. In 1990, when they moved back, up to 75 percent were veiled in one way or another. This conservative Islamic trend made many Egyptian Christians feel increasingly threatened; the relational divide between the two had widened.

Soon after arriving in Cairo, three of Mazhar's books were published in the general market. Known as a writer who was passionate about helping Muslims discover the Christ mentioned in their own holy book, the Qur'an, Mazhar had many people come to him with questions, both Muslims and Christians. Daily Mazhar could be found sitting in the popular Cairo cafes, discussing matters of faith. Together with friends, Mazhar would often go to Al Azhar Mosque for a time of private prayer and the study of the Gospels. Sitting together on the beautiful Oriental carpets, they would read the New Testament together, and very often people interested in learning about the teachings and person of Christ would join them.

Mazhar would visit with the sheiks and talk with them about breaking down the walls that too often divide Muslims and Christians. He had a particular concern for the fundamentalists.

One of Mazhar's friends, who was a follower of Christ, was a local sheik at a mosque in the Islamic section of Cairo. Mazhar had met him during his time in Egypt almost fifteen years earlier. Not only was the sheik still loyally following Christ, but he now had over twenty other sheiks studying the New Testament with him. Captivated by the person of Christ, and seeking to live according to his teachings, the sheik recounted to Mazhar what was to him a miraculous experience: how God had helped him in a time of crisis as he prayed for help in the name of Jesus. Once in the middle of the night, his daughter suddenly began to hemorrhage in a life-threatening way. As there was no local medical service, they rushed her to the nearest clinic, knowing that it typically either had long lines or was closed. Some years earlier, a relative of the sheik had hemorrhaged to death in the waiting room of just such a clinic. As they drove through the city, the sheik, afraid for his daughter's life, cried out to God in the name of Jesus for help. It just so happened that a doctor was standing at the door as they arrived at the clinic and immediately attended to her, saving her life.

Once when a group of American students studying comparative religion was in Cairo, Mazhar took them to visit with sheiks at Al Azhar Mosque. However, as it was a public holiday, the mosque was closed to everyone except tourists and no sheiks were around. With the prayer room almost empty, they sat barefoot, and in that quiet atmosphere Mazhar began explaining the tenets of Islam and religious practices. Soon a lone worshipper approached and started listening in. Mazhar warmly welcomed him and invited him to join them, learning that he was a schoolteacher and sheik from Yemen that had studied Islam in Saudi Arabia. Instead of Mazhar continuing to share about Islam, he requested the Yemeni sheik to answer the American students' questions. To their surprise, he began to give them some unusual answers to their questions, and even criticized the lack of freedom women had in Yemen. During their discussion, Mazhar asked him if he had ever read the Gospels (al Injil). He responded that he had always wanted to, ever since hearing a verse from the Gospels that said, "Forgive us our sins as we forgive those who sin against us." However, when studying in Saudi Arabia at an Islamic seminary, he was told it was forbidden to read the Gospels and that the seminary teachers instead would tell him everything he needed to know about Christ. "Since then I have wanted to know for myself why they forbade me to read the Gospel. And every time I travel outside Yemen I look for a copy of the Injil, but I have never found one. I even asked here at Al Azhar and they couldn't give me one." Mazhar took him home that day and gave him a copy of the New Testament in Arabic. Reading was not easy for the sheik as one of his eyes was diseased, paining him greatly and watering constantly, but he stayed at Mazhar's home and read for ten hours straight before returning to his hotel by the mosque.

Every remaining day of his stay in Egypt this sheik visited with Mazhar, discussing Christ and his teachings, sometimes in the mosque, other times over meals at their apartment. In order to learn more about Christ, he extended his stay in the country. So enthusiastic was he about what he was learning, that once on the telephone, he loudly announced to Mazhar that he should come to the mosque and teach them about Jesus, "as they don't know anything about him here." Mazhar did his best to advise him of the sensitivities, as freedom to change religion was not permitted in Egypt. However, all attempts to encourage him to be more circumspect fell on deaf ears. After studying the New Testament for several weeks, he announced that he would like to be baptized as a follower of Christ. Encouraging him to reflect more on the potential negative ramifications of such a decision only led the sheik to insist all the more on his immediate baptism. "I have been searching for the truth of Christ for thirty years and now I have found him; I don't want to lose any more time. I am going back to Yemen to share what I have found." Aware that no church in Cairo would baptize him due to the sensitivities with the Muslim authorities, and being far from the Mediterranean, he ended up being baptized in an apartment. Just before his baptism, he said, "Give me my glasses. I want them baptized as well so I can always see God's newness of life." So the glasses were baptized also.

During the sheik's remaining time in Cairo, he spent most of his time studying the Scriptures and praying, and visiting the Al Azhar Mosque to share about Christ. His eye condition continued to worsen, making it difficult for him to read for extended periods of time. He then began to use audiocassettes of the New Testament, which enabled him to listen for hours on end. Finally, he left to return to Yemen, needing to stop over in Saudi Arabia on the way for eye treatment. While in Saudi Arabia, he discovered his eye was cancerous and that it had to be removed. The Mallouhis received one letter from him while he was in Saudi Arabia, and this was the last time they heard from him. As the Gulf War broke out then, being in Saudi Arabia with a Yemeni passport most probably caused him some difficulties. They never knew whether he actually made it back to Yemen. Two years later, while Mazhar was visiting Yemen, he went to look for the sheik in his hometown, but could not find him.

With the rise of Muslim fundamentalism, the Egyptian authorities were very concerned to eliminate anything that might potentially "disturb or destabilize society." In addition, with the likelihood of war between the United

States and Iraq in the near future, the Egyptian government decided to pre-empt any local tensions by rounding up and imprisoning those they considered a possible threat. Thousands of Muslim fundamentalists were arrested, while others were falsely implicated along with them. Some simply disappeared. Many Egyptians had family members in prison who had no link whatsoever with the fundamentalists. Even foreign Arabs were detained or arrested upon entering the country, apparently simply because their beards made them look like the stereotypical Islamic fundamentalist. The arrests became so widespread that some people were afraid to pray in a mosque, and instead did so in their homes.

The Christian communities also suffered. Egyptian followers of Christ from Muslim backgrounds were beginning to be officially harassed. Many were called in for interrogation by the secret police. Some were arrested and imprisoned. Tragically, among those locked up, some were subject to systematic beatings and torture. Even a number of foreign Christians were deported, often after spending some time in jail. Friends of the Mallouhis were threatened with "disappearing" by the secret police if they didn't disclose all the information the police wanted—names of followers of Christ from Muslim backgrounds. A number of their friends were on the authorities' wanted list. A tense environment of fear and suspicion emerged. Many Christians and Muslims with family members or contacts in the West began the process of emigrating out of Egypt.

Finding a sensitive meeting place for their motley crew, composed of both Christians and followers of Christ from Muslim backgrounds, was not an easy task. Meeting together in their homes became dangerous, as the authorities were beginning to clamp down on house meetings. Instead, they would often meet on a felucca, a Nile sailboat. Over an Egyptian feast, twenty-five to thirty of them would sing, pray, and study the Scriptures as they floated up and down that great river.

The Mallouhis continued to live their lives generously, open to all. A rainbow variety of people would float through their home each week. Yet from the time of their initial return to Egypt they knew they were under tight surveillance. Three months after their arrival, Mazhar received a summons to report to the local police. Pulling out their old security file on him, they questioned him about his friends and relationships outside of Egypt. Sensing their phone was tapped, they became aware their home was one of many being watched. They surprisingly found it very difficult to keep their house help, going through nine different women in a few months. With unemployment high, and the pay good, they initially couldn't understand why these women always left. Only later did they realize that the police, of whom the house help were very afraid, were forcing them to spy on the Mallouhis.

One incident involving Mazhar most certainly drew the authorities' attention to him as a potential "disturber" of society. As Mazhar and his friends were sitting in Al Azhar Mosque meditating on the Gospels, others nearby noticed that they were reading from the Bible. They started inquiring about the Gospels and Christ, which resulted in a friendly and open interfaith dialogue. Other Muslim worshippers eventually joined in and the group swelled to thirty people, all sitting in a circle around the Bible, discussing Christ and Islam very naturally. After some time, another worshipper walked in, and, seeing the Bible open, reacted very aggressively and began yelling at the top of his voice, while beating his head and body, "Allahu Akbar, al Injil fil Azhar, Kafrun" (God is Great! Blasphemy! The Gospel is in Al Azhar). The Muslims in the circle attempted to quiet him down with no success. Soon a large crowd began gathering and the local mosque police were summoned. The Muslims in the group explained to the police that they were having a quiet discussion and this stranger had come in and did not understand what was really happening. They went on to say to the police, "We just want to know about the truth of Christian belief. We have the right to know." Promptly told by the police that they would be the ones to tell them what to believe, they were ordered not to talk further with Mazhar or his friends. Evicted from the premises, Mazhar and his friends, followed by some Muslim worshippers, went to a café. The Muslims, embarrassed by the way Mazhar had been treated, apologized for what had happened, and asked him to continue coming to the mosque to share with them. However, this incident was most likely recorded in Mazhar's file with the Ministry of Interior.[7]

As in previous situations, the opposition Mazhar experienced did not just come from conservative Muslim circles, but also from the local Christians. The deportation of a key Arab Christian leader who was serving among Muslims shocked the Christian community. It was soon learned that there was concrete evidence that other church leaders were part of the reason for his deportation. Government informants were often planted in the churches and one was never sure exactly who they were. Fearing the authorities, some pastors and priests, in order to protect themselves, would report Muslims who were inquiring about Christ. The head of the Protestant Federation of Churches vocalized his displeasure among the Christian community with Mazhar's overt work with Muslims. At the same time, one of the most prominent Protestant church pastors in the country told people attending his church, both Christians and followers of Christ from a Muslim background, to stay away from Mazhar, spreading the rumor that he was part of the Egyptian intelligence. Mazhar hardly knew the pastor, but realized that within Egypt these were serious charges, so he did his best to keep away from that pastor's territory. Nevertheless, those from a Muslim background attending this pastor's church continued to seek out Mazhar, not feeling fully welcomed or at home in the church, as it was such a culturally Christian context.

Eventually, Mazhar was called in to the police a second time for questioning. Not long after, during one of their felucca meetings on the Nile, someone shared about how four young men from Muslim backgrounds who were following Christ had recently been called into the police and had not been seen again. Afraid that they might be being tortured, they asked for Mazhar's help, as their local church would not get involved. Mazhar went with them to the police station, requesting to see the imprisoned young men. The police did not admit they were being held, but did record Mazhar's name. The church community hired a lawyer to represent the prisoners, and Mazhar and others with ties to Western diplomatic circles called for pressure to get these young men released. They were held for two months, undergoing great trials. Following their release, the lawyer notified Mazhar that his name, and those of some of his friends, had come up with the Egyptian intelligence service during the investigation.

One afternoon while the Mallouhis' ten-year-old son, Tarek, was in their apartment with a friend, an undercover policeman barged in and began to search through their home office. Ever since the assassination of President Sadat, the government of Egypt had implemented a state of emergency rule, which gave the police and security forces the right to search homes without warrants and also to arrest people without formal charges. While looking through their files, he questioned their son about who his parents' friends were, among other subjects. In totalitarian regimes, authorities often question children to glean information with which they can formally charge their parents. Young Tarek did not answer the questions and did all he could to force the man to leave, even going so far as to pull out a curved dagger, a curio from another country, and threaten him with it. Eventually the man departed, leaving a summons for Mazhar to appear at police headquarters.

Following this incident, the Mallouhis, together with others, began to talk about the possibility that one of them might be imprisoned, even going so far as to prepare items they might want to take with them, as the situation in the Egyptian prisons was so miserable. Developing a contingency plan seemed like the wise thing to do. They also began to learn of other foreigners being expelled, making them wonder if they too might be asked to leave. Christine recalls Mazhar telling her, "They won't expel me because they know I love them." She rightly warned him, "Love is the most powerful weapon. They cannot fight love." It was a prophetic response.

A few weeks later Mazhar received a summons to report to Egyptian security headquarters. When he didn't return by midday, his friends went to find him, discovering that he was under arrest. Telephoning Christine a few hours later, Mazhar said he was being immediately deported, and requested of Christine his passport and enough money for a plane ticket. In dismay and a state of shock, Christine, together with friends, put together the items Mazhar needed. Upon arriving at the security office, Christine found Mazhar arguing with the senior official over the cause of arrest. Mazhar said, "If I have something against Egypt then take me to the court and sentence me. If I have done anything to harm Egyptians then I deserve punishment. What are the charges?" The senior official looked at him and simply responded, "You know." The security policeman assigned to Mazhar was a kind man and seemed ashamed by the proceedings. Together with an armed guard he sent Mazhar and Christine to purchase an airline ticket. The first flight out was to be the next day, which would mean that Mazhar would spend the night in jail.

Returning to the headquarters, the senior officer ordered to have Mazhar sent straight to jail until his departure the following day. These plans would not allow him to say goodbye to their two sons. Thankfully, Mazhar was able to convince the sympathetic guard put directly in charge of him to kindly agree to take him by the apartment on the way to jail. By this time the word was out on the streets that Mazhar was being deported, and when he was brought by to see his sons, their home was full of people wanting to be supportive and helpful in the crisis. Others were there realizing that they were losing someone they considered their "father." Many were crying in grief. The Egyptians were complaining, saying, "How can they do this to a friend of Egypt? What will become of us when they throw out the good people and keep the criminals?" Everyone brought food, and as Christine describes that evening, "It was a cross between a wake and a going away party." Even the Egyptian guard, who was risking getting in trouble with his superior by stopping at their home, ended up taking a group photo for them. However, not compromising his honor, he refused to accept any food offered him, knowing he was part of the apparatus that was deporting Mazhar. Following a short time of private encouragement and counsel to Christine and the boys, Mazhar left with the guard. One of the young followers of Christ from a Muslim background for whom the police were searching was so distraught about Mazhar's expulsion that he overcame his fear of being arrested and accompanied him to the airport.

Mazhar spent his last night in Egypt in a jail sleeping on the floor in his suit. Most of those in the cell with him were Muslim fundamentalists. When they asked him why he had been jailed, Mazhar shared that while he was not certain, it seemed to him that it was because he was discussing his faith in Christ with other Muslims. Hearing this, an elderly and bearded fundamentalist Muslim sheik kindly shared his blanket with Mazhar and another, bearded and skullcapped, shared his food with him. The following day, November 13, 1990, Mazhar was escorted under armed guard to the airplane; he was officially deported. No charges were ever pressed. His passport was simply stamped "overstayed visa," even though the visa issued in that same passport was good for many more months. To this day he has not been allowed to reenter the country.

It was decided that Christine should stay with the boys in Cairo for another seven months so they could finish their school year. Many continued to express deep sadness at Mazhar's arrest and deportation. In their apartment, visitors sat around crying. The landlord of the apartment inquired about Mazhar and said, "We are really shocked that our country has come to this point of expelling her friends. Poor Egypt, where are we going?" A well-known Egyptian Muslim author sent Mazhar a message apologizing on behalf of his government. The support from Muslims greatly encouraged Christine; "These Muslims' messages of support and sympathy displayed the difference between regimes and people. Some regimes made life difficult, but Muslim individuals respected and supported us."[8]

As the Gulf War loomed, Christine began to put the pieces of her life together for a phase without Mazhar's presence. Mazhar began to plan a travel itinerary that would take him throughout the Arab World during that same period, helping those working to bridge the gap between Islam and Christianity through the person of Christ. Two short months later, the Middle East would become a war zone, capturing the Western world's attention as perhaps never before. And Mazhar would soon be entering the final phase of a faith journey that would take him home, geographically, culturally, and spiritually.

Discovering Home

3

In the desert is an oasis that is the hope of him who has lost his way.

—SHEIK ABD-RABBIH AL-TA'IH (THE SAINTLY SUFI SHEIK
CREATED BY NAGUIB MAHFOUZ IN HIS WRITINGS)

In the Land of St. Augustine

ST. AUGUSTINE OF NORTH AFRICA, the renowned early fifth-century Christian bishop and prolific writer closely associated with the ancient city of Carthage, penned these words about his experience with God, "You have touched me and I have been translated into your peace."[1] Little did Mazhar know how profoundly those words would reflect the developments in his own spiritual pilgrimage with God as he arrived in the city of Tunis/Carthage in what is today the country of Tunisia.

After the unsettling experience of being deported from Egypt, during a time of transition and separation from his family, Mazhar received an invitation from Christians living in Tunisia to come and assist the newly developing groups of Tunisian followers of Christ from Muslim origins.

This was a much different Tunisia than that of St. Augustine's time. A small progressive Arab Muslim country, Tunisia is often considered a pacesetter in today's Islamic world. As a former protectorate of France, Tunisia has been strongly influenced by French culture through its educational and legal systems. Proud of its liberal heritage, Tunisia's goal is moderation in all things, even in religion. Consequently Tunisians are against any form of fundamentalism or fanaticism. Tunisia's first post-colonial president, the visionary Habib Bourguiba, led the march for the emancipation of women, outlawing polygamy and opening the way for their education, resulting in Tunisia today being the only Muslim country where monogamy is the law and women have equal legal rights with men. With Bourguiba encouraging education for all, a majority middle class emerged.

On the religious front, while Tunisia is today a Muslim country, both secularism and materialism have significantly influenced the spiritual climate of the country due to its strong association with France for two generations. While there is no historic indigenous Christian presence, as exists in the Middle East, Tunisia nevertheless has a rich Christian heritage, dating from the era of early antiquity. Tunisian history dates back to 10,000 BC with the indigenous Berber peoples. Eventually the ancient Phoenicians, with their seafaring conquering ways, occupied this part of North Africa, and Carthage became their key western port. Following the Punic Wars between Rome and Carthage (263 BC–146 BC), Tunisian territory became the property of the Roman Empire, and Carthage the capital of Rome's African holdings. Agriculture emerged as all-important, and Tunisia's wheat fields became the breadbasket for over 60 percent of the empire. The Romans laid down an elaborate road network throughout North Africa, greatly facilitating travel to the many cities they founded around the region.

It was during Roman occupation that the Christian faith was brought to North Africa; the famous city of Carthage became one of the most important sees of the Church during the first six centuries following Christ's death—alongside the cities of Alexandria, Jerusalem, Rome, Antioch, and Constantinople. During the early days of Tunisian Christianity under the Romans, many Christians underwent persecution. Perpetua and Felicitas, two young women, were the first known Tunisian Christian martyrs, executed for their Christian faith in AD 202 inside the ancient amphitheater whose ruins are still visible today on the outskirts of Carthage. Over the first three centuries after Christ the Church in North Africa grew, first gaining acceptance, then legal status, until Christianity was eventually recognized as the official religion of the Roman Empire. Carthage became the Christian metropolis of Africa and the second see after Rome in the western Church. Some of the most colorful Christian names during that era are associated with Carthage—such as Tertullian, St. Cyprian, Aurelius, and St. Augustine of Hippo. Notably, it was at the famous Council of Carthage held in AD 397 that the first complete canon of the New Testament books was published.

After the fall of Rome in 412 BC, Tunisia was overtaken first by the Vandals, and then by the Byzantines of Constantinople, who ruled there for 150 years. Due to their exploitative policies, however, they alienated themselves from the indigenous Berber population. It was also a time when the ramifications of the Christian Church's many years of preoccupation with fighting against purported theological heresies and other schisms began to show, permanently weakening it. The Church in North Africa was essentially Roman in culture, and therefore Latin in language. It had never truly become indigenized among the Berber peoples. With the fall of the Roman Empire, the Church found itself increasingly lost, as if without a parent, and consequently its influence in society diminished significantly. Islam burst on to the scene in the seventh century, sweeping eastward out of Arabia, quickly conquering Egypt. In AD 642–643 the Muslims began their invasion of North Africa, taking control of the region by the end of that century. Conquering Carthage in AD 698, the Muslim invaders set up the city of Kairouan in Tunisia as the North African capital of the quickly expanding Islamic empire ruled by the caliphs in Damascus. The local Berber peoples eventually adopted Islamic religious teachings and Christianity began its decline. By AD 1100 only a handful of bishoprics remained. While there is evidence that a Christian community of some sort lived on in Tunis until the sixteenth century, Christianity in effect slowly ceased to exist in North Africa.

In the late 1800s and early 1900s, both Catholic and Protestant church missionaries moved to Tunisia and began work among Muslims. The Catholic White Fathers were the most widespread and far-reaching in their efforts. Due to the foreign church's missionary efforts, at various times small groups of followers of Christ from Muslim backgrounds formed. However, as a result of having been introduced to Christ through Westerners, the followers very often did not remain culturally rooted in their own Arab society. Consequently these groups tended to be short-lived and never gained momentum or cultural authenticity. Following Tunisia's independence from France in 1956, Christian missionaries were no longer officially permitted in Tunisia, and while allowing freedom of religion for those of other faiths, the country declared Islam as the state religion.

In 1991, Mazhar and his family moved to the capital city of Tunis/Carthage, and he immediately found his milieu in the various writers' clubs and societies. As an Arab follower of Christ in a completely Muslim Arab country, he was somewhat of a novelty. Not long after his arrival, a well-known Tunisian journalist brought him to the attention of the local media by quoting Mazhar in his column on international affairs, identifying him as an "Arab Christian writer living in Tunis." Mazhar's novel, *The Long Night*, was subsequently reviewed in the local press, and this, together with the various articles he had written, resulted in his recognition in Tunisian literary, artistic, and intellectual circles.

Mazhar initially planned to be associated as well with the Western Christians living in Tunisia and local Tunisian followers of Christ, who called themselves "Christian," albeit unofficially. The majority of the Western Christians working and living among Tunisians were from Protestant evangelical backgrounds, and as Mazhar's own theology began to mature, he felt increasingly uncomfortable associating with them. This growing distance was due to the uneasiness he felt about their attitudes toward Muslims and their approach to witnessing about Christ. Sadly, he saw these same perspectives and practices adopted by the local Tunisian "Christians." He found many in both groups seemingly focused more on just obtaining "converts," using a pragmatic approach toward relationships with Muslims, and often seeing the relationships as a means to a very narrow end. Mazhar's belief was that one should be focused on naturally and relationally demonstrating the way of Christ in authentic friendships that have no ulterior "agenda," and sharing Christ's teachings with those who are genuinely interested, leaving the rest to God.

It was also during this time that Mazhar began to consciously develop his own philosophy concerning the sharing and following of Christ in the Arab Muslim world; to Mazhar this entailed a respect for the individual above all else, the necessity of honoring the indigenous culture, and guaranteeing that a foreign religious system is not imposed on them. Mazhar believed that his efforts toward seeing Christ becoming genuinely naturalized in an Arab Islamic society required taking a long-term perspective, perhaps as long as decades or even centuries.

One writer who significantly influenced Mazhar's thinking was E. Stanley Jones, the Methodist minister and close friend of Mahatma Gandhi, who spent most of his life working in India. Having himself been greatly influenced by Gandhi, Mazhar felt a kindred spirit with Jones, who not only loved Gandhi, but respected both Islam and Hinduism while in India, embodying a humble and gentle disposition toward their followers. Jones's primary focus was introducing people to the Christ of the Gospels, whom he experienced as a living person, as opposed to seeing people become part of another religion or religious institution. Jones, a gifted and prolific writer, remains one of the few authors Mazhar has read in English.

While Mazhar increasingly distanced himself from the local Christian community, he did develop a close friendship with the American priest of St. George's Anglican Church, the local international church in Tunis. Mazhar, who has a low view of ecclesiology (see chapter 9), and does not often attend Christian churches, even accepted an invitation to give the sermon one Sunday morning. St. George's Church was filled to capacity. Against the backdrop of beautiful stained-glass windows commemorating the third-century Tunisian martyrs Perpetua and Felicitas, Mazhar shared profoundly from Psalm 23 about God being our "Good Shepherd" in times of trial, and did so as only a Middle Easterner with a Bedouin shepherding background could. The freshness of his interpretation of the Scriptures, and his ability as a Middle Easterner to see in them that which Westerners culturally cannot, captivated the congregation.

Most of Mazhar's time in Tunis, however, was spent with the Muslim community, forming some of his deepest life friendships. Mazhar has been known for his "coffee get-togethers" wherever he has lived, and a typical day in Tunis would find him in a local Arab café, surrounded by Tunisian friends, mostly Muslim, writers, lawyers, artists, professors, publishers, historians, and literary critics, discussing politics, literature, art, religion, and faith. Often the conversation would naturally turn to Mazhar's experience of Christ. At one such coffee time, as Mazhar was sharing from the Gospels about Jesus, he noticed a secret plainclothes policeman sitting nearby, attempting to listen in without being observed. With nothing to hide, in typical Mazhar fashion, he stopped his sharing and graciously invited the man to come closer and join their group so he could hear more clearly.

Mazhar's relationship with the Tunisian intelligentsia enabled him to advise the Ministry of Education's committee responsible for revising the standard school history textbooks. Up until that time, Tunisia's Christian history was not highlighted in the teaching of Tunisian history to students, which instead focused on the developments from the seventh century onward, following the Islamic invasion of the country. A growing movement of educators, however, desired that all of Tunisia's history be equally addressed in their educational system. For Christ to be naturally accepted in the Arab world, Mazhar sees it as critically important that we help correct any misunderstandings people have been taught about Christ. As he often says, "You cannot cook the meat if you do not warm the water around it." In this way, Mazhar's passion for Christ dovetailed with the educational agenda Tunisian Muslim leaders had for their own country. An excellent article by Tunisian Latif Lakhdar highlights the changes made in the Tunisian educational system, as he contrasts their education with that of other Muslim countries like Saudi Arabia and Egypt. In such places, he shares, Islamic education "instills in the younger generation a religious fanaticism, which entails a phobia toward dissimilarity and a rejection of the other, even to the extent of killing." Lakhdar goes on to explain that in Tunisia they are now attempting to teach comparative religion in a manner that demonstrates the lack of a monopoly on faith, and that change is inherent in a religion's historical development. He further elaborates on the approach now used at Zeitouna University, the highest institution of religious teaching in Tunisia. At Zeitouna, students are taught about Islam's moderate teachings and traditions, including that "Islamic consciousness must reinstate the other, particularly the Jew and the Christian." At the university there are now courses on Judaism and Christianity "in a manner which respects the words of their founders," as well as on the Christian Bible. Even in final graduation exams the students are required to elaborate on the "question of accepting the other who is different in religion."[2] Interestingly, the late Muslim professor of comparative religion at Zeitouna University, Dr. Ahmed Mechraqi, was one of Mazhar's dearest friends, and instrumental in his literary efforts to help Muslims study Christ more clearly. Moderate Islam and tolerance of the other is possible when Muslim societies teach their children that it is legitimate. The rewriting of the Tunisian textbooks, which now address the authentic Christian history of the country during the pre-Islam era, has far-reaching ramifications toward Tunisians seeing faith in Christ not as something foreign, but as an integral part of their own cultural history. This significant change in the Tunisian governmental attitude toward Christianity over the last decade is evidenced by the Ministry of Culture's recent joint sponsorship with the Catholic Church of an exhibition in Carthage on the life and faith of St. Augustine of North Africa.[3]

Another significant advance brought about by Mazhar's relationships and efforts was to see the Christian Scriptures made available officially in Arabic. Until then, the only Christian Scriptures legally allowed in Tunisia were those in foreign languages, notably French, English, and Italian. Importation of Arabic-language Bibles was not permitted, as is often the case in Muslim countries that do not have an indigenous Arab Christian presence. The only Arabic Christian Scriptures available were those brought in illegally by Westerners. Ethically against smuggling, and believing that the distribution of the Bible should be through legal sales channels, Mazhar began working with book wholesalers to obtain government approval for the official importation and sale of the Arabic Bible in the mainstream Tunisian market. Otherwise, any Arabic Bible one obtained bore the mark of smuggled contraband and Western-produced Christian literature. Remarkably, for the first time since national independence, the government granted permission for the Bible in Arabic to be sold legally throughout the country's bookshops.

While Mazhar lived in Tunisia, several individuals played a significant role in shaping his life and work. Near the beautiful beach suburb of Carthage lived the late Honorable Dr. Muhammad Fadhel Jamali, the once royal prime minister of Iraq (1953–1954) and at that time the only original signer of the United Nations Charter still living. Dr. Jamili, a Muslim, was a respected friend of the West and yet exemplified the best of Arab nationalism, modeling the spirit of tolerance. As a respected Iraqi statesman and a gifted diplomat, he had played a major role in international politics and was recognized as a great humanitarian the world over. Following the coup d'état in 1958, the military court of Iraq's dictatorial government sentenced him to death. While in prison under the death sentence (1958–1961), he wrote profound letters to his son about the Muslim faith, which were later collected and published under the title *Letters on Islam; Written By a Father in Prison to His Son*. Needing to flee Iraq, he was warmly welcomed by Tunisia, and he made his home in exile there until his death in 1997. Mazhar found Dr. Jamali to be one of the most gracious, humble, and yet brilliant individuals he had met; he became a mentor to Mazhar. Every Friday evening, Dr. Jamali would host a soiree for intellectuals and writers at his lovely yet simple home. They would meet and discuss the events of the week—political, religious, and cultural—while tapping Dr. Jamali's wisdom and vast experience. Together they would stroll through the nearby flowering fields and hills, encircling the elderly Dr. Jamali, who carried his walking stick in hand, and learning from him. Married to a Christian American, Dr. Jamali had a great respect for Christ and knowledge of the Christian faith. He was to Mazhar one of the most Christ-like individuals he has known. Their admiration for each other was mutual. Dr. Jamali once introduced Mazhar as the "best example of a Christ follower he knew." Today, every time Mazhar visits Tunisia, he makes a point of visiting Dr. Jamali's simple grave outside of Carthage, offering a prayer of thanks to God for his life and meditating on the example he set for all.

The Palestinian Connection

Mazhar was also deeply influenced by a visiting Arab Christian to Tunis. Together with St. George's Anglican Church, Mazhar and Christine invited Abuna (Father) Elias Chacour to give a series of public lectures. A Palestinian Melchite Catholic priest from Galilee and a global ambassador for non-violence and Christ's Sermon on the Mount, Father Chacour is known around the world for his work of peace and reconciliation between Israeli Jews, Palestinians (Muslims and Christians), and Druze in Israel and Palestine (he is now the Archbishop of Galilee). For many years he started kindergartens, elementary schools, community centers, and libraries in Palestinian villages. Having been nominated for the Nobel Peace Prize several times, he founded the Mar Elias Educational Institutions (MEEI) in Galilee to enable Palestinian young people, together with Israeli Jews and Druze, both at the high school and college level, to enjoy the opportunity of a good education that could give them hope and a future, whilst teaching about the reconciliation, forgiveness, and peace that comes from Christ's teachings. As the only non-Jewish college in Israel, the MEEI now has an enrollment of over 4500 Palestinian, Jewish, Muslim, Christian, and Druze students.

Mazhar invited Father Chacour to Tunis because he felt that his presence would help to break the Tunisian stereotypes of Christianity as being exclusively a Western faith, and therefore culturally foreign. As an Arab Christian in an Arab Muslim country, Father Chacour was viewed as an anomaly by most Tunisians: for them to be Arab means to be Muslim. Speaking at numerous public meetings about the Sermon on the Mount, Father Chacour's visit was a spectacular success, covered by national and international media. As far as one is able to access, he was the first Christian speaker in the Tunisian public domain for over 1,400 years. Yet it was perhaps on Mazhar himself that Father Chacour had the greatest influence. Up to this point, Mazhar's personal friendships with Arab Christians had largely been with Protestants or Roman Catholics, both of which are culturally Western Churches, and therefore less than fully Arab in their expressions of faith. Father Chacour was the first Middle Eastern Christian from a historic church that Mazhar had come to know well. A true Arab, who can trace his family's Palestinian roots back almost to the time of Pentecost, Father Chacour's Middle Eastern spirituality opened Mazhar's eyes to another culturally authentic Arab expression of faith in Christ. Referring to Christ as "his compatriot from Galilee," Father Chacour and his faith resonated with Mazhar's soul, ministering to him deeply.

Father Chacour's visit to Tunis took place just after the signing of the Oslo peace accord on the White House lawn. The Palestinian Liberation Organization (PLO), which had been headquartered in Tunis following its expulsion from Lebanon in 1982, was planning to relocate to the West Bank soon. Therefore the PLO authorities were very interested in hearing Father Chacour's perspective on how the Palestinian people in the West Bank, Gaza, and Israel were reacting to the news of the peace agreement and the imminent return of chairman Yasser Arafat to Palestine. The special timing of Father Chacour's visit allowed Mazhar and Christine close interaction with Mrs. Suha Arafat, the wife of the late Yasser Arafat, also then living in Tunis. While her late husband was a Muslim, Suha comes from a Greek Orthodox Christian background and is very proud of her Christian heritage. She was so interested in Father Chacour's visit that she co-sponsored some of the public lectures Mazhar and Christine had set up for him. Throughout Father Chacour's busy visit, the Mallouhis were in frequent contact with Suha Arafat, from diplomatic receptions to hosting her at small dinners in their own home. The Mallouhis and Father Chacour were also invited to a private dinner with Mr. and Mrs. Arafat in their modestly furnished home. In the fashion of true Arab hospitality, a gracious Mr. Arafat personally served them. A special relationship developed between Suha and the Mallouhis, with Suha inviting them to live near her husband in Palestine, promising to provide them a house. This invitation would later cause them to seriously consider moving to the West Bank. The unique interaction with both Father Chacour and Suha Arafat instilled in Mazhar and Christine a desire to assist the many oppressed Palestinians who suffer unjustly, a suffering often perpetuated in the name of God and with the blessing of Western Christians. Taking it upon themselves to vicariously, through prayer and advocacy, help shoulder the burden felt by the Palestinian people, they became determined to be involved in the future in some practical way toward righting their injustices and alleviating their pain.

Passionate about the Gospels, Mazhar would often encourage his Muslim friends to read them in order to discover Christ for themselves. However, after beginning to read the Gospels, they would often give up because they were not able to understand them at first reading. Among the various reasons for this difficulty: the published presentation is seemingly foreign to them. For example, the publication's physical appearance does not look like an Arab "sacred book" and therefore does not encourage Muslims to respect the Scriptures, and it is also filled with culturally Christian Arabic vocabulary and expressions. In Tunis, Mazhar's Muslim friends challenged him to help them by publishing the Scriptures in a format they could more readily approach and understand, echoing the Ethiopian eunuch's cry in the Book of Acts, "How can I understand unless someone explains it to me?"

Thus Mazhar developed a vision for a commentary on the Gospels especially suited for Muslim readers, and in Tunis he began in earnest to work on a re-presentation of the Gospel of Luke for Muslims. An initial systematic survey was conducted among hundreds of Muslims to ascertain the difficulties they had in understanding the text. Mazhar asked Muslims for their help in explaining Christ's teachings in a clear way to them, and all cooperated at every level, even overseeing the survey process for him. Mazhar's Muslim friends were especially honored that he was willing to put so much effort into this endeavor for their sake. After five years of hard work, this representation of Luke's Gospel was published, titled *An Eastern Reading of the Gospel of Luke*. A Muslim-focused publication, it includes the text of the Gospel of Luke together with a commentary that seeks to address the common Muslim misunderstandings and prejudices. It is packaged in a fashion that conveys great reverence, as Muslims are accustomed to with their own holy book, the Qur'an. The enthusiastic reception throughout the Arab World of this publication laid the foundation for the shape most of Mazhar's future literature work would take (see chapter 7).

After years of frustration with what they viewed as unacceptable literature, either offensive or irrelevant, published by Christians for Muslim readers, Mazhar and Christine decided to take a proactive approach and publish, in addition to Mazhar's own writings, literature in Arabic that would shatter stereotypes, overcome prejudices, and illuminate, resolve, and explain typical Islamic misunderstandings of Christian faith by presenting Christ and his teachings in a culturally acceptable way. In order to facilitate this objective, in Tunis Mazhar founded Al Kalima ("The Word" in Arabic), a non-profit publishing association that publishes spiritual books of this genre and distributes them through one of the largest secular Arab publishing houses. The aim of all these publications is to help Muslims and Christians in the Arab World understand and respect each other, and to introduce the teachings and person of Christ, whom Mazhar found to be the Middle Eastern Prince of Peace. Under the editorial oversight of Al Kalima, which includes Christians and Muslims, they have published numerous books in Arabic, including, among many others, *The Gospel in Dostoevsky* (selections from Dostoevsky's writings), collections of Leo Tolstoy's short stories, *Blood Brothers* by Elias Chacour, and *Justice and Only Justice* by Naim Ateek.

After several encouraging years in Tunis, Mazhar and Christine decided to take a sabbatical year in the U.S., where their oldest son, Faris, was finishing up his high school education in Arizona. Almost from the outset, Mazhar found living in the U.S. a deep inner struggle. As a result of the Gulf War, through which the average American was awakened to the existence and complexity of the Middle East, he experienced a strong anti-Islam and anti-Arab sentiment.

In addition to this, having just come through a period of close relationships with Palestinian refugees in Tunis, Mazhar found it very difficult to observe firsthand how many American Christians uncritically supported Israel's occupation of the Palestinian territories and even theologically justified the injustices committed against the Palestinian people. Tragically, they more often than not branded as terrorists the terrorized Palestinians, who were people simply desiring a peaceful life like everyone else. While living in the U.S., as they thought about where they might return to live in the Middle East, Mazhar and Christine made a couple of exploratory trips to the West Bank in Palestine. Building upon the many close friendships they now had with Palestinian religious and secular leadership, they researched the possibility of setting up a ministry of compassion for Palestinians in Gaza or the West Bank.

Mrs. Suha Arafat had also renewed her invitation to them to live near her, offering them a home in Gaza. On one of their visits, they were invited to have dinner with the Arafats at their new home. Mazhar and Christine were prevented, however, from keeping the appointment due to an escalation of violence. An Israeli soldier had been kidnapped by Palestinian militants, and in retaliation the Israelis sealed off the Gaza strip, positioning their tanks around Gaza city. The office at the Oriental House in Jerusalem suggested they not try to enter, with the Palestinian Authority office in Gaza confirming that the situation was explosive. Unbeknownst to them, as the Mallouhis headed back to Jordan, another Gaza office had sent a car on behalf of Suha Arafat to the checkpoint to wait for them. Sadly, they were not able to reconnect with the Arafats. While in Israel/Palestine, they also spent time with Father Elias Chacour, and with Rev. Dr. Naim Ateek, the Palestinian Anglican theologian and director of Sabeel, an advocacy ministry for Palestinians. As they investigated the various options, they did not sense a natural opportunity or an open door. Nevertheless, the experience reinforced in their minds their commitment to continued involvement in alleviating the suffering of the Palestinian people from wherever they resided.

Imprisoned in Syria

Living in Arizona, Mazhar soon began to feel like a traitor to his own culture. As an exile, it is natural to cling to one's homeland with a sense of deep loyalty accompanied by a sense of wonder. And while safety exists in exile, it nevertheless breeds a sense of profound loss and alienation. Mazhar refused to accept the counsel given by the main character in Amin Maalouf's excellent novel, *Leo the African,* Hassan al-Wazzan, who had to journey again and again looking for a new home: "A lost homeland is like the corpse of a near relative; bury it with respect and believe in eternal life." The challenges of living in the U.S. during a post–Gulf War era caused Mazhar to pine once again for his lost country, Syria. Even though his country, thirty-five years earlier, had imposed undue suffering on his life, forcing him into exile, he still had a great love and respect for his homeland. While lost to him many years previously, he did not feel released from Syria's grip. Mirroring another great exiled writer, Joseph Conrad, who left Poland at the age of seventeen only to return thirty years later, having always felt his country's "shadows crowding upon him," Mazhar decided to attempt going home to Syria. Better to die in Syria than lose his soul in the U.S., he felt.

With the strong impression in his heart that he should return to Syria, and strengthened in his faith in God's protection, Mazhar used his Australian passport to cross into Syria by land from Lebanon without being detected.[4] Heading straight to his family in his hometown, he experienced a beautiful reunion. Many, amazingly, said they had recently had dreams that prepared them for his return. He found his family and the local neighborhood irresistibly drawn to knowing more about his faith, and he shared from the Gospels about how Christ, whom he addresses as "my Lord," had transformed his life and guided him all the many years of their separation from each other. One neighbor even visited his sister, a Muslim, pleading to be given a Bible.

But not all was plain sailing, for Mazhar also discovered that there were three warrants out for his arrest. Concerned about his safety, his family accompanied him to the border. Mazhar introduced himself to the border police, who, after realizing who he was, were shocked that he had managed to enter the country undetected. They urged him to leave immediately and to have someone important and respected by the Syrian authorities write on his behalf to the president of Syria, His Excellency Hafez al-Assad.

Determined to clear his name with the Syrian government, Mazhar decided to return a second time in May 1995. This time, prior to entering the country, former U.S. senator Charles Percy, a close friend of Mazhar's and someone well acquainted with the Middle East and the Syrian president from his time serving as chairman of the Committee on Foreign Relations, sent a letter ahead to President Assad.

> "My purpose in writing [wrote Senator Percy] involves a good friend that I have known for many years . . . Mazhar Mallouhi . . . a writer who has diligently promoted the Arab case to the West for over twenty years. . . . On our project in Tunisia . . . Mazhar was a facilitator in many facets of our work. As a writer he commands great respect from those familiar with his efforts, and he is steadfastly non-partisan in any political sense, reaching across many different ideologies to make friends and to help others. The problem is that he had been banned from returning to Syria for over 25 years. . . . Mazhar now has shared with me that he very much wants to return to his native country, that he loves, to live. I have the greatest respect for him, both as a professional writer as well as a superb human being and friend. I appeal to you to grant Mazhar amnesty. He will, I assure you, be a model citizen, a man of good character and a true credit to your very beautiful country as you open more to foreign investment and various cultural exchanges. . . . I look forward to our next visit."[5]

On the day Mazhar re-entered Syria, Christine went to a local Roman Catholic church in Phoenix, Arizona, to pray for Mazhar's safety. Joining the small group at mid-week worship, she felt Mazhar's safety confirmed in her heart as she discovered that the Scripture reading for the day was on the dialogue that took place between Moses and God in the Sinai. Moses objected to returning to Egypt, believing it was not safe to do so because he was a fugitive from the royal court. But God answered his concern with these words, "You are not going alone, nor on your own authority. I will be with you and bring you safely to Pharaoh's court."

Upon arriving in Syria, having once again not been stopped by immigration officials, Mazhar went directly to the Intelligence Service, and surrendered himself to them, requesting his case be investigated and that he be given the chance to prove his innocence. A friend of Mazhar's, the minister of petrol at the time, happened to be at the security headquarters and noticed him. Four men carrying machine guns arrested him. Blindfolding him and shoving him into a car, they raced through Damascus, taking him to an underground prison, where they directly ushered him into the interrogation room.

"When I heard the charges," says Mazhar, "I felt utterly hopeless. I thought I would never see my family and friends again." Accused of spying for the

Israelis with Massood, the British with MI6, the Americans with the CIA, and for the Iraqis due to his past connection with the Baath Party; of speaking against the Syrian regime; of changing religion; and of exhorting and paying people to become Christians, Mazhar knew that Syrian friends of his who had been accused of less serious crimes had simply "disappeared." He was reminded of his Muslim friend from his hometown, the writer Ahmed Swayden, who for simply saying, "I see Syria could end up as a police state," was picked up by the secret police two days later and imprisoned for almost fifteen years, ending up permanently blind in one eye. For the next eighteen days Mazhar was kept in solitary confinement in a small underground cell, with nothing but a thin blanket on a concrete floor. Sleeping on the hard floor for three weeks caused permanent nerve damage, with numbness still in his legs today. Cut off from the outside world, his only company was a rat and cockroaches. Mazhar says, "The eighteen days were full of darkness and suffering. I was repeatedly and harshly interrogated. Blindfolded, I was forced to stand for hours in the cell. Attempting to break me, they deprived me of sleep by playing tapes of other prisoners being tortured. They also continuously played loud rock music to prevent me from thinking and praying." He attempted to cope with the interrogators by using humor, wanting to touch their human side. They would have him write down his life story, everything he could remember, and then aggressively interrogate him, only to then have him write down his life story again, in order to compare it with what he had previously written.

Mazhar began to fast, drinking only water, which angered the police at first, who threatened to beat him if he didn't eat. He was finally able to convince them it was for spiritual reasons and not for coercion. The first eight days were absolute misery, and Mazhar became very bitter toward God. Around the ninth day, he experienced the presence of God reaching out to him, in such a direct way it was as if God was physically in the cell with him. He began to see that God desired to transform this prison experience into a spiritual gift and blessing. Recalling the experience, Mazhar says, "I drank deeply of the Father's love and suffering for us. And I felt as if I was released from my dismal surroundings and from my personal internal prison. It was an experience of deep internal healing, and I felt completely free. God gave me a profound sense of restfulness, and I ceased to wrestle internally. All fear I was experiencing left. I stopped hating the Muslims who were bringing this suffering on me, and began to see them as victims of an evil government, instead of victimizers." It was a type of conversion experience and it dramatically changed Mazhar's life (see chapter 6). His wife, Christine, shares that following this mystical prison experience, "the anger and bitterness he felt toward some Western Christians was gone, and there was a new sense of deep calm and peace in his inner spirit." Still being kept in solitary confinement, just after this spiritual experience Mazhar was taken to a worse cell, where he underwent even more intimidating interrogations for another seven days.

He had no contact with the outside world, so no one had any direct knowledge of his situation. He had told Christine that if after two weeks she hadn't heard from him, then she should assume he was in serious trouble. Word leaked out about the status of his case. After two weeks, the Syrian Embassy in the U.S., shocked to learn that Mazhar had actually returned to Syria, warned Christine that the case could take a long time. There was a considerable amount of political pressure at the time on Syria from the U.S. regarding the issue of human rights. Mazhar's family in Syria began to discuss options to pressure his release, and contacted Christine, saying that they believed the government wanted a bribe, an idea that she agreed to endorse. With still no word on what had happened to Mazhar, on the eighteenth day concerned friends in various countries, unbeknownst to each other, felt led to gather for special prayer. In Aspen, Colorado, one such group alone numbered over eighty people. On the morning of the nineteenth day, the secret police began to talk with Mazhar about their openness to releasing him if he cooperated with them, asking him to spy on Christian missionaries and Syrians criticizing the government; he immediately refused.

The next day Mazhar was unexpectedly released without explanation, on the conditions that he had to report to them in Damascus every two weeks. He had to walk to two relatives' houses before he found someone home. Opening the door, his niece didn't even recognize him, as he was heavily bearded and dirty after almost three weeks without washing and sleeping on the filthy cell floor. As Mazhar shared with them what had happened, he told them about the experiences he had had with God in prison, and they were deeply moved. The spiritual freedom experienced during his imprisonment was so powerful that two days later, when Mazhar saw on the street one of the prison guards who had treated him very harshly, he was able to go up to him, introduce himself and share with him that he had forgiven him and did not hold anything against him, giving the guard a Middle Eastern embrace of peace.

The Syrian Embassy in Washington D.C. was very cooperative. The ambassador's representative was aware of Mazhar from his writings from thirty years earlier. They assured Christine that Mazhar had been released because he had been proven innocent and that the case was now closed, apologizing for the length of time it had taken.

Christine joined Mazhar in Syria that summer. With his reinstated citizenship and a new Syrian passport, the plan was to reside in Syria on a permanent basis, thinking this would be their "promised land." Living initially in

Mazhar's hometown of Salimeyia with his oldest brother's family, their presence was definitely seen as a celebrative family homecoming. The house was constantly full of people, with singing and dancing every night. Over 150 family members gathered with Mazhar and Christine for a large welcome party, as is done for bridal couples in the Middle East, the couple positioned high up in front of everyone in gold gilded chairs, while songs were sung in their honor. Belly dancing and traditional folk dancing such as the *debka* took place until the middle of the night. It was a very special occasion, with all generations of Mazhar's family dancing and celebrating together. Their lost son had come home.

The living conditions at Mazhar's brother's home in Salimeyia were simple and the family lived in very close quarters. The main living area was spread with a mat and pillows around the walls for socializing with guests during the day. For meals a cloth was spread on the ground and everyone ate out of a common bowl. At night, sheets helped to turn the mats into beds. Mazhar and Christine stayed there for one month, and being viewed like celebrities, everyone tried constantly to keep them happy, allowing them no time to be alone. Understanding that this setup would eventually suffocate them and cause undue strain on his brother's family, they moved to Damascus, renting a small studio with a little Arab tiled courtyard, just below the minaret of a downtown mosque. Hearing once again the beautiful and melodious Syrian calls to prayer filled Mazhar's heart with a deep sense of the joy of coming home.

Waking up early for pungent Arab coffee in their little courtyard, Mazhar and Christine would then walk for several hours a day, taking in the old city of Damascus. Walking from Bab Toma (St. Thomas Gate) to the famous Straight Street where St. Paul's conversion culminated, through the narrow, crooked alleys of the Hammidiya Souk, passing the great statue of Saladin (the great medieval Arab leader), and then back by the Salhiyah quarter, they would admire all the historic Christian and Muslim sites of this ancient city. Their afternoons were filled working on various writing projects. Three branches of Mazhar's family lived in Damascus, and they spoke with each daily, visiting them weekly. Monthly they would return to visit Mazhar's brother and extended family in his hometown of Salimeyia.

Unbeknownst to his family, Mazhar was required to report twice a month to the National Security police. He had to report in detail where he had been, with whom he had spoken, and what each conversation had been about. They would also harangue him for not trying to solicit negative comments from others about the Syrian regime, renewing threats to imprison him again. Mazhar knew that any even slightly disparaging comment about the Syrian president or his regime would automatically lead to his being considered a traitor. And thousands of such "traitors" were either in prison or had "disappeared." Seven different departments of secret police not only spied on the Syrian people, but on each other as well. Mazhar and Christine were literally followed everywhere, and their phone and apartment were assumed bugged. Every time they wanted to discuss something privately, they would go into the courtyard and play loud radio music to cover their voices. The continual harassment and the around-the-clock surveillance severely restricted their movements. When they wanted to visit some Western Christian friends, in order to lose the "tails" of the secret police, they would have to walk through the Arab souk in a circuitous route for several hours at night. They began to develop a sense of paranoia from living under this continual stress. They purposely isolated themselves from other Christians, and largely only saw their own family members, not wanting to have to report conversations with friends, or have their friends' names put in the police files. Christine was not able to get close to other Syrian women, as Mazhar could not afford to get close to their husbands. While Mazhar had been released by the Syrian intelligence from solitary confinement, they had effectively put him into another prison—their apartment. Every time Mazhar wanted to leave to travel outside Syria he needed to obtain special permission. And each time he departed, he would be detained at the airport and told, "You are under arrest," and then be taken to a private room for questioning. When Mazhar and Christine decided to travel to Australia to spend Christmas with their sons, upon his departure he was detained. Prior to leaving the country he was first required to visit several different state security departments. One of the departments, when looking at his file, immediately told him that he should be in prison. Evidently the previous pardon had not been entered into his files. His case was passed onto a higher level, requiring him to wait. Returning to stay with his relatives, Mazhar prepared for the worst: possible re-imprisonment. A few days later, he was granted special permission to leave the country.

During this time of difficulty Mazhar telephoned his old friend Greg, requesting that he come and encourage them. While Greg's colleagues warned him that it was too dangerous for him in Syria, he told them "I have to go as my brother needs me." His visit was instrumental in helping to break their paranoia.

Early in the new year of 1996, the situation worsened. It was evident that the secret police were becoming more hostile and demanding that Mazhar cooperate with them by informing on others. While the Syrian authorities had in effect declared Mazhar innocent, it was clear that they were not going to allow him to live in peace. Determining that they could not continue to live in such isolation and under constant pressure, they requested special permission to leave the country. Again Mazhar was pulled aside and taken into a secret room for interrogation. Eventually, they allowed him to board the plane with Christine, and as she writes, "It wasn't until we were airborne that the tension in our muscles began to uncoil. With very mixed emotions we thus joined the millions of other refugees in the world."[6]

Refugees Again

Emotionally and physically exhausted, Mazhar and Christine headed to the country that had been their home and had served as a place of refuge to them several times before, Morocco. Their friends who picked them up at the airport in Casablanca thought they were coming for a short visit, only to see them disembark with all their belongings—arriving this time as refugees. British Christian friends graciously hosted them for six weeks. Settling in Rabat, the beautiful, tranquil Moroccan capital on the Atlantic coast, they were both spiritually discouraged. They had had such high hopes and expectations for their return to Syria, but their dreams of a new life there after many years in exile had now been shattered.

Over the next two years Rabat became for the Mallouhis an oasis in the desert, serving as a place of peace and recuperation, physically and emotionally. It was also a time of renewing and refocusing their spiritual vision and calling. While in Morocco they worked on two new book projects. Mazhar began a Muslim-focused publication with commentary on the Biblical book of Genesis. Again his editorial team consisted of Muslims and Christians. Similar to his earlier publication for Muslims of the Gospel of Luke, this new venture was a major publishing initiative that would take several years to complete. Published in 2001 by Dar al Jil in Beirut, *Genesis: The Origin of the World and Humanity* became a bestseller throughout the Arab world (see chapter 7). At the same time Christine began to work on a book for a Western audience titled *Waging Peace on Islam*, which advocated a nonconfrontational approach by Christians toward Muslims. In Rabat, Mazhar did not have much contact with Christians, but the Mallouhis did become quite close friends with Father Jean Pierre Micheau, a French Catholic priest, as well as with the nuns at the Notre Dame de la Paix convent. Father Micheau was especially encouraging to them when Christine's sister tragically died in Australia during that period.

After two years, when their son Tarek finished his high school education in Morocco, the Mallouhis decided to return to Tunis. During their sojourn in Tunis, the president of Syria, Hafez al-Assad, died and was replaced by his son, Bashar al-Assad. Mazhar viewed this as another possible window of opportunity to return to Syria, as the son was initially considered to be more moderate, issuing official statements of opening the country to the outside world. Again, Mazhar passed through the Syrian border without incident. The following week was one of the most encouraging weeks of his life. In his Muslim hometown, there was great eagerness and a corresponding openness to learn about his faith in Christ. Mazhar distributed over 400 copies of his various publications. Family members and friends longed to converse with him about his commitment to Jesus. Mazhar was so encouraged that he felt it would work out for them to move back to Syria.

However, when he returned to the border upon his departure, he was again detained and declared under arrest. The usual explanations from 1995 that his case had been cleared did not work this time. They had "new information" and the old warrants for his arrest were still in place, sharing that a new "more serious warrant" had been added. Aware that one of the previous warrants carried a death penalty, he questioned in his mind what this would mean. Mazhar was detained for six days. This time he was not afraid, for he had experienced this type of intimidation before, and he was bold in his dealings with the secret police. He also found the ability to love and forgive them as they questioned him. They charged him with hosting the Syrian ex-president, ex-vice president, and ex–prime minister in his home in Beirut way back in 1967—thirty years earlier. Amazingly, they even asked Mazhar to recall the specific conversations he had with them at the time. A nephew of Mazhar's, who was near him during this ordeal, was surprised at Mazhar's lack of bitterness toward the police. After Mazhar explained Christ's display of forgiveness, the nephew saw the reality of faith in Christ, and thereby became a follower of Christ. He committed his life to following Christ in the presence of his Muslim parents and with their blessing. Today this nephew is only one of a handful of Muslims committed to following Christ in the entire country.

Describing the frustration of having Mazhar detained once again, Christine writes, "It's like playing Monopoly for so long without winning and returning to GO so regularly, and missing a turn and ending up in jail so often that you forget why you began playing this anyway. But God has many GET OUT OF JAIL FREE cards." The unthinkable then happened. He was told by the authorities to leave the country. Someone highly placed in the government had been protecting him, and advised him, "If you can get out, stay out. They are out to get you on these trumped up charges. Someone is giving them new false information." Mazhar had felt that he would definitely not be allowed to leave, never even thinking that instead he would be told to leave. Eventually, he was allowed to leave, talking his way out at the border and heading into Lebanon. It was clear that even with Bashar al-Assad in power, it would not be possible for him to live in Syria without harassment, as the new president maintained the outlines of his father's regime.

Unsure exactly where to move next, Mazhar briefly considered living in the Gulf. The Mallouhis have long had a passion for the Muslims in the Arabian Peninsula, who have very few opportunities to learn about Christ, due both to the conservative nature of Islam, and to the fact that there are so few indigenous Christians in the region. However, the literary circle in the Gulf is not as extensive as in other Middle Eastern countries, like Egypt or Lebanon. In their many moves, the Mallouhis had never considered Lebanon, largely because Mazhar had many memories there, some not so positive, from his early days as a follower of Christ. At the same time, Lebanon is the hub for the intellectuals and writers of the Arab world. And Beirut serves as the literary capital of the Middle East today, with many of the most prominent publishers based there. Living in Beirut would allow Mazhar access to what was moving and shaking in the Arab world, thereby enhancing his literary projects. After much reflection, the Mallouhis moved to Beirut in 2001, with the plan to make it their permanent home and operating base in the Middle East.

Home Base Established: Al Kalima is Born

Settling in Sunni Muslim West Beirut was in many ways a homecoming for Mazhar, who had begun his journey with Christ in this beautiful city. It was also the place where he had first sensed the calling to write novels for Muslim audiences about the person and transforming power of Jesus. Quickly finding his daily place, Mazhar discovered a setting in which he was able to do what he had dreamed of doing for years. Close proximity to Syria also enabled good contact with his family, whose members visit them from time to time.

Mazhar still lives in Beirut today and thrives in the cultural and religious diversity of Lebanon. His close friends represent a mosaic of adherents from most of the religious groups in the Middle East: Sufi mystics, Sunni and Shia Muslims, Druze, Alouite Muslims, Chalcedonian Orthodox, Maronite Catholic, Jesuit priests, Anglican Christians, and the list goes on and on. Mazhar naturally plays an active role in various interfaith dialogue programs. The Mallouhis soon found opportunities to assist Palestinians in the refugee camps south of Beirut. Seeing the desperate and hopeless situation in the camps, which fuel revenge, hatred and violence, they have helped set up public reading rooms with books that encourage the way of peace and loving our enemies. They found that providing books as gifts for graduating Palestinian students, such as *Blood Brothers*, offers a message of hope, reconciliation, and forgiveness in Christ.

Mazhar's main focus in Beirut is on the world of literature. From the beginning he entered into a bookshop partnership with a Muslim friend; their shop is located in the heart of the shopping area of Beirut. Near the American University of Beirut, it serves as a kind of "drop in" place for Lebanese intellectuals. Mazhar's specific passion, though, is the numerous publishing projects of their Al Kalima association, which was founded in 1991. The mission of Al Kalima is to publish spiritual books for Muslim audiences about the person of Christ and his teachings through some of the largest secular Arab publishing houses. Al Kalima's publications exist to shatter stereotypes Muslims have about Christ and Christian faith, and then illuminate and explain typical misunderstandings Muslims have of the Scriptures. This nonconfrontational approach is one of its unique distinctions and strategic emphases. Al Kalima asks Muslims for assistance, and seeks to affirm the insights and values incorporated in their culture. Coupled with the use of normal, legal distribution channels, and having taken a mutually reciprocal teachable position when Al Kalima challenges the traditional perceptions and prejudices against which Jesus is, Mazhar finds Muslims demonstrate a spirit of appreciation and openness to genuine dialogue and to the person of Christ. Al Kalima's greatest local support comes from Muslim readers. Their purchases, which are their "paid endorsements," are financing multiple reprints, besides the more important spiritual impact on the readers' own lives. Mazhar's goal in Al Kalima is to educate influential Arab Muslims as to what Christians really believe and to enable them to meet firsthand the Christ of the Gospels.

Al Kalima's publications include Mazhar's own novels, works by Russian novelists Leo Tolstoy and Fyodor Dostoevsky, Muslim-focused Biblical commentaries, books by Arab Christian writers that help change the stereotype Muslims have of Christians, and titles about the Bible and Christ with the Muslim reader in mind, such as *The Stranger on the Road to Emmaus* (an introduction to the Bible well suited for Muslims), *The Master: A Life of Christ*, *Seeking Peace* by Johan Arnold, and *Journey of Light* (a chronological approach to the Biblical story published for an Arab Islamic context). The Al Kalima publishing association has begun working to develop an interactive website for those within Islam wanting to know about the person of Christ. While Mazhar serves as the chief editor, there is an editorial team composed of Christians and Muslims, with a Sufi group assisting as well.

Mazhar's primary desire today is to make the Scriptures available to Muslims with a contextualized commentary for them in easily accessible, legally available places. His most important projects therefore focus on re-presenting the Scriptures as the ancient Middle Eastern sacred writings that they are— returning them to their authentic cultural origin. The Muslim-focused "Easternized" commentary publications of the Gospels of Luke and the book of Genesis, mentioned earlier, have become very popular, with *An Eastern Read-*

ing of the Gospel of Luke being their most widely read title in the Arab world. It has gone through numerous printings and is one of the bestsellers at international Arab book fairs. It is also used as a textbook on comparative religion in two well-known Islamic universities (see chapter 7).

The success of the Muslim-focused Eastern presentations of the Gospel of Luke and the book of Genesis encouraged Mazhar and Christine, once in Beirut, to work on a similar publication of the Gospel of John (the most mystical of the Gospels) for Muslim mystics, traditionally called Sufis. After several years, with assistance from Muslim and Christian scholars, and groups of Sufi mystics that helped shape and field-test the material, *A Sufi Reading of the Gospel of John* was published to high acclaim, obtaining outstanding reviews by Muslims and Christians alike (see chapter 7).

Mazhar's most ambitious project to date is a new translation and commentary of all four Gospels and the Book of Acts for Muslim readers, to be titled in Arabic, *An Eastern Reading of the Gospels and Acts*. Existing Bible translations in Arabic have all been done by Christians, and largely for the minority Christian population of the Arab world. The terminology used in these translations can often confuse Muslim readers, for it is extremely difficult for an Arab believer from a Christian background to understand the Muslim worldview sufficiently to clearly convey the meaning of Scripture to a Muslim reader. Mazhar, with the encouragement of Muslim academics and in consultation with professional Muslim and Christian translators, is working to see all four Gospels and Acts translated into modern Arabic for the Muslim reader.

Al Kalima books have infiltrated the markets across the Arab world. Arab magazines and newspapers often publish Mazhar's articles, providing a hearing for his most important literature projects. Much public interest is generated when articles written by other Arab Muslim academics highlight his unique publications of the Scriptures, such as *An Eastern Reading of the Gospel of Luke*, as an exemplary model of bridge-building between Muslims and Christians.

Travel continues to be a frequent occurrence in Mazhar's life. He spends much of his time attending the primary Arabic book fairs throughout the Arab world. Not only are his books bestsellers at each of these fairs, they also provide an occasion for Mazhar to meet with publishers from other countries to facilitate distribution of his Al Kalima titles in their local markets. He frequently receives invitations to visit groups of Muslim followers of Christ, like himself, to share his experiences and years of learning. One such invitation came from a group of Shia Muslim sheiks who have come to faith in Christ through Mazhar's publications.

Committed to helping bridge the gap of misunderstanding between Muslims and Christians, Mazhar teaches at Middle Eastern theological institutions about the responsibility of followers of Christ to love their Muslim brothers and sisters. He gives seminars or retreats to encourage Muslim followers of Christ, such as those in Sudan, who are facing persecution. Mazhar loves his many opportunities to coach and train thousands of Christians throughout the Muslim world on culturally appropriate, sensitive, and effective ways to share and demonstrate the person of Christ. He is also found participating in various Christian/Muslim dialogue gatherings, adding his particular experience of how the life of Jesus and his teachings can provide a framework for peaceful and meaningful relationships.

Mazhar believes he is called to a ministry of reconciliation that seeks to facilitate people drawing closer to God through the person of Christ, where he has experienced hearing the voice of God most clearly. Taking a grace-filled approach, he is a unique gift to the Muslim world. From Mauritania to Malaysia, his life, writings, and ministry are making a strategic impact on the Muslim peoples. His passion is that Muslims, from Morocco to Indonesia, are all given an opportunity to learn about Christ without the Christian religious baggage that so often surrounds him, in order that they too may be given the possibility of becoming Christ followers. Having gained respect among Muslim leaders and popularity with Muslim readers, Mazhar has come to hold a position of great influence for the name of Christ in the Muslim world for such a time as this.

BRIDGING TWO WORLDS

II

As they pass through the Valley of Baca. . . .

(PSALM 84:6)

Salaam on Islam

4

> *Out beyond the ideas of wrongdoing and rightdoing,*
> *There is a field. I'll meet you there.*
> *When the soul lies down in that grass,*
> *the world is too full to talk about.*
> *Ideas, language, even the phrase "each other"*
> *doesn't make any sense.*
>
> —JALAL AL-DIN RUMI,
> A THIRTEENTH-CENTURY MUSLIM SUFI MYSTIC

> *All truth, by whomever it has been said, is from God's Spirit.*
>
> —ST. AMBROSE (WHO BAPTIZED AND DISCIPLED
> ST. AUGUSTINE OF NORTH AFRICA)

THE CHRISTIAN WEST IS OFTEN SEEN by Muslims as generally immoral and supportive of a regime which they perceive as having for decades humiliated both Muslim and Christian Palestinian people. Most Muslims know the God of Jesus Christ through the Western countries' foreign policies and military actions in Sudan, Iraq, and Afghanistan—and they know the God of Moses through the oppression of the Palestinians. Many Arab young people are angry about Western political policies, and see them in their minds as "Christian" and therefore unjust. In the war in Iraq, both Western Christians and Arab Muslims prayed for God to give their respective side victory—seeing it as a moral or holy war.

Over the centuries, both East and West have talked about war in religious terms. The Crusades of the Middle Ages were one such example, with both Christians and Muslims fighting each other in the name of God, and both sides maintaining they were fighting a holy war against unbelievers. As Christine Mallouhi, Mazhar's wife, says, "The love of God and the love of war became confused." Christians were focused on reclaiming the Holy Land for Christ, then under Muslim Turks. The Church's leaders used inflammatory stereotyping of the enemy. Mazhar says, "The most beautiful part of the Gospel . . . the cross—became a weapon used against us in crusader's hands (crusader in Arabic means "cross-bearer"). The cross, where God had embraced humanity, had become a sword."

In perusing titles of Christian books about Islam, which often include key words like "targets" and "strategies," one would think Christians were at war with Muslims, albeit meant in spiritual terms. Much of the Christian literature written for Muslims attacks the Qur'an and the Prophet Muhammad, seeking to alienate the individual from Islam. This literature all too often uses militant anti-Islamic language. Some Christian groups organize prayer marches through Muslim countries to "reclaim the land" and "capture Islamic strongholds." It is clear that many Christians see Islam as the enemy camp, as if they are a religious block at war with God.

Muslims are of course hurt by this approach, further alienating them from Christians. Articles by Muslims that focus on Christian mission activities aimed at Muslims speak of the Christian hatred and contempt for Islam, how they are targeted and boast of successes. They feel Christians use deception in trying to make Christianity acceptable to them. Some even go so far as to describe Christians as new crusaders in a war with Islam.

In the last century, Christians' communication about Christ in the Arab Middle East has often taken a confrontational approach, using apologetics. To Arab Muslims, this approach has been associated with and reinforced by the cultural prejudices of Westerners and even the stigma of the colonial era. A tragic example of this was the French seizure of the Grand Mosque of Algiers, in the North African country of Algeria, and its forced conversion into the Cathedral of St. Philippe, with the French flag and the cross on its minaret. Actions like this, and others far more subtle, convinced Muslims that Christianity had come to colonize their lands and convert Arab Muslims.

Christians are in danger of repeating harmful periods of history when the West has gone to war on the Muslim East to conquer, physically or spiritually, in the name of God. Muslims rarely hear "Good News" from Christians; instead they feel targeted as enemies in a new war. As Christians, we must honestly ask ourselves, Do Muslims know we are Christians by our hostility? It is time to lay aside warfare rhetoric and antagonistic strategies; this only creates an unnecessary enmity between us. The Christian faith will continue to be suspect to Muslims while the Christian West sees the Muslim world as an enemy.

Muslim writer Ziauddin Sardar concluded his book *Why do People Hate America?* with the prayer of St. Francis of Assisi: "O Master, grant that I may never seek so much to be consoled, as to console, To be understood as to understand, To be loved, as to love, with all my soul." Sardar's wise counsel for the West is to put down the crusader's sword and unwrap ourselves from national flags and envelop ourselves instead in the Prayer of St. Francis.[1]

Due to the Western media's preoccupation with terrorism and Christian leaders' exaggerated pronouncements concerning Islam, many Western Christians today are afraid of Muslims. This mentality is based on a lack of genuine understanding. Ignorance often breeds unnecessary fear and violence. Many Western Christians approach Muslims as if they are from another planet. Yet they are people just like Christians—with the same needs and desires, created in the image of God, and wanting to be respected and loved as Christians do.

The tendency to depersonalize Muslims dehumanizes the individuals and their beliefs. Most Westerners wouldn't talk about a colleague from France by using a category such as, "my colleague, a secular humanist." Instead they would use their name and see them as a person. We need to give Muslims the same respect. They are "persons" who believe in Islam.

While the Western Christian world harbors resentment toward Muslims for the harsh and unfair treatment of Christian minorities in some countries, most Muslims are not in a war with Christianity. Most are peace-loving toward Christians, incredibly hospitable, gentle, and kind. However it has to be said that the Christian media rarely reports the many positive things that are happening between these two faiths in the Islamic World. Mazhar recalls two controversial activities that took place while he was living in North Africa. The first was the illegal mass distribution of Christian films by a Western church group and the second was a large Bible smuggling operation. Both circumstances were reported in the Western Christian media, which painted the local government and Islam in a very negative light and the Western Christians as heroes persecuted for their faith. Yet the Christians were actually breaking the law in this particular country.

"Muslim" can mean many things, as there are many kinds of Muslims, so generalization is not wise. When some Christians say to Mazhar that they hate Islam, he asks them, "What Islam do you hate?" Mazhar goes on to say, "There are so many expressions of it. . . . I cannot afford to hate Islam, or anything. For me, hate connects with fear, desire for revenge and unforgiveness. These things are debilitating and constricting. . . . . Waging a war takes a huge effort and God doesn't need us to defend Him. Islam actually does this from time to time,[2] and it's not one of the things I want to take on. It conveys a fear of not being right. I want all my energy to be given to the quest to live in a spirit of openness and forgiveness."

Christ gave his followers a simple mission related to the Other and to others: "Love God with all your heart, and love your neighbor as yourself." God's love is indiscriminate. Christ was all about breaking down the ethnic conflict between "Jew and Gentile." Jesus was all about fighting any type of evil with good: "If we treat others the way they treat us, or only show compassion . . . when our friends and family suffer: how are we different from others?" Christ's Sermon on the Mount provides the foundation for loving our "enemies."

Christians need a grace-oriented approach to Muslims. Jesus focused on overcoming fear with love, for as St. John writes, "perfect love drives out fear" (I John 4:18). The enemy is not the other—whether Muslim or Christian; instead we have common enemies—evil, injustice, intolerance, and so forth. As the late Virginia Cobb, a respected Western Christian leader who lived in Lebanon, said, "We have centuries of Christian enmity and harshness and rejection of Islam to atone for and undo; we have walls of prejudice built up through the centuries to break down; we have deeply engrained attitudes in both Christians and Muslims to change."[3]

From Family, to Foe, to Friend

Growing up in a Syrian Sunni family, Mazhar was culturally and religiously raised a Muslim. However, his earliest recollections are of feeling quite negative about Islam as a religion for two distinct reasons. First of all, as a naturally spiritually-oriented young man, his first attempt to fill the void he felt was through knowledge of the Divine. However, he found God as presented in Islam, taken largely from the Qur'an, much too transcendent and distant for his liking. Second, the Qur'anic school he attended from a young age was influenced by the Muslim Brotherhood, an Islamic fundamentalist movement, and therefore the Islam that he first become acquainted with was one of strict legalism, as opposed to one of grace and love.

At the same time, Mazhar was "poisoned" against Christianity by the local Muslim community. In the context in which he was raised, Muslims saw Christians as their enemies and vice versa. Ironically, following his commitment to Jesus Christ, the Arab Christians he began to associate with in Syria and Lebanon "poisoned" him against his own religious background, inspiring him to hate Islam. For a short period of time, Mazhar even went so far as to pray for Israel's successful occupation of Palestine—the last thing any Arab Muslim would do. Hugh Thomas, the managing director of the Christian publishing house in Beirut where Mazhar worked, recalls Mazhar being very antagonistic to the symbols of Islam, like the Kaaba (the holiest site in Islam). Looking back, he now sees that one of the main reasons his family ostracized him at first, after his decision to follow Christ, was that he took a confrontational approach toward them that was aggressive, critical, and arrogant— attempting to "set them straight."

Mazhar was so poisoned against Islam during his early years within the Christian community, which saw Islam as a religious counterfeit, that he continued to demonstrate elements of hostility toward the religion of his birth for over twenty years. For quite some time, he refused to adopt Islamic practices in the living out of his own faith in Christ. He would quickly admonish Christians who used the Qur'an side by side with the Bible when attempting to share about Jesus Christ with Muslims. The Reverend Dr. Harold Vogelaar, a former pastor in Cairo, knew Mazhar when he lived in Egypt in the late 1970s. Mazhar often exhibited to him a negative disposition toward Islam. Dr. Vogelaar recalls him once saying, "There is a lot of honey in the Qur'an, but there is also a lot of poison." Dr. Abdullah Turkmani, a researcher for the PLO living in Tunis, remembers that when he first met Mazhar he was "very anti-Islam in his orientation," and considered him too aggressive in his approach toward Muslims. Mazhar even used to get upset with Western Christians who contextualized their approach to Muslims by calling themselves "Muslims who follow Christ," saying it was dishonest.

As Mazhar slowly began to rediscover his own religious and cultural roots he became more loving toward his fellow Muslims and more generous in his perception of Islam. While remaining initially guarded about his changing attitude, little glimpses could be seen that perceiving Islam negatively may not have been his most deeply held view—such as his appreciation for the great Sufi teachers, his use of the Qur'an in sharing about his faith in Christ, his usage of the standard "Muslim" Arabic greetings and phrases, the carrying of Muslim prayer beads, and his visits to the mosques to meet and interact with people.

Retrospectively, it is clear that this evolution in Mazhar's attitude toward Islam and Muslims came through various channels and was due to specific life experiences. Mazhar was very influenced over the years by Christians whom he admired who demonstrated a love for Muslims and genuine respect for Islam. One such individual is the Reverend Dr. Harold Vogelaar. Dr. Vogelaar and Mazhar would go to the mosques, such as Al Azhar in Cairo, to dialogue with Islamic leaders. While Vogelaar was theologically more liberal than Mazhar at the time (today Mazhar would use the word "generous" as opposed to "liberal"), he was immeasurably impressed with his love for and openness with Muslims. Over time, they began together to use the Qur'an with Muslims to talk of "Muslim reasons to take Jesus seriously."

Perhaps the most significant step taken by Mazhar in regard to Islam resulted from his prison experience in Syria. In solitary confinement in a small prison cell, Mazhar found himself a broken man. This brokenness tenderized his heart toward all people—regardless of religion, race, or rank in society. He emerged from prison a gentler, kinder, and more compassionate person. Fundamentally, his time in prison served to profoundly reinforce to him that all people are made in the image of God. Consequently he became more appreciative of Islam as a possible signpost actually directing people to Christ.

This positive evolution in Mazhar's attitude toward Islam and his relationship with Muslims brought him into conflict at times with other Christian leaders. Many of the Arab Christian leaders in the Middle East take a confrontational approach in their work among Muslims, attempting to disassociate themselves completely from Islamic culture. Some would even forbid their staff to have any direct contact with Mazhar. Once in Cairo, a Muslim saw Mazhar reading the Injil (the Gospels) at a café and asked if it was true that it says in them, "Don't throw your pearls among the pigs." Mazhar asked this Muslim why he was asking. His response was, "Because I saw a Christian the other day reading the Injil and I asked him to read it to me, and he said the Injil said, 'Don't throw the pearls to the pigs.'" Mazhar, with sadness, remembers meeting a Christian military officer at a book fair, who, having realized that Mazhar's publication of the Gospel of Luke was oriented especially for Muslims, told him, "Muslims don't deserve *our* Savior." These are examples of how great the resentment from Christians toward Muslims can be. One of the key Christian Arab leaders in Tunisia, a convert from Islam, shared with me that while he loves Mazhar as a person, he is "against 80 percent of Mazhar's concepts and approach." Mazhar's positive approach, which is not apologetic or antagonistic, he sees as "playing with fire." Ironically, just after this man became a follower of Christ, he testified that Mazhar's Muslim-oriented Scripture and commentary publications played a significant role in bringing him to faith in Christ.

Theologically, Mazhar increasingly became more "generous"—seeing Muhammad and the Qur'an as potential signposts pointing toward Christ. He says, "I believe that God has set his witness in the center of Islam. I love the symbol of the mural of Jesus and Mary reputed to be still on the walls of the Kaaba today." Though Mazhar would not exactly use this terminology, there is a sense that he sees Islam as a sort of sect of Christianity, like other sects that existed in late antiquity, such as Arianism, Gnosticism, and Monophysitism. In this regard, he can see how Muhammad could be viewed partly as a victim of nonorthodox Christian beliefs that were prevalent at the time in the region. "For me," says Mazhar, "Islam has light, while I believe Christ is the fullest light I can know."

However, Mazhar has never really been attracted to Islam, or religion, for that matter, and is therefore rather uninterested in engaging it. I have never heard Mazhar debate a point about Islam with a Muslim. He refuses to get into theological arguments and is against pushing one system over another (i.e. Christianity vs. Islam). His focus is instead on the person of Jesus Christ and what Jesus means to him. If someone asks him about the Prophet Muhammad, or Islam, Mazhar will often tell them to ask someone, such as a Muslim sheik, who can give them a far better answer than he is able to. However, if they want to learn about Jesus, he will eagerly spend all day helping them do so. As he explains, "I desire to be a person of honor who treats Muslims with respect, and I don't want to get sucked into debates." A prominent imam in Oman, on the Persian Gulf, vividly remembers that Mazhar would not engage them in debate, but kept returning to the topic of Jesus. "The Qur'an is like the Bible to me—without Christ, it is just a book—for me the difference is Christ," says Mazhar.

When challenged by his fellow Muslims on aspects of his faith in Christ, Mazhar keeps his focus on asking them to "help him" find the truth, as opposed to attempting to give them the truth. If a Muslim says to him, "How can you read the Bible? It's been changed and corrupted," (for traditional Islamic teaching is that the Gospels have been corrupted and are therefore no longer reliable) he will respond, "Friend, you could be right. Please help me understand more fully how the Bible may have been changed. How do you know that it's been changed?" Then Mazhar may tell a story about an Egyptian pound note: "How can you tell if it is forged? You have to compare it to an original. So if someone claims the Bible has been changed, are they saying they have the original? If so, please get it and help me better understand it."

Over the years Mazhar began to sympathize more with Muslims as individuals than with Islam as a religion. He tells the parable of a Bedouin who came in from the desert for the first time. The Bedouin of course knew the desert very well. However, when he entered the city, he went through a red light and was stopped by the police for running through it. His response was "What red light?" as he had no knowledge of what driving in a city was all about. While Mazhar actively affirms the good in Islam, he also sees it as an ideology or religious system that at times victimizes its followers. In this sense, over time he has become less and less tolerant of Islamic fundamentalism, which prioritizes law over relationships and distorts something that he believes was meant to be simple and nonjudgmental. Within the Muslim community he identifies most easily with Muslim liberals and Sufis (mystics).

Certainly, the two groups with which Mazhar still has the most difficulty are Muslim fundamentalists and Christian conservative evangelicals: those who are "too black and white on truth" and who in his mind do not therefore reflect the spirit of Christ. "There are many things in the Qur'an I say yes, yes, yes to—and there are many things in Christianity I say no, no, no to." Unlike many Christians, Mazhar does not call Islam "evil," but rather sees Muslims (and Christians too) as being "incomplete" until they grasp the radical message of God in Christ above all earthly, political kingdoms, whether Islamic, Christian, or secular. Seeing Islam in a neutral and, at times, positive light, greatly shapes how he relates to Muslims. One of the foundational principles that he seeks to put into practice at all times is honoring their culture and religion.

One opportunity to honor Muslims is to allow them to share directly about their own faith with those who wish to learn about Islam. Mazhar does not condone Christians living in Muslim countries who bring in Western scholars to teach on Islam, when there are actual Muslim scholars in the same country. Once when he was teaching a course on sharing Christ with Muslims at a seminary in Jordan, he invited the general secretary of the Ministry of Islamic Affairs, a prominent Muslim sheik, to give a lecture to the theological students. This, of course, initially stretched their comfort zone. However, this Islamic leader actually ended up challenging the students to share their Gospel with boldness, love, and patience with Muslims. Winning the students' hearts, the sheik was more inspiring to them than any local Christian pastor would have been. Most students had never had such close contact with a Muslim sheik before. One of the Iraqi theological students shared with me the impact of Mazhar's teaching on him. He found himself crying for three days as he realized how profoundly prejudiced he had been against Muslims all his life. By introducing the students directly to Muslims and by exemplifying a genuine love for them, Mazhar had given this student at least a new heart for Muslims.

Mazhar's openness to learning from Muslims and journeying toward God with them is illustrated in a beautiful little story shared with me by someone living in the Gulf States in the Middle East. He observed Mazhar talking once with a Muslim peasant about Jesus. The man noted that Jesus was very hospitable—after all, he said, didn't Jesus make sure there were a lot of leftovers when he fed the 5,000? Mazhar's spontaneous response was to thank this simple, "uneducated" Muslim man for giving him a new perspective on the life of Jesus, as he had never thought about Jesus's miracle in those terms before.

Often, when moving into a new neighborhood, Mazhar will seek out a respected Muslim spiritual leader in the community and share with him that he has no spiritual mentor in his new community and that for him "the Bible contains guidelines to live according to God's desire." Then Mazhar will ask, "Can you please read these Scriptures in order to help me live up to them? In other words, I would like you to observe me as I live in your country and am accountable to you." Asking his Muslim friends to help him journey closer to God requires that he be vulnerable with them—allowing them to see his weaknesses.

Honor is one of the highest virtues in an Arab Muslim society, and Mazhar above all else seeks to honor Muslims. He shares a story of a young North African convert to Christ from Islam who overtly refused to fast during Ramadan (the Islamic month of fasting), because he was now a "Christian." So, at lunchtime, his sister would cook something for him to eat. When telling this story, Mazhar's question is invariably "Who was the better representative of Christ? The young man, or his Muslim sister?" For Mazhar the main question is "Are we honoring the Muslim families among whom we live and with whom we share our faith?"

Another way in which Mazhar honors Muslims is by first asking the father's permission when a young person approaches him wanting to study the Gospels. Often the father, or even the entire family, will then also want to be in on the opportunity. Choosing to honor the parents does not dislodge the young person from his family, and actually at times draws them all in instead.

While being quite sympathetic toward Muslims, Mazhar is often critical of many Christian mission approaches among Muslims. His experience is that some Western Christians befriend Muslims only with an agenda of conversion, which is not true love or friendship. He recalls a Tunisian Muslim intellectual asking him—knowing he was a follower of Christ, and reflecting his previous experience with some Western Christians—"I am not going to become a Christian. But will you still be my friend?" "Of course," responded Mazhar. Years later, this man's wife reads the Gospels in their home, and their children have been softened to the idea of Christ. Due to Mazhar's authentic friendship and his having no ulterior motives, Christ is being "naturalized" in their household.

Once, following Mazhar's attendance at a conference for Arab and Western Christians living and working in Muslim countries, he wrote the following in a letter to one of the conference participants:

> When I came to the conference . . . and heard the stories they shared I felt so devastated and hopeless. . . . The stories were about someone who went from United Arab Emirates to Switzerland and met an Emirati (someone from the UAE), or from Bahrain to London and met a Bahraini, or an Egyptian going to be trained about Islam in London, etc. Why are the Christian Arabs willing to go outside their own countries and especially Europe to meet Muslims but not in their own country? Where is the life lived with people in the daily routine, where we share our life with Christ naturally? What is wrong with us Arabs that Western Christians don't want to be our friends? I really feel I want to burst into tears.

Instead of trying to bring Muslims to Christianity, Mazhar tries to bring Christ to where Muslims are. And he looks for ways in which Arabs can stay culturally Muslim while following Jesus as their Lord.

Mazhar is all about making allies with Muslims. He attempts to allow the life and teachings of Jesus to provide a framework for his building of meaningful long-term relationships. He has little patience with those who want to make polemical war with Muslims. He emphasizes loving them, having compassion for them, and when it comes to sharing his faith in Christ with them, focuses on touching their hearts—sharing about how much God loves them.

The late Dr. Ahmed Meshraqi, professor of comparative religions at the Islamic University of Zeitouna in Tunis, described Mazhar's interaction with Islam as being "not for Islam or against Islam." There is a sense that Mazhar appeals to Arabs more on the basis of Arab culture than on the basis of Islamic faith. In general, he is critical of religion as an institution, seeing it as divisive. Instead he attempts to see people as people, not products of their religion. Therefore, Muslims, to Mazhar, are fellow pilgrims seeking to journey toward God.

Appreciation for Christ and his acts of mercy for individuals in need, irrespective of their religion, is what overshadows Mazhar's views on Christian or Muslim religious practice. Saladin Ben Ohbed, Tunisian lawyer and university professor, sees Mazhar's openness to Muslims as partly due to his return to his roots: "Mazhar was a young man during the period of Arab nationalism, which bred a culture of tolerance—it was the 'school of thought' of Arab nationalism at the time. And influenced by the legacy of this avantgarde perspective, Mazhar can spontaneously bridge the two—Islam and Christianity."

In addition to encouraging a greater sensitivity toward Muslims, what Mazhar sees as the most important need today is for Christians to enter into genuine friendships with Muslims as they attempt to live out the way of Christ among them. This is the way Muslims will most fully experience Christ and it is a critical part of seeing Christ naturalized in the Arab Muslim world—requiring a long-term perspective. As Mazhar says, "The light we see from the stars at night comes from stars that are quite far away. These stars may no longer even be in existence, but their light still shines on us. Even so, the memory of Christians lives on with Arabs they knew and loved . . . even if they are no longer there in person."

Mazhar's life journey with Islam has led him to have a paradoxical relationship with it. Today, when he hears the Qur'an read, the beauty of its literary language can send chills down his spine. At the same time he sees Islam as a religious system that can keep people away from God unnecessarily. His best advice is "instead of attempting to get rid of anything one sees as darkness . . . it is better to light some candles." In looking at Mazhar's life and ministry, we are able to glean some effective ways of "lighting candles."

Waging Peace on Muslims

Salaam on Islam. *Salaam* is the Arabic word for peace. In regard to relating to the Islamic world, Mazhar advocates a peaceful and sacrificial attitude, one that is nonconfrontational in nature and focused on relationship. His approach is perhaps best described as one that "wages peace on Muslims."[4] With this as his working philosophy, he has been a powerful force for reconciliation between Muslims and Christians—"'un homme de paix' between the two faiths," as a prominent Tunisian Christian describes him.

A peaceful approach has long been one that Mazhar's family demonstrated to him throughout their rich heritage. When the twentieth century opened with the Turks and Kurds massacring the Armenians, Mazhar's grandfather took in seven Armenian families who survived and arrived in a terrible state in his Syrian hometown.

Mazhar considers that if Muslims are to be enabled to see the Christ of the Gospels, they must first see the likeness of Christ in his followers. "If the Christian message is spread in an un-Christian manner, is it still Christian?" asks Mazhar. Historically, Christian activity in the Arab Muslim world prioritized the proclamation of their faith—preaching, literature, education, starting churches, etc. However, today the greatest need is of "demonstration," toward enabling Muslims to "see Christ" in Christians. Christine Mallouhi, in her book *Waging Peace on Islam*, tells the story of St. Francis of Assisi, who during the height of the Crusades traveled to Egypt and visited the Sultan Kamil (the nephew of the great Islamic leader Saladin). Francis came in humility and peace, in contrast to the conquering Crusaders. His approach and attitude so impressed the Muslim Sultan that he invited Francis to send his Little Brothers throughout his territory. It is out of this experience that we have perhaps Francis's wisest counsel: "Preach the Gospel at all times, and if necessary, use words." He saw the dignity of God in every Muslim person. Such grace toward Muslims was radical in his day, and still is in ours.

Reflecting on Mahatma Gandhi, so influential in his spiritual journey, Mazhar shares, "Gandhi has taught me more of the spirit of Christ than perhaps anyone else." He challenged Christians to make love their "working force," adopting it as a total way of life, "for love is the center and soul of Christianity." He urged Christians to "live more like Jesus Christ . . . put your emphasis on love."[5] This advice fits with an early picture we have of Gandhi, as reported by C. F. Andrews. Andrews, a respected Scottish Anglican priest serving in India, once visited Gandhi at the Phoenix Ashram in South Africa, where he found him surrounded by children, whom he loved. A baby girl belonging to a family that in India was considered untouchable was in his arms, along with a little Muslim boy who was an invalid. Gandhi's tenderness toward the smallest thing that suffered pain was part of his devout search for truth, or God.[6]

Gandhi would constantly say to Christians, "Don't talk about it. The rose doesn't have to propagate its perfume. It just gives it forth, and people are drawn to it. Live it, and people will come to see the source of your power."[7] Because of Gandhi, a non-organized "Christ-following" arose in India apart from the church. The leading ideas of this movement were love, service, and self-sacrifice.

Gandhi's humility and sacrificial nature were particularly evident in his relationships with Muslims. At the age of seventy-eight, during the riots in Calcutta between Muslims and Hindus, he chose to stay in a Muslim home in the very center of the riot district. There he welcomed the former Muslim premier, called "The Butcher" by Hindus because they believed he had incited the riots, to stay with him. In order to stop the brutalities, Gandhi went on a fast until death. As a result, after seventy-two hours both sides came to him to guarantee the lives of the opposite community with their own lives, laying all their weapons at his feet. Later, at the even greater Hindu-Muslim riots in Delhi in early 1948, he drew up eight points on which all had to agree, or he would fast until death. All eight points shamelessly favored the Muslims, including returning 117 mosques that had been converted into Hindu temples or residences. On the sixth day of the fast, the parties signed the "Pact of Peace."

Gandhi's last pilgrimage was to Mehrauli, a Muslim shrine seven miles south of New Delhi. Muslim women who had been fasting with Gandhi had complained to him that Hindu violence had kept them from going alone to Mehrauli. Gandhi chose to accompany them on their journey. Once they reached the Muslim shrine, which had been vandalized by Hindus, Gandhi promised that it would be repaired. Three days later he was murdered by a Hindu fundamentalist who was incensed at his kindness toward Muslims.[8]

In like spirit, in relating to his fellow Muslims, Mazhar doesn't use Islam as a bridge, but rather uses love and compassion. Muslims often say to him, "I can't figure you out. Why are you going to so much trouble to help us?" His response is simply, "If I see a chance to do good and don't help, it is a sin. The opposite of love is indifference." Consequently his encouragement to Western Christians is not necessarily to study more about Islam, but rather to proactively love Muslims. Mazhar gives the sad example of a Western priest living in the Middle East, who speaks fluent Arabic and yet does not exhibit love for the Arabs, so consequently does not have true Muslim friends. Loving Muslims can be demonstrated in many ways, even embracing and enjoying the unique aspects of Middle Eastern culture: the literature, art, food, and dance.

We need to learn how to love our neighbor, the other, in a way that he or she will recognize that we give them value, respect, and recognition as a child of God, whom God wants to bring closer to himself. For as Mazhar shared in an interview for *Assahafa* (a daily Tunisian government newspaper), "The Scriptures say that the person who does not love does not know God, for God is love." Connecting the love for God with our love for our Muslim brothers and sisters, he raises the question, "Suppose I tell you that I love you dearly, but when I encounter your children in the street, I treat them harshly. Would you believe me?"

Throughout the Islamic world, hundreds of Christians have shared with me that Mazhar taught them to love Muslims. In 1979, one of Mazhar's Moroccan neighbors was a militant Muslim sheik who was also always verbally attacking Christians. He would even tell Mazhar that he was going to hell, to which Mazhar would respond with humor, "If I do, I will certainly miss you there." Instead of moving apartments, as many Christians would do, Mazhar decided to focus on building a relationship with him by serving their local community. If, for example, anyone was sick or delivering a baby, he would make sure his car was always available to be of assistance, regardless of the time of day or night. Eventually, this sheik came to eat in his home and vice versa. Commenting on this experience, Mazhar asked, "After two years, do you think he continued to speak negatively about Christians? No, he couldn't—as people would see him as a hypocrite." Sometime later, a Muslim *hijab*-wearing (veiled) woman friend of the Mallouhis shared with them her desire to read the Christian Scriptures. She shared how she had first gone to the local sheik to ask his permission, and that he had responded, "Yes, you may do so, for I know a fine Arab follower of Christ in town." She would most probably never have been allowed to read the Bible if Mazhar had not cultivated the relationship with that sheik by serving the community.

Mazhar says, "If you look at someone as your enemy, you make him your enemy. A stranger can be an enemy or a friend you haven't yet met. We seek to treat Muslims with the same respect with which we Christians would like to be treated." Many Westerners brand Arab Muslims as terrorists, when in reality the Muslims often feel they are the ones being terrorized. For example, they feel helpless at times when Western culture is indirectly imposed on them. Paul Tournier, the late Swiss psychologist, once wrote in *To Understand Each Other*, "It is quite clear that between love and understanding there is a very close link. . . . He who loves understands, and he who understands loves. One who feels understood feels loved, and one who feels loved feels sure of being understood." Putting ourselves in their shoes helps us to understand what they are experiencing. Imagine how we Westerners would feel if our children only wanted to watch Arab Muslim movies and began dressing like Middle Easterners.

The church in the West, instead of setting an example of Christian love as Mazhar did, is at times noted for its hostility toward Islam. As Mazhar says, "When the only tool you have is a hammer, every problem you encounter resembles a nail." In regard to relating to Muslims, he attempts to give Christians more tools to understand them, so there is less hammering. Mazhar frequently draws attention to the way Jesus treated the Samaritans—whom he considers the "Muslims of Christ's day." The Samaritans aggravated the Jews because they shared the same religious story, prophets, and holy places, but had their own differing interpretation. "Muslims are our Samaritans," says Mazhar, "and Jesus refused to wage war on them. Such was his encounter with the Samaritan woman: he responded to her thirst for God and left us with one of the most beautiful stories of grace and love in the Gospels." Mazhar has a beautiful way of describing this encounter between Jesus and the Samaritan woman: "Two thirsty people at a sacred well, who meet and journey together."

Through respect and reciprocity Mazhar has found an amazing openness to his publications about Christ. A veiled Shiite Muslim woman doing the typing for Qur'anic verses in his publication of the Gospel of John for Muslims was much impressed with the material. "It is not attacking," she said, surprised. As a result she not only saw the similarities between Islam and Christianity, but also then felt comfortable enough to discuss questions raised in her mind. She shared that she could feel the presence of Jesus with her. During this time she became pregnant and decided to name the baby either Mary or Jesus (Isa).

The words of the late Virginia Cobb in a brilliant paper at a 1969 historic conference in Tehran, Iran, for Christians working among Muslims, left an indelible impression on Mazhar. The entire thrust of her prophetic paper concerned the importance of demonstrating the spirit of Christ among Muslims, and therefore exhibiting graciousness, generosity, love, peace, and respect.

> We are not *warring* Islam. If we were, we couldn't afford to give any quarter, to let anything go unchallenged, to admit any good or truth. We would be happy to damage it as much as possible, to show every weakness or inconsistency. But this is contrary to the spirit of Christ. And a major error in any struggle is to pursue the wrong enemy. Our enemy is evil, God's enemy. Islam teaches love of God, supreme loyalty to Him, great reverence and high principles of character.

> ───

> Christianity, like Islam, has produced wars, persecutions, bigotry and empty forms; we cannot therefore war against it but seek a truer understanding of it.

Love. Christ's love was a genuine concern for the total welfare of those he came to save. It was demonstrated, not spoken. It . . . included healing, moral teaching, crossing of social barriers, comforting, calming, freeing, touching the untouchables, and befriending sinners and outcasts . . . To love as he did means seeking the good of others in every sphere, actively and without reciprocation, without even appreciation, without conversions. It means accepting the inconvenience or hurt they may cause us without lessening our positive efforts on their behalf. Perhaps the only way we can prove—to ourselves or to others—that we love in this way is to be really concerned about the "this-worldly" welfare of some who reject the message [of Christ], to feel real friendship for some outside the circle of [Christians], to keep on serving those we feel will not be won.

———

Therefore, there must be *some concrete demonstration of love*. It can be personal, in the relationship between friends, or institutional—schools, hospitals . . . reading rooms, community centers . . . and publications that are directed to real human needs.

———

We must have an attitude of love and acceptance, and strong faith in the power of the truth.

We must get into the midst of people, identify with them, and love them in deed not word, in some concrete ways.

———

Many years of friendship, love, service with reciprocation . . . may be required.[9]

In order for Muslims to be "acclimatized" to Christ walking down their road, it is now time to "wage peace" on them, as Mazhar exhorts us. For they, like us, are made in God's image. *Salaam* on Islam.

Building on the Dark Side of the Moon

Waging peace on Muslims requires that we build on the "dark side of the moon." The Islamic symbol is a lunar crescent, the small part of the moon that reflects light off the sun. However, the majority of the moon is dark—shadowed due to the lack of reflected sunlight. This lunar crescent and dark side of the moon can be a beautiful analogy for our relationship as Christians with Islam. The narrow crescent can represent the differences between Islam and Christianity, and the dark side, which of course is much larger, can represent all that we have in common. In the midst of the increasing chasm of discord and misunderstanding between the "Christian" West and the Islamic East, there has never been a greater need for a new movement of Christians to build on what we have in common with Muslims, hence "building on the dark side of the moon."

Laying the foundation for this approach, the former archbishop of Canterbury, Lord Carey, in an address at Beit al-Qur'an in Bahrain, said, "One can, I believe, be a Christian, as I am, wholly convinced of the uniqueness of Christ and his abiding relevance to human kind, and still affirm that other faiths possess value, significance, and integrity. That recognition sets us on the path of dialogue, a dialogue which is not just a matter of trading ideas but of sharing our deepest convictions and concerns, and opening our hearts to one another."[10]

It is critical that we recognize what we Christians have in common with Muslims, and build our relationships with them on those commonalities. Over the ages there has been a kinship between the two faiths, which is not often mentioned in our contemporary polemical literature. The Qur'an actually calls Christians "nearest in love" to Muslims. Indeed, during Islam's expansion in the Middle East following Muhammad's death, many Eastern Christians welcomed the Arab Muslim armies as liberators, as they were being oppressed by the Byzantine Christian West.

By spending time among Christians in the Middle East, we become aware of how much early Eastern Christian tradition formed the foundation for the basic practices of Islam. The Muslim form of prayer, with prostration and bowing, comes from the ancient Syrian Orthodox Christian tradition and is still practiced today. The month-long fast of Ramadan is an Islamization of our Lent, and some Eastern Churches still practice an all-day fast. The architecture of the earliest minarets, square instead of round, was derived from the church towers in Byzantine Syria. Their pilgrimage, creed, and prayer five times a day facing their holy city likewise all have Christian origins. If a Christian from sixth-century Byzantium were to return today, he would find much more that was familiar in the practices of Muslims than in a contemporary Protestant evangelical church.

In our relationships with Muslims, we can proactively build on the guiding principles of Christianity and Islam. Discussing the basis for a healthy dialogue between Christians and Muslims, Lord Carey comments, "First and foremost is the theological basis of a common humanity. Both Islam and Christianity have a very high view of what it is to be a human being, made in the image of God. We have a shared sense of the sheer wonder of creation by God, and also of the dignity of our vocation as human beings. Both faiths resist racism and all other attempts to deny the equal dignity before God of all people. From this base other things can develop. Indeed, from this flows our common spiritual quest. Our journey is a shared one . . ."[11]

If we truly look through the lens of Jesus, we will see Muslims as children of God who are on a journey of faith as we are. The renowned Islamic scholar and Arabist, Anglican Bishop Kenneth Cragg, writes, "The differences, which undoubtedly exist, between the Muslim and Christian understanding of God are far-reaching and must be patiently studied. But it would be fatal to all our mutual tasks to doubt that one and the same God over all was the reality in both."[12]

Christianity and Islam indeed have much in common and we need to rediscover our family connections. Each is monotheistic, and each claims universality. Each fosters strong traditions of piety, social action, and justice. Each even claims to be a religion of peace. Both honor the authority of Moses and the Hebrew prophets, believe in the Creator God of Abraham, and know that God desires that we exhibit justice, mercy, and humility before him.

One effective approach is to build on the commonalities within our respective theological beliefs. Rev. Colin Chapman, Anglican priest, Islamist, and author of *Cross and the Crescent,* suggests we can build on what we naturally agree on together: God Creates, God is One, God Reveals, God Loves, God Forgives, God Judges, God Rules—though we may of course differ on how God does each. Another approach is to begin by building on our similar worship practices: traditions, liturgical practices, pillars—fasting, pilgrimage, charity, creed, prayers.

As Christians, perhaps the most obvious commonality on which to build is the mutual respect for Christ. Islam's preoccupation with Jesus is unique among the world's great non-Christian religions. Islamic culture gives us the richest images of Jesus in any non-Christian culture. As Cambridge University professor Tariq Khalidi, a Muslim, says, "no other [non-Christian] religion has devoted so much living attention to both the Jesus of history and to the Christ of eternity." Muslims have a profoundly reverential picture of Christ. In the Qur'an Jesus is called the Messiah, the Messenger, the Prophet, the Word, and Spirit of God. Mazhar's experience is that the Qur'an, for many Muslims, can be a path to Jesus.

Building on what we have in common requires that Christians take a positive view of Muhammad and all he was attempting to do. Beginning with this foundation, everything changes in how we see Islam. As Mazhar says, "Muhammad was partially a victim of Christianity at the time." Christianity as it reached Arabia included a mixture of heresies—preaching not the Trinity, but a triad of God Father, God Mother, and God Son. Muhammad challenged this idea and made his central message *"la illah il-Allah"*: there is no god but God. Throughout history, many of the Middle Eastern Christian figures, while not agreeing with all of Islam's theological tenets, nevertheless applauded the way Muhammad converted the Arabs from idolatry and poly-theism, and admired his single-minded emphasis on worshipping one God. In many ways, Muslim fundamentalists have misrepresented Muhammad to the world. Mazhar says, "What Christians have often done to Christ, Mus-lim fundamentalists have done to Muhammad—speaking and distorting his message and purpose." Muhammad was based in Mecca during his first four-teen years of ministry and focused solely on a spiritual reformation, preach-ing to the residents to return to following the one true God—away from their idolatry and polytheism. During this period he underwent significant persecution. This is often called his "Meccan phase." Then, due to persecu-tion and rejection, he fled to the city of Medina, seeking a refuge and a place to form a base on which to build. It was in Medina that his spiritual message became associated with power and authority, and he himself became a polit-ical and military figure, uniting the various Arab tribes around a common belief and mission. After eight years, Muhammad's platform and following was strong enough to return and conquer Mecca. This later period is often referred to as his "Medinan phase." Interestingly, a similar thing happened to the Christian church. Prior to Constantine, the Christians did not have political influence or military might. On the contrary, they were often per-secuted and forbidden to exist. From AD 76 to AD 303 there were ten sig-nificant movements of persecution against Christians. Hence, they often were forced underground. However, in AD 312, when Constantine, the Ro-man Emperor, converted to the Christian faith, he not only made the church officially legal, but put Christianity on the path to becoming the state reli-gion and began to fight wars in the name of Christ. This association with might and power distorted Christ's original message. Mazhar believes that Christians should build upon the first period of Muhammad's ministry, the Meccan phase, as that is when he was focused uniquely on the spiritual di-mension of worshipping God. As Bishop Kenneth Cragg says, "One mission Christians can have to Islam today is to help them rediscover the heart of the Meccan message of Muhammad."[13]

Mazhar's interaction with Muslims demonstrates the importance of build-ing on the commonalities between the Christian and Muslim faiths. He sees God's fingerprints on Islamic thought, believing, as Justin Martyr said in the second century, that "all truth is the Lord's." And therefore he capitalizes on this idea of truth and goodness to point Muslims to Christ, who is truth and goodness. Yet he does so while also communicating a strong sense of submis-sion (the world "Islam" in Arabic means "submission"), and testifying that he has found the most excellent Master (Christ), who deserves our submission. Some have shared with me that they have seen Mazhar so extol this Master that Muslims beg to know who this Master is.

Perhaps most important of all, by building on the commonalities between following Christ and Islam, Mazhar affirms all the Christ-like insights and values that have been incorporated into the Muslim faith and Middle Eastern culture. Reflecting Mazhar's perspective, Christine Mallouhi says, "As people seek to serve God in line with Jesus's teaching (whether they know it or not) by loving God and loving their fellow humans, then they are worshipping the same God regardless of cultural, ritual or human understanding of attributes or doctrine."

While Mazhar in his heart sees the teaching of Islamic fundamentalists as far from what Allah has in mind for his children, he is careful not to criticize Islam or to cause Muslims to lose face or become defensive. Instead, he always looks for common ground until he finds it. He loves to focus on the Qur'anic verse (50:60) that describes God as being nearer to man than his jugular vein. "If people do not have the revelation of God in Christ, this of course does not mean that they do not know God," says Mazhar. Here, the words of the late Virginia Cobb, addressed to Christians, are as pertinent as ever:

> We are *not debating* with Islam to prove that our views are correct and theirs incorrect. Were we, we might rely on polemics, logical proofs, etc. But no one is won by this method or convinced against his will. This approach makes the basic mistake of acting as if Christian faith were credence rather than commitment to a Person, an act of the intellect rather than of the whole person. It ignores the fact that our doctrines came about as an attempt to explain in comprehensible terms our experience, i.e. they follow rather than precede experience.

> ——

> Our attitude should be one of *love and acceptance.* God accepts and loves them [Muslims] as they are. He is already reconciled to them. . . . If we . . . are "reconciled" to them, we will accept them as persons as able as ourselves, and as deserving of respect and a hearing for their views. We will not go to straighten them out or tell them all the answers. If we are reconciled to them we will be able to appreciate all that is true, good, commendable and worthy in their lives as individuals and in their culture and religion.

> ——

> We must talk openly, freely and respectfully of religious matters, whether in regard to our religion or theirs, and emphasize the responsibility of the individual to God, to act according to his own best light. [14]

Yet unfortunately today it is all too often not the similarities but the dissimilarities between us that concern most Christians and Muslims. However, as Christians, if our heart's desire is that Muslims be introduced to the Christ of the Gospels, it is critical that we build upon any kinship and proximity between the two, rather than act and speak in ways that create further alienation. Realizing what we have in common with Muslims and building on those commonalities ("the dark side of the moon"), provides us with a foundation from which we can then address our legitimate differences ("the narrow crescent").

A Guest Posture

Building on what we have in common with Muslims in order to be able to most effectively address the true differences between our respective faiths, we must assume the posture of a guest. I am reminded of that well-known story of Jesus's encounter with Zacchaeus, the chief tax collector.[15] Zacchaeus was reaching for God and somehow sensed truth in this Jesus who was passing through his city. However, while greatly desiring to see Jesus, every imaginable wall existed to prevent him from truly seeing Jesus for who he was. Physically, he was short, and therefore could not see over the crowds. Socially, as "chief tax collector" he would have been the most hated person in the area, as tax collecting was considered a very dishonorable profession because those who did it worked with their occupiers, the Romans, and were viewed as enriching themselves by cheating their own people. Zacchaeus would therefore have been greatly alienated by his own community. Consequently, from the religious standpoint of that time, he would have been viewed as one of the greatest "sinners"—those who most displeased God. Tax collectors were in fact so despised that they were barred from the Temple.

Zacchaeus was attracted to Jesus and desperately wanted to discover him, but every barrier existed to keep him from doing so. In this Gospel story we see Jesus break these barriers down: "When Jesus came to the place, he looked up and said to him, 'Zacchaeus, hurry and come down; for I must stay at your house today.'" Jesus stopped and said, "I *must* stay at your house," not "I would like to stay." This is a very strong expression, meaning not only visiting him, but fully being Zacchaeus's guest. Jesus is saying to Zacchaeus, "I want to be your guest." As he went to Zacchaeus's home, our Gospels tells us that Jesus was criticized for "being the guest" of such a despised person.

This "guest posture" was very much Jesus's approach to breaking down the barriers that prevented others from seeing who he was. Most important, being someone's guest requires allowing oneself to be vulnerable and dependent on the host. And this requires the guest to humbly and willingly receive from the host. We see this happen again with Jesus during his encounter with the Samaritan woman at the well. Jesus asked her for a drink—an unthinkable thing for a Jew at that time to do to a Samaritan, let alone a Samaritan woman. Jesus is crossing all the lines of difference: gender, ethnic, religious, social, and political. Yet Jesus approached her out of need and weakness, and with respect. Consequently, she asks Jesus, "*How is it* that you a Jew ask a drink from me, a woman of Samaria?" Jesus's approach opened doors that would normally have remained closed. He was then able to share with her about the living water he provides.

In our relationship with Muslims, this is the posture we are encouraged to take as followers of Jesus. As Father Louis Massignon, the late Christian priest and renowned Islamic scholar from France said, "To understand the other, one does not need to annex him but to become his guest."[16] We need to ask Muslims, "Can I be your guest?" It is this posture that breaks down the walls. To what extent do we try to alienate Muslims, as opposed to acting as guests in the House of Islam? As to the manner and spirit of the presentation of our faith, we should consider of the highest importance that penetrating statement of Rabindranath Tagore, the Bengali Indian poet who won the Nobel Prize for Literature in 1913: "When [Christians] bring their truth to a strange land, unless they bring it in the form of homage it is not accepted and should not be."[17]

As a follower of Christ, Mazhar's orientation within an Islamic community is that of being a guest. In this sense he attempts to see and encourage all that is positive in Islam, while at the same time sharing the truth he has found in Christ. From this perspective, he had no problem with his children growing up in schools where they were taught Islam and the Qur'an. This guest posture means that Mazhar leaves to Muslims the open critiques of Islam or Muhammad and allows himself to be vulnerable by sharing with them his own struggles—such as when the Church does not reflect Christ. He even believes that we should openly seek to discover from Muslims why Christian activity among them over the centuries has all too often been perceived negatively.

Adopting a guest posture naturally requires that we respect and honor the other's culture. A Westerner shared with me after having left the Middle East how shocked Mazhar was that she was going to be fairly hard in her critique of the Muslim mind-set in a speech to an American Christian audience. "Mazhar wanted me to remember how graciously and kindly I was received while I was a guest in their countries," she said. "He did not want me to feed the hostility that was growing in post-9/11 America. Humbled, I therefore reworked my talk."

Mazhar once learned of a Christian group sending booklets about the Christian faith to people in Algeria to try and convince them of its truth. Mazhar does not endorse this kind of activity, yet knowing he cannot stop them he nevertheless shared with them that a more honorable way, a way that would exhibit the love of God, would have been to simply send a letter saying, "I was recently in your beautiful country of Algeria and while there I often experienced how our Scriptures came to life before my eyes as the culture of the Bible is still kept alive in your country as in many Arab countries. I saw how the shepherd gently led the sheep and gives himself to them day and night. It reminded me of Christ's words that he is the shepherd of God's people. Many Algerians hosted me in their homes and I was reminded of Jesus's teaching of the story of the Good Samaritan. I want to thank Algerians for their generosity and for living out this parable to strangers like me." Mazhar's counsel to this group echoes his actions whenever a Muslim asked him for a Bible. When giving the Scriptures to Muslims, Mazhar often asks them to pray for him so that he can more effectively follow the teachings in this book, "as following Christ is not easy without God's help."

All too often Christians, even Middle Eastern Christians, do not embody this sensitivity to Islamic culture. Mazhar shares about an Arab Christian couple living in the Arabian Gulf who, on arriving at a Westerner's house, noticed piles of shoes at the front door. According to the local custom, people remove their dirty shoes and walk barefoot in the house, or are given house slippers, in order to keep the floor clean. The living room is filled with large cushions propped around the walls; when it's time to eat a tablecloth is spread over the carpet and they eat from communal plates while reclining on the cushions. The Arab Christian couple stood at the door and angrily pointed to the shoes, "What is this, a mosque?" they asked. The American hosts invited them to do what felt comfortable for them. They remained the only guests to have walked on the carpets in their dirty shoes—and all because they did not want to "do as the Muslims do." The relational divide between Christians and Muslims is very wide in some places, and often this is due as much to the actions of Christians as of Muslims. In Egypt, for example, some Coptic Christians will not even purchase a car from a Muslim. By contrast, Mazhar actually enters into business partnerships with Muslims.

The fundamental characteristic of a guest is being open to receiving from the hands of the host. In regard to being the guest of Muslims, this means that we are to be open to learning from them. There has never been a time when the need has been greater for Christians to recognize the positive among Muslims—to learn from them. E. Stanley Jones, the famous Christian Methodist minister in India and a close friend of Gandhi, whose writings have mentored Mazhar, once asked Gandhi, "How can we [Christians] see Christianity naturalized in India?" Gandhi's brief answer included, ". . . study the non-Christian religions and cultures more sympathetically in order to find the good that is in them, so that you might have a more sympathetic approach to people."[18]

In this regard, some Christians believe they have the whole truth and therefore assume others can have no truth at all. However, as Mazhar says, "We do not own the truth; the truth owns us." Consequently, Mazhar is very grateful for all truth found anywhere and is about stretching out beyond the religious borders and sacred texts to find truth that gives light to Jesus *wherever* it is found. Elaborating further, Mazhar shares, "If we cannot step out of the boxes of our own religion, how can we present ourselves to be open to the truly Other? My soul guide is the spirit of our Lord Jesus." Khalil Gibran, the late best-selling Lebanese author, put it another way: "Say not, 'I have found the path of the soul.' Say rather, 'I have met the soul walking upon my path.' For the soul walks upon all paths. The soul walks not upon a line, neither does it grow like a reed. The soul unfolds itself, like a lotus of countless petals."[19]

"Our Muslim friends have more to teach us than we could ever imagine," Mazhar says. And indeed we need to learn from each other. Through Muslims, God will certainly teach us new things about himself. Mazhar questions, "What if I want to go to Pakistan, but I start wandering through Libya. Would I like it if someone came to me and called me stupid or looked down on me? Wouldn't it be much better if they said to me, 'I also want to go to Pakistan. Let's journey together.'" Ironically, Muslims are the ones who actually challenged Mazhar to publish a readable biography on the life of Christ, because no suitable publications for Muslims in Arabic existed in the secular market, even though Christ is such an important figure in the Qur'an.

In every way possible we need to look with eyes that seek to receive from the faith and practice of Muslims, toward benefiting our own faith in Christ. The opportunities for this are numerous—from continuing our own spiritual formation, to deepening our theological understanding of God, to helping us live in more Christ-like ways. Growing up in Muslim-majority Senegal, I recall being challenged to take advantage of the Islamic call to prayer from the minaret for Muslims five times a day, and to use it to remind me throughout the day to be dependent upon God. To this day, every time I hear the call to prayer (as long as it isn't blaring into my bedroom early in the morning at a high volume), I find myself thinking of God.

An excellent illustration of a Muslim helping us grow in our theological understanding of Christ is Kamel Hussain's book, *City of Wrong*, which explores the various events in Christ's life on Good Friday. A devoted Egyptian Muslim, the late Kamel Hussain leaves an atmosphere of mystery concerning what really took place that day. His depiction of Jesus, however, and of the suffering he experienced, draws us as Christians powerfully nearer to understanding this mystery of Christ's suffering as presented to us in the Gospels.

Concerning the other end of Christ's life, his birth, Mazhar shares about how a Muslim friend of his so beautifully described what took place in that event: "Christmas is about God joining us in the life journey to lift us up to God."

Mazhar queries a Christian's openness to learn from Muslims by asking, "If the Muslim Arab invites you into their home, and they feed you and give you drink, and are kind to you, do you go back to your Christian community and tell them, 'I want to thank God for using these Muslims, for showing me love and hospitality . . . showing me things that you, God, have wanted to show me all these years?'" In this regard, I recall the moving words that Carl R. Raswan wrote in his book titled *Black Tents of Arabia: My Life among the Bedouins*, about his experience of living among the Muslim Bedouin in the desert for 22 years: "I claim one thing, however: that during my sojourn in Arabia, I lived entirely as a Bedouin. I had never any need to deny my race or my creed amongst the Arabs. I was never once the butt of their mockery or suffered at their hands any discourtesy."[20]

Affirming the guest posture, Mazhar says, "Our openness to all they stand for opens them to all we stand for." And by assuming the guest posture with Muslims, he has found an amazing openness among them toward his faith in Christ. For this whole approach elicits from Muslims a spirit of appreciation, openness, and genuine dialogue concerning the person of Christ. Anglican Bishop Kenneth Cragg, in his book *Sandals in the Mosque*, writes of how when you enter a mosque you must do so barefoot, and uses this illustration to remind us that we need to approach that which to Muslims is holy in a spirit of humility and reverence (even when it may not seem holy to us), or we will find all doors closed to us.

As Lord Carey said in his address at Beit al-Qur'an in Bahrain, "Christians and Muslims engaged in that kind of dialogue may thus approach their own faith in a new way, a way which opens up new and exciting opportunities. . . . to have one's own faith enlarged and deepened."[21] On another occasion, in a joint article in the *London Times* with the principal of the Muslim College in London, Zaki Badawi, Dr. Carey wrote about the importance of continuing dialogue and expressed the opinion that in our day "one of the key challenges is how to handle difference. The 'dignity of difference' is a challeng[ing] but exciting reality we must all address in the conviction that our faith will not be diminished but enhanced. . . . We can discover much that is good and true in those who are different from ourselves and at the same time can come to a deeper understanding of our own tradition."[22]

As Christians we can find the deeper roots of our own faith in Christ when we are immersed in a world of another religion—such as Islam—and this can help us understand our own faith's depth and heritage in a transformed way. Paradoxically, Jesus is often revealed most clearly in environments that seem contradictory to who he is. Some of the deepest writings on the Christian faith are a result of followers of Christ living in the midst of another faith, where these individuals, as a result of their environment, see Jesus anew and afresh and often quite differently than the traditional understandings of Jesus that they brought with them.

The faith stories of both Father Louis Massignon and Charles de Foucauld, two Christians known throughout the Islamic world for their beautiful demonstration of Christ among Muslims, are moving examples of how God used Islam to draw them in a deeper way to Christ. Father Louis Massignon, the famed French Islamist and Christian (d. 1962), during a trip to the North African desert among the Tuareg Muslim nomads, wrote, "It seemed to me that for the first time in this nomadic life of the desert, I had really seen men render homage to the divinity." Later, through his study of Hallaj, the Sufi Muslim mystic and martyr, Massignon was drawn to Christ. During a crisis, while studying about Hallaj, he felt himself invaded by a mysterious presence and called it "the visitation of the Stranger." This experience led him back to the church, and ultimately to become a priest in the Melchite Catholic Church. He writes, "In 1908, I had become, through the apprenticeship of Arabic, the liturgical language of Islam . . . converted to Christianity by the witness to God implied by the Muslim faith."23

Charles de Foucauld (d. 1916), explorer, missionary-monk, Christian mystic, and founder of the Little Brothers, a contemplative community order that is now active worldwide, had his faith in Christ similarly enhanced through Islam. As a young explorer in North Africa, the young Frenchman was profoundly affected by his encounter with Islam. As Zoe Hersov writes, "He was impressed by Muslims' constant repetition of the name of God, their prostrations in prayer in the open desert and the haunting call of the muezzin. . . . He admitted that Islam had disturbed him deeply, and that 'the sight of this faith, of these souls living in the continuous presence of God, has made me aware of something greater and more true than worldly preoccupations.' At the very least, this experience made him see the emptiness of his life and prompted him to undertake his own spiritual journey."24 This experience of seeing Muslims revere God had a lasting impression on Foucauld, beginning a spiritual journey of returning to the faith of his childhood.

> As he wrote, "My exposure to this faith [Islam] and to the soul living always in God's presence helped me understand that there is something greater and more real than the pleasures of this world." An irresistible force was drawing him—where, he could not say. But over and over, as he restlessly roamed the streets of Paris, he repeated a prayer: "My God, if you exist, make your existence known to me." In the fall of 1886, after finally overcoming his inhibitions, he made his way to the church of St. Augustine, where he sought out

Abbé Huvelin, a famous spiritual director. Finding Huvelin in his confessional he described his predicament and asked the priest to recommend some Christian reading. Huvelin, with inspired insight into the character of this seeker, told Charles that what he needed was not to be found in books.[25]

His conversion to Christ, brought through the irregular channel of Islam, led Charles to eventually serve as a missionary-monk in Tamanrasset, in the Algerian desert, among Muslim Tuaregs, witnessing to the love of God.

As we seek to adopt the posture of the guest toward Muslims, the late Virginia Cobb's words are again most relevant—words that had a profound impact on Mazhar's approach:

> [Concerning the] Law of *reciprocity*, Jesus clearly taught that we are in some measure able to control, and therefore responsible for, the type of response we elicit. . . . If we give genuine friendship, openness to all that is good, respect and sensitivity for all that is dear to others, we may expect the same. If we go with closed minds, rejection of their ideas, suspicion, fear or superiority, we may expect the same. If we refuse to listen in the truest sense, can we expect them to listen? The example of our attitude toward Islam may set the pattern for their attitude to Christianity.

> Here *attitude is all-important*. For if we . . . have Muslims in our institutions or services, and then show an attitude of superiority or condemnation or enmity, or show disrespect to what is sacred to them, we not only lose them but create further animosity. Our relationship with them should be such as to inspire confidence in our sincere desire to serve them, our fair-mindedness, sensitivity and appreciation of all that is good.

> We should emphasize every point of agreement, encourage every true direction, praise all that is praise-worthy, put the best possible interpretation on every teaching or practice.

> We must do these things patiently for many years, regardless of the . . . results.[26]

The growing divide between Christians and Muslims today requires Christians to see Islam differently, to approach Muslims in ways that draw us to them as opposed to creating further alienation—so that we might find open hearts. In our attempts to do this, we are also able to learn from Muslims. Islam is a culture of pilgrimage. One of their five pillars is to take the hajj (pilgrimage) to Mecca once in a lifetime. Following their return they are then called El Hadj (pilgrim). Instead of viewing this as having just accomplished the pilgrimage requirement by journeying to Mecca, devout Muslims see their pilgrimage to Mecca as the beginning of the final, and most intense, phase of their pilgrimage to God. This is a beautiful concept.

As Christians, we do well to recall that our Scriptures also refer to us as needing to be like pilgrims, for we are a "people of pilgrimage" spiritually journeying toward God. Perhaps nothing is more critical than fully understanding that we are all pilgrims, for people familiar with journeying tend to usually be more open to new horizons—and more open-minded to learning new things and meeting new people. As followers of Christ, we have therefore not "arrived"; instead we are on a continual journey toward the new horizons of God through Christ. Such a pilgrimage mindset lays the foundation for us to be able to see Islam and Muslims with new eyes. With this perspective we can be open to new ways of approaching Muslims that will not only enable them to more clearly see who Christ is, but will also more importantly assist us in following Christ more faithfully.

A Muslim Disciple of Christ   5

> *Though it is out of the east that the sun rises . . .*
> *It burns and blazes with inward fire*
> *Only when it escapes the shackles of east and west*
> *. . . it may subject all horizons to its mastery.*

—MUHAMMAD IQBAL: JAVID NAMA

> *A person who has a yearning for the spirit feels like an exile in*
> *this world, no matter how much he serves it.*

—SEYYED HOSSEIN NASR

THROUGHOUT HISTORY, CHRIST FOLLOWERS within the Arab Islamic world have typically been encouraged by Christians, both Arab and Western, toward radical discontinuity with their Muslim culture and society. This has resulted in their experiencing a deep sense of rupture from their environment, which more often than not causes a severe crisis of identity, with dire consequences, as they are then often doomed to a life of isolation and loneliness as a result.

In addressing this important subject, Mazhar frequently shares the parable of the monkey who was seen urgently pulling fish out of a pond and hanging them on a tree. When someone came walking by and saw the monkey carrying out this bizarre action, he asked him what he was doing. The monkey replied with great enthusiasm and confidence, "When I looked into the pond, I saw all the fish, and I am pulling them out and hanging them on the tree as quickly as I can to save them so that they don't drown."

Similarly, Christians, in their desire to spiritually "rescue" followers of Christ from Muslim backgrounds, when they encourage them to separate themselves from their culture, family, and society, they are often unnecessarily bringing profound emotional, social, and spiritual hardship upon them.

Identity is of supreme importance in Arab culture. There is an Arab proverb that says, "Don't tell me who you are. Tell me who your friends are." Arabs in the Middle East and North Africa live in a society where the individual is important only as he or she belongs to a community (called the "ummah" in Arabic). The foundation of Arab society is not the individual, but the community; first, the family, then the extended family or clan, then the religious community, and sometimes then the nation. Arab society does not culturally function with the belief that the individual is free to make his or her own choices. All important decisions are made within the family or community.

Consequently, when one individual in the community causes some offense, it reflects the whole community—not just the person concerned. If the individual publicly causes shame, then the whole community is shamed—the honor of the family or community is at stake.

Therefore if someone from a Muslim family or community joins the "Christian" West (which is what they assume becoming a Christian means), they see this as a transfer of communal affiliation. This in turn publicly shames their community, as it is seen as an act of hostility toward their culture and social background. Out of a sense of family or community honor, they feel they must respond.

This is one of the primary nontheological reasons that help to explain why Arab Muslims hold Muhammad in such esteem. He gave the Arabs an identity to be proud of and rally around. In pre-Islamic literature, such as in Arab poetry, one finds the question asked, "Why can't we have a prophet for the Arabs?" The Jews had their prophets, the various other Christian countries had theirs (e.g. Mark for Egypt, Matthew for Ethiopia), but the Arab tribes did not have someone with whom to religiously identify. The small groupings of Christians in Arabia during the time of Muhammad were not indigenous, as it was a Christianity associated with the Byzantines, a foreign culture. The whole cultural atmosphere at that time was prepared for someone like Muhammad to come and serve as their own prophet, someone from and for them. As the Right Reverend Riah Abu El-Assal, the former Anglican Bishop of Jerusalem, and a friend of Mazhar, says;

> Islam had the advantage that its teachings were in Arabic, whereas the leaders of the Christian churches in the seventh century were foreigners, Greek-speaking Byzantines and others. Hellenistic thinking, Aramaic thinking, Roman thinking and Judaism influenced those Arabs who had been converted to

Christianity. This influence came through reading the Scriptures and repeating the liturgies, and led to Arab Christians adopting foreign customs and habits such as giving their sons and daughters Christian names, which were originally Hellenic and later Westernized. Some of them became part of an imperial system which looked down on the local Arabs. Colonialism does not occupy land only, but also infiltrates the spirit and the mind. It shook the confidence of Arab Christians in their own Arab identity. It was no wonder that many Arab Christians welcomed the early Islamic conquests which were, in essence, Arab conquests.[1]

In this sense, Islam could be viewed as originally an Arab contextualization of the monotheism of the Jews and Christians.

The situation is made all the more complex because in the Muslim mind, to be an Arab means to be Muslim. Islam is not just a religious faith separate from ethnicity, cultural tradition, and social, economic, and political aspects of life. Their religion is a part of all of life. In their thinking, to use the term "Arab Christian" is like speaking about an air-breathing fish, or dehydrated water. For Muslims, culture, politics, and religion are inseparable, making changing one's religion a total break with society.

Additionally, during the colonial era of the nineteenth and twentieth centuries, the traditional view of Muslims toward Western Christians living and working among them is that they focused on denigrating and defaming Islam while promoting Western culture instead, thereby endangering their Arabic-Islamic culture. In the larger context, Christianity was seen as a product of Western imperialism, not only focused on turning Muslims into Christians, but also working to acculturate Muslims to Western ways.

Christianity is therefore often seen as being about Islamic deculturation. Muslims came to view Protestant Western activity during the colonial period in the Middle East and North Africa as having "a sense of overpowering . . . duty to spread a nation's vision of society and culture to an alien and often subjected people," according to Muslim writer Samir Khalif.[2] Western writers, like T. O. Beidelman, also support these assertions, believing that Western Christian workers were actually more of a threat to Arab Muslims than anyone else, as they "invariably aimed at overall changes in beliefs and actions of [local] peoples, at colonizing of heart and mind as well as body."[3] The overriding concern of Muslims about Westernization was that they become "Christianized" culturally and socially, thereby losing their distinctive identity. This is why when Mazhar was interrogated in Syria during his imprisonment, the officials were more concerned about any contact he may have had with Western missionaries than his having become a follower of Christ per se.

The colonial era of mission greatly influenced the current Arab Muslim perspective of Christianity. Even in Tunisia, considered to be one of the most open-minded and tolerant of Arab Muslim societies today, the liberal Muslim intellectual Muhammad al Talibi, one of the founders of the University of Tunis and an advocate of Muslim/Christian dialogue, describes current Christian activity in the region as "cultural-religious imperialism" and sees this as an "attack on the dignity of humanity."[4]

The word "Christian" can therefore carry very negative Western cultural connotations. As a result, accepting Christianity is seen by most Arab Muslims today as cultural destruction. True to form, much Western Christian mission activity has prescribed cultural disengagement and isolation for Muslims who wish to follow Christ. The result is that these individuals from Muslim backgrounds go through a cultural transformation, and end up imitating Westerners, even to the point of attacking Islam (as Mazhar experienced), and "try[ing] to destroy their own society and mock[ing] the foundations on which it is built."[5]

From Muslim to Christian to Muslim Disciple of Christ

Mazhar believes the core issue is that we all too often confuse spiritual identity with cultural identity. Within the complexity of this cultural and religious tension, Mazhar and his life experience teaches us a great deal about how someone from a Muslim background may follow Christ without having to leave his Arab and Islamic culture and community. He is an example of someone who has kept his Islamic culture *and* Christ as his Lord, presenting us a distinctive example of a Muslim following Christ—remaining culturally fully "Arab" and not dislocated from his "birth" culture.

As both a committed follower of Christ for four decades and also an insider in Islamic circles, Mazhar's approach is not one of radical discontinuity from his Islamic Arab culture. Mazhar, who calls himself a "Muslim follower of Christ," says, "Islam is my heritage. Christ is my inheritance." As it is almost impossible to separate Islam and Arab culture, he is therefore instinctively Muslim. Yet as he is also at the same time a follower of Christ, he challenges our religious and cultural presuppositions.

Living within the clash of cultures and beliefs and having had to negotiate between identities all his life, he provides an example that Muslims who desire to follow Christ need in order to visualize how they too can retain their cultural identity.

Mazhar's spiritual journey has taken him from being completely dislocated from his community to once again becoming very much an insider in Islamic society. Having grown up in a conservative Muslim family that planned on his becoming a Muslim cleric, he initially left his Arab Islamic culture and society to enter a "Christian community" in order to follow Christ, only to begin a slow, but steady, return journey to his Arab and Islamic roots, all while maintaining his loyalty to Christ.

When Mazhar became a follower of Christ, Arab Christians told him that he needed to leave his cultural past behind, so he dislocated himself from his Islamic culture (family, community, etc.) and attempted to take on a "Christian culture." They encouraged him to change his name (to take a "Christian" name), to stop socializing in cafés (the primary meeting place for Arab Muslim men), to stop attending his family's religious celebrations, to keep his distance from mosques and Muslims, to cease fasting, to pray in a different posture (not bowing or prostrate), to use "Christian" as opposed to Islamic Arabic greetings and words when speaking (such as "good morning" instead of "peace be upon you"), and even to eat pork to prove he was converted.

Desperate not to be alone, as in Islamic society people who are alone are suspected of being mentally ill, Mazhar aggressively adopted a Christian culture and ended all relationships with Muslims. He became a "churchian" because that was the only option presented to him. Desiring to be accepted in his "new family and community," he even went to extremes in order to please them. The local Christians tried to put upon him all their traditions and views, such as inspiring him toward hating Islam, encouraging him to denigrate his own religious and cultural background, and even to embody Zionism, praying for the success of the new State of Israel (something completely contrary to Arab society). Furthermore, he was encouraged by the local Christians to emigrate to the West, or to a country like Brazil, where he could be free to be a "Christian."

Uncomfortable with the way he was being indoctrinated, Mazhar faced a deep internal struggle. He knew that not to be a "Christian" culturally would be tantamount to denying Christ to the Christian community that had taken him in. Yet, ironically, no matter what he did, due to having come from a Muslim background, he still was not fully accepted by the local Christian community as one of them. This explains why, for many years, he found himself still having a deep craving for respect and friendship from Western Christians.

As Mazhar quickly became alienated from his family and all his former friends, he faced a profound crisis of identity. He was on the road toward destruction—spiritually, emotionally, and psychologically. This is sadly the case for many followers of Christ from Muslim backgrounds who have become culturally "Christian" and therefore dislocated from their own communities.

Mazhar recalls a friend who had a similar background and experience. He ended up so indoctrinated by Christians against his Islamic past that he became irrationally paranoid about Islam and mentally unstable.

Many Christ followers from Muslim backgrounds struggle the rest of their lives, never fully fitting into a Christian culture. Consequently, they regretfully end up following Christ in lonely places. In 1991, when Mazhar was required to leave Egypt, one such young man wrote him, "I looked at you as a son looks to his father. The day you left I . . . lost a father. . . . I am not exaggerating to tell you I became like a dirty sick donkey everyone avoids being near. . . . My fellowship is limited to myself, my wife and my little daughter."

In explaining the challenge followers of Christ from Muslim backgrounds face and the damage it causes to their persons, Mazhar shares a short story about a turtle and an eagle. Once there was a turtle who asked an eagle to teach her how to fly. The eagle at first refused, but after repeatedly being asked by the turtle, the eagle took the turtle between his claws and carried the turtle up and then left her to fall. The turtle of course fell and broke her shell. Just like the turtle, Muslim followers of Christ are led to believe they can fly like the eagle, and yet in attempting to do so they end up seriously wounded and scarred.

When Muslim followers of Christ leave their cultures to become "Christians," they can often end up in an even worse faith condition. Mazhar loves to tell the well-known Arab parable about how crows came to waddle when they walk. One day the crow became jealous of the hud-hud bird (a bird in the Middle East that walks with a dignified strut). The crow therefore tried to imitate him. However, the crow was unsuccessful and as a result lost the ability to walk correctly, thereby being stuck with a waddle forever.

Regardless of how much Mazhar assimilated himself into a "Christian" culture and appeared to be Christian, he never felt truly at home. He often found himself feeling he was betraying his heritage and people. Even years later, while attending the National Prayer Breakfast in Washington, D.C., during the time of the Gulf War in 1991, he felt himself to be a "traitor" to his culture and people by just being present, as the West had become so anti-Arab and anti-Islam. It put him into a state of delirium.

Mazhar's struggle of identity continued for many years. He recalls being deeply influenced in this area by the writings of E. Stanley Jones, the Methodist minister who served in India in the first half of the twentieth century. Jones loved the Hindu and Muslim cultures in which he found himself, and respected them, demonstrating a spirit of humility. In Jones, Mazhar sensed a kindred spirit. To this day Jones is still one of the few authors he has read in the English language.

Over the years, Mazhar slowly realized that following Christ does not require him to be against his own self, but rather that following Christ is all about enhancing and fulfilling his true identity. Reflecting today on his experience, Mazhar tells the parable of the Middle Eastern donkey who wanted to be a lion. The donkey tried to be one by dressing like a lion, walking like a lion, talking (roaring) like a lion, and eating like a lion. However, in the end, he was eaten by a lion. The point, of course, is that changing one's outside appearance does not actually change the essence of who and what one is. For example, Mazhar's official identity papers still list him as a Muslim, as the Syrian government does not allow a change in one's religious identity.

After a long and arduous journey, Mazhar rediscovered his roots, albeit returning to them in a fresh way. It was a process of gradually beginning to see and call himself "culturally" a Muslim and "spiritually" a Christ follower. He realized that following Christ does not mean denying his loyalty to Middle Eastern culture and becoming part of an alien "Christian" culture. Though he follows Christ, he now deeply embraces his Middle Eastern, and even his Islamic, roots. Tunisian Muslim writer Jalel El Mokh describes Mazhar as "someone with Christian faith that is culturally Islamic."

Today Mazhar is very proud of his heritage and identifies himself as a Muslim according to his family, people, and culture, and enjoys breathing that air. Yet he also openly shares that he loves and follows Christ. He enjoys praying and meditating in the quiet reverent atmosphere of a mosque, where he sits on the carpeted floor and reads his Bible and loves to talk with people about his and their faith. While there, he often visits the sheiks and imams, who are his friends. He has kept a lot of the Muslim practices, from using "Muslim" greetings and prayers, to fingering his Islamic prayer beads, to reciting the character of God (or meditating on sections of the Scriptures, such as the Psalms, particularly phrases like "the Lord is my shepherd"), to spending a lot of time in Arab cafés. Interestingly, cafés in the Arab world are often exclusively the milieu of Muslims. (In Egypt, Mazhar recalls an Egyptian Christian declining Mazhar's invitation to go sit in a café, saying, "If someone in my church sees me, they will kick me out of the church." This shows the divide in religious cultural practices.) He leads most of his studies of the Gospels with others in the Arab cafés or in mosques. Mazhar, after all these years of following Christ, still feels the pull of the culture when he hears the call to prayer or the Qur'an melodiously chanted.

Some Westerners might incorrectly assume that Mazhar's return to being an insider in Islamic circles is a means of becoming contextualized to more effectively share his faith in Christ with his fellow Muslim brothers and sisters. Yet for him it is not a means to an end, but rather a "coming to rest in his true identity," discovering who he really is, a finding of his way home.

Today Mazhar is deeply immersed in all strata of Muslim society in the Arab world. Looking retrospectively, he realized how heavily influenced he was by Christians during his early years as a follower of Christ, and sees how this has been detrimental to the work he wanted to do among Muslims. Even in his writing and oral communication of Christ with his Muslim brothers and sisters, he was molded by a Western Christian approach to Islam. Some Western Christians recall him strongly criticizing them for their more contextualized approaches to Islam. In the early days of being a "Christian," Mazhar condemned people for their use of the Qur'an and did not even feel comfortable using the word Isa for Jesus (the word for Jesus in the Qur'an). For a while, he even went so far as to believe that it was dishonest to call oneself a Muslim after making a decision to follow Christ.

Nevertheless, inwardly he was attempting to process and deal with this identity issue. Dr. Harold Vogelaar, a seminary professor in the U.S. and a former pastor in Egypt, recalls talking to Mazhar in Cairo about how a Muslim might stay within Islam and how the Qur'an might be able to be viewed by Muslims who follow Christ like the Old Testament is by Christians. Together they would try to picture how Jesus might come today if he came within Islam, as he did within Judaism during the first century.

However, the greatest influence toward change for Mazhar was the experience of continually seeing how Muslim followers of Christ were unnecessarily being dislocated from their families and community, and how as a result many of them were either disappearing or eventually ceased to follow Christ as they had no legitimate identity or support community. Slowly he began to change his philosophy toward imagining and helping these followers of Christ stay in their Muslim community.

During the last thirty years Mazhar has been able to embody a new approach that encourages followers of Christ from Muslim backgrounds not to leave their families, people, or culture. Increasingly, he has difficulty with the methodology of Western missionaries, and jealously protects Muslims who were following Christ from cultural "contamination" by them. He has worked to help them become disciples of Christ without having to join the "Christian" West.

Mazhar emphasizes that following Christ does not require taking a Christian name, wearing a different type of clothing, using the symbol of the cross (which was not used by the early church), changing the day of public worship (Sunday instead of Friday), adhering to a different style of worship within a church building, eating different foods, drinking alcohol (Muslims do not drink alcohol, whereas many Christians do), using pictures of Christ (most incorrectly illustrate a Jesus of European descent), or ceasing to fast.

In the West, the word "Christian" refers to someone who believes in Christ, while a "non-Christian" is someone who does not. However, in many parts of the Middle East the word "Christian" means something totally different. In countries where there is no indigenous Christian presence, "Christian" means "foreigner" and Christ is more often than not seen as a product of Western Christianity. Therefore "converts," who are often encouraged to stop all Muslim practices, are seen by their families as having deserted all the good values of their culture.

Mazhar recognizes now that his family's rejection of him at first was not because he was following Christ, but rather because of the way Christians had told him to act and to explain his new faith. So when he told his family that he had become a "Christian," it didn't sounds like *Good News* to them at all. They understood it as him joining the enemy. In their eyes he was turning his back on family and community values in favor of Western individualism, on a monotheistic faith for polytheism, and on strong moral traditions to follow what they would consider morally lax Western styles of behavior—basically abandoning the whole essence of Arab culture itself. This was the greatest shame imaginable to bring on his family.

Related to the stereotype Muslims have of Christians, Mazhar tells the story of something that surprised him during one of his first visits to the U.S. many years ago. As a new follower of Christ, he remembers being in a gas station and seeing girls in skimpy bikinis driving a car that had a big sticker on it saying "Jesus is Lord." Mazhar recalls being shocked at seeing this; indeed, someone from a conservative Muslim background would find these two sights very difficult to reconcile.

Regrettably many Arab and Western Christians continue to extract new followers of Christ from the Muslim context. As a result, in their external appearance they sometimes end up becoming more Western-looking than Westerners themselves—feeling that they need to adopt Western practices. Culturally they stand out. Mazhar explains, "It is almost like seeing the Hare Krishna in the West."

Mazhar humorously shares about a "convert" in North Africa, where everyone drinks green tea. However, this man would only drink "black tea," because an Englishman introduced him to following Christ. More seriously, he recalls deciding to take a Yemeni sheik who had begun following Christ to visit a large church in Cairo. Immediately, other Christians felt the sheik should change his clothing to wear something Western (many Arab Protestant churches in the Middle East resemble churches in American culture). Mazhar of course countered by declaring that the sheik was acceptable to God just as he was. As they entered the church compound a church leader approached them to bar their entry; they ended up being allowed to sit in a place where no one would see them. As Mazhar knew that the sheik would not be warmly greeted and welcomed at the church by the Christians, and desiring that the sheik have a good first experience with a Christian church, he prearranged with some Christians who attended that church to come up and greet him after the service and to take him to a party—albeit a "prearranged" party.

Today Mazhar's primary desire is to communicate God's love as shown in Christ to Muslims in their own culture and environment. In so doing, he is able to get into the hearts of Muslims. He realizes that many of our images of God and ideas are more cultural than they are about the God who reveals himself through the Jesus of the Gospels.

Throughout the Middle East and North Africa, Mazhar works to assist these unique followers of Christ in finding ways to remain in their culture and society. One Westerner recalls Mazhar encouraging a young follower of Christ in the Gulf to be proud of his Muslim heritage and culture. A young North African who has left Islam and is now culturally "Christian," he recalls meeting Mazhar at a book fair and being asked right away by him, "Why do you say you are a Christian? Instead you should say you 'haven't left Islam but have gained Christ.'"

Magdy, a Syrian follower of Christ from a Muslim background who is now working in Europe with a Christian organization, [6] found Mazhar's wisdom, counsel, and example life-changing. Having known about Mazhar through his novels, he recalls with great affection the opportunity of spending a couple of days with him. "I had been in a crisis of identity most of my adult life," shares Magdy, "and Mazhar encouraged me to first discover who I really am. He helped me to discover my unique and authentic identity as a Muslim follower of Christ, and to be proud of my heritage. It has brought about a total transformation of my world view."

Mazhar shares the story of a Muslim sheik who had obtained his PhD in Islamic law and worked in a well-known mosque in North Africa, who had become a follower of Christ. The sheik felt he had to worship as Christians do. After several months he came to Mazhar and said, "I feel so cheap. When I was a Muslim I gave God everything and totally dedicated myself to him in worship. Now as I pray I do not feel as dedicated. My whole being—body and spirit, is not worshiping God. This means nothing to me. I feel like I am cheating God. I should be giving God more and I am giving him less." So Mazhar encouraged him to use whatever postures felt like worship for him and to read the Psalms out loud as prayers. He was even given an Anglican prayer book in Arabic to help provide a reverently based worship structure, to which Muslims are accustomed. While living in North Africa, Mazhar even began to experiment with the chanting of the Scriptures in an Islamic style.

Assuming the identity of a Muslim follower of Christ is of course not without its challenges. Both Christians and Muslims may find it either confusing or unacceptable. While Mazhar lived in Egypt, some of the most prominent Protestant ministers were very against him and his approach. Some even spread the rumor that he was a spy with the local intelligence service. Others, such as "converts" (those from a Muslim background who have become culturally "Christian") are usually against Mazhar being an insider in Islamic culture. They see it as if "he is playing with fire," as one young North African convert put it. Believing that "Islamic worship is devised by the devil," the convert feels that followers of Christ should be separate from and not attached to their Muslim past.

Upon first meeting Mazhar, some Arab Christians, such as Dr. Ekram Lamie, an Egyptian Church leader, could not tell if he was Muslim or Christian, as he still embodied so much of Muslim culture. Even some Muslims find Mazhar's and others' identity as "Muslim followers of Christ" confusing. For example, when the secret police forced their way into his apartment in Cairo when only their son was present, they kept asking their son, "Is your father a Muslim or a Christian?" They found it difficult to put him into one category or the other.

That was also the case with the late renowned professor of comparative religion at Zeitouna University in Tunis, Tunisia, Dr. Ahmed Mechraqi, himself a Muslim. His impression was that Mazhar, if asked directly, most probably would not identify himself with either religious group. Dr. Mechraqi's perspective on Mazhar is that he sees Christ as Christians do, but doesn't use Christian language or culture. "He is theologically Christian, but culturally Muslim," said Dr. Mechraqi. Dr. Mechraqi preferred to call him an "anonymous Muslim" (like some Muslims are "anonymous Christians")—a phrase taken from Catholic theologian Hans Küng.

Christ versus Christianity

There is a growing number of Muslims that follow Jesus who cannot declare themselves "Christian" because this is tantamount to their renouncing their culture and therefore their families in favor of Western culture. As Ali Merad, a Muslim and a professor of Arabic literature and civilization at the University of Lyon in France, wrote concerning Charles de Foucauld's ministry among Muslims (the late missionary-monk in the Algerian desert among the Muslim Tuareg people), "For it was one thing to seek the friendship of the Muslim population, even to teach them, and to summon them ceaselessly to make them better. It was another thing to try to shatter their certainties in order to induce them to get rid of all, or part, of their beliefs and to give up their ancestral faith. Such a renunciation would have meant *the 'unraveling' of the intimate fibers of their being*."[7] It is critical that the culture and heritage of new followers of Christ from Muslim backgrounds be honored and that they be assisted to find ways to stay rooted in their Arab society.

This is why Mazhar doesn't call people out of Islam, but rather toward Christ, seeing himself as a fellow spiritual pilgrim alongside them. He reminds us that Jesus himself did not call the Samaritans or Gentiles to convert to Judaism. Because most Samaritan followers of Christ did not become Jewish, they most certainly carried on with their religious practices, even though Jews might have found them heretical. Nevertheless, God poured out his Spirit on them. Furthermore, Mazhar points out that it is important for Christians to remember that the early Jewish followers of Christ remained in the Temple and synagogues. Speaking of Muslims who follow Christ, the late Virginia Cobb echoed this in her excellent Tehran address, "They have severe 'culture shock' and need dependable, understanding friends. Since the national churches . . . are very slow to provide this, and the Muslim often remains a relative outsider . . . some . . . may feel they can do more good by remaining within their own community. . . . Jesus called no one to leave Judaism, and the Christian remained in synagogue and temple for some time."[8] Mazhar also highlights the early counsel of St. Paul to the new followers of Christ in Corinth (1 Cor. 17–24) not to separate from their society, but to stay where they were and live in it in a new way.

Mazhar turns our attention to the Jew-Gentile tension that existed within the early church, where Jewish followers of Christ first expected Gentiles to adopt Jewish religious customs and practices in their following of Christ. In this sense, Arab and Western Christians certainly need to avoid the dogmatic judgmentalism of those in the early church who could not see past God's work in their own religion and culture.

Instead of calling people to another religion, Jesus called them to himself. Following him and his way was what mattered to him. Jesus's primary concern was the establishment of the new life of the Kingdom of God, not the founding of a new religion. Addressing responsible Christian activity in the Middle East, Virginia Cobb highlights this theme: "We are *not trying to change anyone's religion*. Religion consists of affiliation with a group, culture, ethic, dogma and structure of authority—clergy, book, orthodoxy. . . . It is possible to change all of them without knowing God. If we stress these we may give the impression that these *are* the Christian faith."[9]

According to Mazhar, what has happened over the years is that Christians living among Muslims have tried to get them to change their religion. Mazhar instead sees his Lord, Christ Jesus, inviting Muslims to him without requiring them to leave their culture for a foreign Western religion—Christianity.

Mazhar shares the parable of a Sufi master in "Zawea" (a place in the house dedicated for meditation). One day while the Sufi master was speaking to his disciples a black cat kept walking around, distracting and annoying him. So the Sufi master tied the cat to the chair every time he spoke to his disciples. Years later, the black cat died. And the disciples ended up bringing another black cat to tie up every time their Master addressed them. Eventually their master died and a new master comes and every time he speaks to them they first tie up a black cat—as this had now became part of their tradition. As Mazhar says, "The Christian faith has so many 'black cats tied up' in our tradition of worshipping God."

The late E. Stanley Jones from India, whose writings have mentored Mazhar, in speaking about the cultural Westernization of the Christian faith, wrote, "But just as a stream takes on the coloring of the soil over which it flows, so Christianity in its flowing through the soils of the different racial and national outlooks took on coloring from them. We have added a good deal to the central message—Jesus".[10] It is critical that Christians in the world reconsider their approach toward Muslims when communicating Christ. As Mazhar says, "No wonder some Muslims say, with Mahatma Gandhi: 'Take away your Christianity and give us your Christ.'" This is exactly how a well-known Muslim Tunisian book distributor named Babay sees Mazhar: "To me he is someone who has kept the values and traditions of Islamic Arab culture, but who has taken the basics of Christ's teaching, without all the trappings."

In the West, Brian Maclaren, a leader in what has come to be termed the emergent church movement, in his book *A Generous Orthodoxy,* addresses this same issue with great clarity: "I believe a person can affiliate with Jesus in the kingdom-of-God dimension without affiliating with him in the religious kingdom of Christianity. In other words, I believe that Christianity is not the kingdom of God. The ultimate reality is the kingdom of God, and Christianity at its best is here to . . . lead people into that kingdom, calling them out of smaller rings, smaller kingdoms. Christianity at its worst . . . holds people within its rings and won't let them enter the kingdom of God. Jesus diagnosed the religious leaders of his day as doing this very thing."

Instead of seeing Muslims brought into Christianity, Mazhar tries to bring Christ to where Muslims are—so that they can stay culturally Arab, and even Muslim, as they follow Christ. He believes it is critical that Muslims do not get the impression that they have to become anything other than who they are in order to follow Christ. After all, Mazhar asked, "What makes someone a follower of Christ?" He goes on to say, "We have corrupted the simple truth that Jesus shared with all the Christian doctrine. The thief on the cross simply said to Jesus 'remember me.'" Once again the words of Virginia Cobb ring true:

> What of doctrines related to Christ himself? Jesus didn't insist on a certain view of himself as prerequisite to discipleship. He called [people] to follow him unconditionally, and after two years of living with him, asked what their conclusion was. . . . It is safe to leave people to draw their own conclusions after sincerely seeking to know Christ and experience him. . . . "Seek first the kingdom" means that all else can be and must be sacrificed for the highest goal. We have many valued truths and emphases that may have to be left out of our efforts with others. . . . Many of our institutional forms as well as the details of doctrine hinder more than they help people coming from a different way of life, while Christ and his teachings attract with power. We must lay aside the weight of non-essentials for the sake of the essential.[11]

As a Muslim follower of Christ, and therefore free from ecclesiastical affiliations, Mazhar's simple desire is that Muslims experience Christ. "In some ways, Islam is irrelevant to me," he says. "For me, there are only people experiencing the love of Jesus and seeking to follow his way and those who are not—whatever religion they belong to."

Henri Marchal, the Catholic priest who worked among Muslims in Algeria during the first half of the twentieth century, has a helpful way of looking at this possibility. Marchal saw three types of "conversions": First, he saw a conversion to God—such as conversion from nominalism to a truehearted spiritual concern for God. Second, a conversion to Jesus could take place—experiencing him and following his way. The third conversion was to the Church; a conversion that Mazhar of course does not see as theologically necessary or culturally beneficial for Muslims.

Perhaps the most eloquent portrayal of a Muslim's ability to follow Christ without becoming culturally Christian, and thereby staying within his Arab Islamic culture, comes from Samir,[12] a university professor of English literature in North Africa, and someone who has had a close association with Mazhar for many years. Samir's own story and life experience have much to teach us. He became a follower of Christ while doing his dissertation study on the Sufi mystic al Hallaj, the respected Sufi Islamic martyr who requested to be crucified like Christ. It was during his study of Hallaj that he went through what he calls a "process of negotiation." Samir discovered in Sufism a spiritual dimension, a mysticism, which he felt was lacking in orthodox Islam. Hallaj, he learned, focused on the interior life, on internal transformation.

During his time of studying Hallaj, he was introduced to Mazhar as someone who could tell him more about Sufism. From the beginning he was fascinated by his knowledge of Arab culture and literature. He turned to Mazhar's novels during this period in order to learn more of his faith. Mazhar talked about Christ with him and encouraged him, without any pressure, to follow Christ. However, Samir found himself instinctively pulling away from Mazhar, as he was seriously concerned about losing his Arab identity. In his North African country, local "Christians" (all local Christians in this country are "converts" from Islam, as there is no historic indigenous church in North Africa) are viewed like those who have AIDS, as they are believed to have rejected their heritage and joined the West, which in turn is considered to have been an oppressor of the Arabs. Interestingly, the rejection of these "Christian" converts has little to do with Christ himself or faith beliefs per se, but is largely due to cultural reasons. Eventually, Samir resumed active contact with Mazhar, who helped him during his early phase of believing in and following Christ. It still had not occurred to Samir that he could keep his Arab and Islamic culture and follow Christ. He recalls Mazhar practicing this, but he also knew Mazhar was from another country—Syria. His only local examples were Christians (converts from Islam) who he observed were now denigrating their own culture and modeling themselves after Westerners.

Samir continued to study Sufism and came to the conviction that the essence of Christ's teaching, and also the heart of Sufism, was of self-sacrifice for God. During this period he sometimes went to the mosque and yet because of the Christian views he found himself slowly absorbing, he felt guilty attending. At the same time he felt himself deeply drawn to the mosque to pray. Samir's faith in Christ continued to deepen and he stayed in contact through letters with Mazhar (who by this time had left his country). Today, as an academic, he is a believer in Christ who has remained in his Muslim context and is not part of a "Christian" community. For his own spiritual growth he uses the beautiful verses of the Qur'an, the Gospels, and the Psalms. As he has not been uprooted from his own religious culture, he fully understands the dangers of extraction and has an excellent grasp of what it means to stay in his local cultural context. At the university, he lectures in halls that have large numbers of students, and he encourages students to go to the source of a great deal of what they study in English literature—the Bible. He feels very comfortable inviting people to believe in Christ, since they do not need to become "churchians."

Samir wrote an outstanding essay on the critical need for followers of Christ from a Muslim background not to be dislocated from their religious and cultural community. Below are excerpts of his essay titled "Transformation versus Rupture" that he sent Mazhar:

What we call the failure of the Christian message in the Muslim world is rather a failure of the mediator of such a message. . . . It is a failure that does not affect the content of the message but its mediation. The early missionaries made the critical mistake of neglecting the vital issue of cultural identity . . . because they were blinded by their cultural naiveté. . . . The [Christian], well versed in Christian theology, deeply rooted in western modernity, sure and sometimes proud of his own cultural identity, seldom takes serious care to know about the culture of the [local people]. If he does so, it is always through the material written about such a culture by western anthropologists, orientalists, travel book writers . . . which amounts to the same narcissistic position. What he learns is either negative or exotic.

What makes things worse is that while learning about the [indigenous] culture, the [Christian] is usually victim to cultural prejudice. By this I mean that the [Christian] learns about the local peoples' culture in order to refute it, demonstrate its blind spots and eventually present Christ's message as the alternative. Such a [Christian], who has always been the typical western [Christian], is not aware that in doing so he distorts reality and misreads Christ's message. Moreover the identification between religion and culture has always been one of the critical fallacies. It is this which causes the [local people] to see the transmission of Christ's message as an attempt to westernize him . . . Christianization, westernization, and colonization sound synonymous in the [local peoples'] mind. . . . The [Christian], who does not distinguish between religion that is specific and culture that is broad and general, thinks that a Muslim should be brainwashed before embracing Christ's message. Not the least trace of Islam should remain if the individual is to be considered a true Christian.

In my life I have pitifully seen the wretched destinies—in the cultural sense— of Muslims who have become Christians. They sometimes personified the concept of total alienation because they seemed to have undergone a process of eradication from their [indigenous] cultural soil. Eradication! Detraditionalisation! Deculturation! Deracination! The whole thing entailed a renunciation of one's culture and traditions.

I have always wondered if it was really necessary to renounce one's own Islamic culture to deserve Christ's message. A renunciation, which in cultural terms means auto-destruction. . . . Culture is built into the heart of the heart. That is why a person who renounces his culture is doomed to remain till the end of his days suffering a terrible crisis of identity.

So to what extent can I embrace Christ's message without denying my Islamic culture and identity? . . . For Christ does not ask a Muslim to deny his own culture. Unlike the culturally naïve [Christian] he did not abuse a single aspect of another's culture. Consider in depth Christ's magnificent words in the Sermon on the Mount: Think not I am come to destroy the law or the prophet: I am come not to destroy but to fulfill. These words are beyond contextualisation because of their striking universality. These are the words of the Lord spoken on the Mount to the whole of mankind. . . . Jesus Christ did not come to destroy the law which is a representative aspect of any culture, but rather . . . to complete it . . . to remedy the soul. . . .

"Each one should retain the place in life that the Lord assigned to him. . . . Each one should remain in the situation which he was in when God called him." (1 Cor. 7:17, 20) In a Muslim context, this means that a Muslim has to remain faithful to his Islamic cultural roots. Moreover, if in Islam as a religion (i.e. a set of religious beliefs) difference of opinion is possible, Islam as a culture has a powerful impact which is impossible to rid oneself of. Thus in terms of culture, a Muslim remains a Muslim despite himself because he has been built as such.

This is why it is a bad approach to try to transmit Christ's message to a Muslim by undermining Islam. (i.e. trying to efface the halo from above the great representative figures of Islamic culture.) . . . It is also a bad approach to make him feel that the mosque, which is a powerful spiritual and cultural space, is a negative and adversary place. It is also a house of God where if he likes he can experience his new relation with Jesus. It is also better to not make him feel that fasting during Ramadan alienates him from Christ's message, but that he can give Ramadan fasting a new spiritual orientation through Christ.

It is also better not to ask him to affect a rupture with his spiritual verbal discourse. Let him in his prayers keep the name that Jesus is given in Islam, because that is the name dear and familiar and close to him: and so with the other Biblical names. Let him keep the basic prayer formulas common in Islamic praying discourse. This will make him feel at home in his new relation with Jesus.

The main objective as might have been deduced is to experience conversion as a *transformation*, not as an experience of systematic deracination. In this respect I view one's experience in Jesus as basically capable by itself of spontaneous transformation which without external interference helps modify if necessary one's cultural view. *Transformation—rather than rupture*, so as to avoid causing people a long lasting shock.

A Way Forward

Increasingly there are groups of Muslims who have come to faith in Christ yet remain officially and socio-religiously in their local Islamic community. Mazhar sees this throughout the Muslim world—from a sheik following

Christ at a mosque in Egypt who didn't see any contradiction in being a follower of Christ and a Muslim sheik, to a group of Shia sheiks who had become followers of Christ and wanted assistance in working through some complex issues as well as encouragement in their faith.

Mazhar's vision is to see the teaching of Jesus taken into the inner chambers of Muslim communities, with the goal of seeing them follow Christ while remaining vital members of their families and society—serving as salt and light within their culture. Seeing Islam as the cultural/religious heritage of 1.3 billion people, he desires that they move *beyond* Islam, as opposed to *from* Islam, to go on with Jesus Christ as their primary form of identity.

Sadly, Mazhar sees the opposite happening in parts of North Africa, where increasing numbers of young men and women leave Islam to become culturally "Christian," and therefore Western—a response seen by many Western Christian groups as encouraging. "The same path is tragically being followed once again in North Africa," says Mazhar. He goes on to say, "Carthage today is only a monument to the Christian faith of early antiquity. What happened? The Christian faith had not become naturalized—it remained foreign—a religion of Rome. This same thing is happening all over again. It is critical that we focus on Christ being naturalized—where an atmosphere is created that is more open to considering following Christ. This of course requires having a marathon perspective, and is in sharp contrast to the fairly shortsighted perspectives that seek to start churches with converts extracted from their communities."

In contrast, Mazhar draws attention to the numbers of Muslims throughout the Islamic world who find themselves saying "yes" to Jesus, but "no" to Christianity. Some people have referred to these as "insider movements"—followers of Jesus from other religious backgrounds who stay in their communities and do not call themselves Christians. There is an increasing amount of literature available on this phenomenon.

In this regard, a fascinating study related to Hindus was done by Herbert E. Hoefer, a former seminary professor in India, which resulted in a book titled *Churchless Christianity*. Hoefer began hearing stories of Hindus who were following Jesus in their homes. He discovered that large numbers (in his view over two hundred thousand) of these families who have never joined a church follow Christ uniquely. They did not call themselves Christians, but *Jesu bhakta*, "devotees of Jesus." Their basis of belief is built on the Hindu bhakti movement that allows Hindus to focus their worship on a specific god, and therefore it is not offensive to the Hindu community for them to choose to worship Jesus exclusively. In so doing they maintain their cultural and social identity as Hindus. When asked, they identify themselves as Hindus, not as Christians.[13]

Modern theologians and missiologists have formulated a categorization for stages of Islamic contextualization for followers of Christ from Muslim backgrounds. Known as the "C1–C6 Spectrum," it compares and contrasts groups of followers of Christ within the Muslim world, starting with low contextualization with Islamic traditions, culture, and belief, to being completely embedded within the Islamic culture. Mazhar personally avoids all such terminology and all theories of categorization, believing that spirituality cannot be systematized, as God works differently in each person's life. However, he does point out that these "insider movements" do not exist to hide the identities of followers of Christ, but instead to enable them to go spiritually deeper within their own Islamic community. Interestingly, as most of the "pillars" of Islamic practice are all adaptations of previous Jewish and Christian forms, many Muslim followers of Christ are adapting the pillars of their Islamic faith to enhance their faith in Christ.

In his book entitled *On Identity,* Amin Maalouf, the Arab Lebanese writer and well-known novelist shares some great counsel that can benefit Muslim followers of Christ. Maalouf writes:

> What makes me myself rather than anyone else is the very fact that I am poised between . . . several cultural traditions. It is precisely this that defines my identity. . . . Identity cannot be compartmentalized. You can't divide it up into halves or thirds or any other separate segments. I haven't got several identities: I've got just one; made up of many components combined together in a mixture that is unique to every individual . . . someone comes and . . . says, "Of course . . . but what do you really feel deep down inside?" . . . I found this oft-repeated question . . . presupposes that "deep down inside" everyone there is just one affiliation that really matters, a kind of "fundamental truth" about each individual, an "essence" determined once and for all at birth, never to change thereafter. . . . It may be said that there are special cases, I don't agree. . . . Every individual is a meeting ground for many different allegiances, and sometimes loyalties conflict with one another and confront the person who harbors them with difficult choices . . . people must be able to accept a dual affiliation without too much anguish, which means remaining loyal to their culture of origin and not feeling obliged to conceal it like some shameful disease, and at the same time being receptive to the culture of their adoptive country.[14]

An Arab Follower of Christ

While it is difficult or nearly impossible to separate Arab culture from Islamic culture, Mazhar would say that he attempts to put the emphasis more on his being Arab as opposed to Muslim. He sees Arab culture more as his bridge and cultural foundation then the Islamic religion. In this sense, Mazhar does make a distinction between Islamic faith and Islamic culture. He rarely speaks of Islam or of Muslims, but often of being "Arab."

North African literary critic Zahara Hamani sees Mazhar first and foremost as an Arab—as opposed to seeing him as a Christian or a Muslim. Her experience is that Mazhar always first identifies himself as an Arab, and that being Christian or Muslim doesn't really matter to him. She sees similar examples in Edward Said (the late Palestinian professor at Columbia University) or Khalil Gibran (the renowned early twentieth-century Lebanese author from a Christian background). However, if Mazhar were required to define himself further, Hamani feels Mazhar would say he is a Muslim.

Saladin Ben Ohbed, a Tunisian lawyer and university professor, considers Mazhar to be a "true Arab," meaning an Arab from the former era of the progressive open-minded Arab Nationalism.[15] Ben Ohbed believes that Mazhar is from the old Arab culture of tolerance, where one culture is not viewed as opposed to the other, and therefore is able to find himself in "two cultures" equally. He strongly recalls going with Mazhar to the Carthage Festival to hear some Sufi singers, and seeing Mazhar crying as he watched them—an expression of the depth of his love for his Arab Islamic culture.

A Sufi Follower of Christ

The critical issue for someone who follows Christ from an Arab Muslim background is what their identity will be. In this regard, Mazhar and others like him feel that Islamic Sufism, or mysticism, might be an acceptable place of identity and belongingness for them. Sufism, with its flexibility and wide variety, might be a way for Muslim followers of Christ to not be dislocated from their Muslim culture.

Over the years Mazhar has developed a growing appreciation for the Sufi/mystic traditions and the great Sufi teachers in Islam. In the last several years he has joined a small Sufi group, and together they even study the Gospels. Sufis have encouragingly assisted him in his literature projects and continue to do so.

During the history of Islam, Sufis like al Hallaj, Sahra Wardi, Ibn Arabi, and Jalal al-Din Rumi, the great Sufi poet, have tried to interpret Islam in new ways. Attempting to bring in new themes, the Sufis have been particularly sympathetic to Christ. They have been regarded as a sect for hundreds of years and gone through periods of intense persecution, as orthodox Islam does not look kindly on innovations to the traditional theological schools. Al Hallaj remains the supreme example of a Muslim who loved Christ and tried to identify with him. He chose Jesus as his model among the prophets. Consequently, orthodox Islam crucified him in AD 922.

Yet Sufism, the mystical tradition in Islam, is very much alive in the Arab world today. Focusing on a different concept of approach to God from that of traditional Islam, the aim of Sufis is union with God. Interestingly, much of Sufism bears a Christian resemblance. Unlike traditional orthodox Muslims, whose primary concern is for the religious practices and forms established by Islam, Sufis focus on the living God who stands behind their religion and on the need to live one's life always in his presence. As Nasr Abu Zaid, the writer and former academic at Cairo University, said of his hero Ibn Arabi, the twelfth- to thirteenth-century Sufi mystic and philosopher: he is "a man for this time; for he has a foot in every camp"—Muslim, Christian, and Jewish.

It is difficult to know how much this mystical spirit has penetrated orthodox Islam. However, if this ever became a dominant view within the Muslim world, Islam would experience a change so significant that it would be comparable to that of the Reformation's influence on Christianity.

Counsel for Christians

Mazhar's approach and life experience can profoundly assist Christians, both Western and Arab, to better understand Muslims with the purpose of knowing how best to live and work among them. According to Mazhar, the Western and Arab Christian world needs to be open to fully accepting Muslim followers of Christ. As the writer Amin Maalouf says so poignantly, "It is often the way we look at other people that imprison[s] them within their own narrowest allegiances. And it is also the way we look at them that may set them free."[16]

If one of the greatest hindrances to seeing Muslims follow Christ is not theological, but rather one of religious cultural identity, then Christians should be devoted to seeking a path that affirms that Muslims can remain Muslim at the same time as living as followers of Christ. As an insider, Mazhar knows where we Christians tend to make our mistakes and how to help steer us away from any land mines. All of this powerfully affects how we live among Muslims. Mazhar believes in the rich counsel of Virginia Cobb:

> *Identification.* Christ in his incarnation came to dwell in the midst of those he came to save, and became like them. . . . This meant a full entering into the life of the people. It meant speaking their language, using terms and concepts they understood, dealing with problems they faced and values they held.

> This principle cannot be applied by setting up a meeting place and inviting people to come. It cannot be applied by living in relative isolation from them, in a separate quarter, or with little day-to-day contact. It cannot be applied by using the terminology Christians have grown accustomed to and others do not know. . . .

It means close association, sharing in everything possible, and an awareness of their concerns, problems, hopes, value system. Speaking their language means not just grammar and syntax but studying their culture and religion to learn the terms and values they comprehend.

Christ presented . . . but never persuaded. He let [people] come to decisions in personal freedoms, and even discouraged some who misunderstood what was involved. We teach the competence and responsibility of every individual and therefore must urge each person to do only and exactly what he is convinced in his own heart he must do. We can only emphasize his responsibility before God to obey his best light. If he feels he should be a more faithful Muslim, we should encourage him to do so to the best of his ability, and to try to understand what that means in the fullest sense. If he feels he should try to follow Christ's teachings, we should encourage that.

For the orthodoxy-conscious Christians, it is vital to understand that the line between heterodoxy and orthodoxy is not as clear as they may wish it to be. In every age, there are those who walk the vital fractal edge, and who sometimes end up as harbingers of spiritual renewal. In this regard, I am reminded of the profound words of Paul Tillich, the renowned twentieth-century German theologian who taught at Union Seminary in New York City. He titled his autobiographical sketch *On the Boundary*. In this short but influential work, Tillich wrote:

The boundary is the best place for acquiring knowledge. . . . The boundary might be the fitting symbol for the whole of my personal and intellectual development. At almost any point, I have had to stand between alternative possibilities of existence, to be completely at home in neither and to take no definitive stand against either. . . . This disposition and its tension have determined both my destiny and my work. . . . Culture is religious wherever human existence is subjected to ultimate questions and thus transcended. . . . In experiencing the substantially religious character of culture I came to the boundary between religion and culture, and I have never left it. . . . The boundary between native land and alien country is not merely an external boundary. . . . It is also the boundary between two inner forces, two possibilities of human existence. . . . The God who demands obedience of him is the God of an alien country; a God not bound to a local soil . . . but the God of history, who means to bless all the races of the earth. This God, the God of the prophet and of Jesus, utterly demolishes all religious nationalism. . . . The real meaning of "homeland" varies according to the situation of the individual. The command to go from one's country [the call from God to Abraham] is more often . . . for "spiritual emigration." . . . The path into an alien country may also signify something wholly personal and inward: parting from accepted lines of belief and thought. . . . In [the Kingdom of God] the boundary between native and alien land ceases to exist."[17]

"Natural Christians"

Mazhar is reminded often of Jesus's parable of the father with two sons whom he told to go and work in his vineyard. One son said he would follow and obey him, but did not do so and went on living his own way. The second son told his father he would not follow him, but then went out and did everything his father had asked him to do. "Which of these did the father's will?" asked Jesus.

Reflecting on his mentor and the person whose life and writings pointed him toward Christ, Mahatma Gandhi, Mazhar says, "I believe Christ spoke of people such as Gandhi in this parable. I see Gandhi as the second son, who said 'I will not' and then afterward went—by demonstrating the spirit of Christ and following his teaching as few Christians have ever done. I believe Gandhi loved Christ but could not afford to be publicly associated with 'Christianity'—being a Hindu by allegiance, but a Christ follower by affinity. And I fully expect to see Gandhi when we are privileged to enter God's presence in eternity."

In Tertullian's sense of the soul being naturally Christian,[18] he views Gandhi as a "natural Christian." Mazhar meets many Muslims who are in the same predicament. "While they cannot envision joining the 'enemy camp,' they love Christ with their whole being and follow him in the cultures where God has placed them."

NEW DIRECTIONS
FOR THE JOURNEY

*"... they make it a place of springs;
the autumn rains also cover it with pools"*

—PS. 84:6

Resurrecting the Eastern Christ: Embracing the Semitic Face of Jesus

6

∽

*We have reduced ourselves to religions, to
denominations, to confessions . . . instead of following
my Palestinian compatriot from Galilee, Jesus of Nazareth.*

—ELIAS CHACOUR (THE PALESTINIAN ARCHBISHOP OF GALILEE)

*Once every hundred year Jesus of Nazareth meets Jesus of the
Christian in a garden among the hills of Lebanon. And they talk
long; each time Jesus of Nazareth goes away saying to Jesus of the
Christian, "My friend, I fear we shall never, never agree."*

—KAHLIL GIBRAN (TAKEN FROM SAND AND FOAM)

MANY MUSLIMS PERCEIVE CHRIST as a Westerner with no relationship to Eastern culture. As Christine Mallouhi has written, "If Christ were walking the streets of his birthplace on the West Bank of Palestine today, I believe he would be mind-boggled by this perception of him. Who is this Christ and what sort of Christianity is this that no longer has anything to say to Eastern Muslims?"[1]

Of the three great monotheistic faiths (Judaism, Christianity, and Islam), Christianity is the only one to have had its center of influence move from the Middle East to the West—to Rome, Canterbury, and beyond. Commenting on the impact of this move westward, Mazhar writes in his publication *An Eastern Reading of the Gospel of Luke*, "A gap was created in the Arabs' understanding of Jesus Christ's message and its significance because of the absenteeism felt by them after Europe became Christian. Since Europe converted to Christianity, the gap between Arab Muslims on one side and Arab Christians on the other grew bigger and triggered a violent and negative reaction against Christianity. As a result, the Arabs overlooked the fact that Christ is an effect of our oriental heritage and that his message and teachings derive from our own culture and values."

Christianity is indeed a Middle Eastern faith in origin, not a Western faith. Born in Jerusalem, it received its intellectual frame in Antioch, Damascus, Alexandria, and Constantinople. At the Council of Nicea in AD 325, where the creed was hashed out, there were more bishops and leaders from Persia and India than from Western Europe. Due to various historical events, Christianity's center of gravity shifted slowly to the West.

Christ was a Middle Easterner. He was culturally much more like today's Arab than like a Western Christian. In this regard, Mazhar serves to effectively bridge this gap. Perhaps his most significant spiritual contribution to this often hostile relationship has been of effectively stripping Christ of his Western trappings and introducing him to Muslims as one who was born in the Middle East, and who lived and died there. This is the Christ that Mazhar met as a young man on the Golan Heights, and this is a Christ that Muslims can understand. In his extrication of Christ from a Western culture and agenda, Mazhar is able to introduce a Christ who is both relevant and attractive to Arabs. By changing the traditional Muslim perceptions of who Jesus is, and introducing him as a Middle Easterner, Mazhar helped thousands of Muslims now see Christ in a new way. Muslims, like Tunisian writer Jalel El Mokh, describe Mazhar as "easternizing" Christ.

Mazhar is understandably proud of his Arab heritage, and his passion is to make sure Jesus comes across as a Middle Easterner. Desiring that Muslims see that Jesus Christ is from their own culture and background, he has built on the common Middle Eastern cultural heritage the Christian faith shares with Islam. Reflecting on this challenge, Mazhar says, "Arabs have lost sight that Jesus was a child of Palestine and was like them." He fully agrees with the words of his friend, the Palestinian Melchite Archbishop of Galilee, Elias Chacour: "They need to see Christ as their compatriot from Galilee—not as a foreign import."

By resurrecting the Middle Eastern Christ, Mazhar is acclimatizing the Arab community so that Christ can be naturalized within it. His approach once again echoes the words of E. Stanley Jones, "the Christ I presented would be the disentangled Christ—disentangled from being bound up with Western culture and Western forms of Christianity. He would stand in his own right, speaking directly to the needs of persons as persons without any canceling disentanglements."

Mazhar presents Jesus as the Middle Easterner that he was, in order that his fellow Arab Muslim brothers and sisters may experience the lasting reconciliation found in the Middle Eastern Prince of Peace that Christ is today. While this theme pervades all of his efforts, such as in his various Middle Eastern presentations of the Christian Scriptures, his daily priority is his attempt to embody a demonstration of the Middle Eastern Christ in the living out of his own life among Muslims. He has much to teach Western Christians about displaying Christ-likeness in the Arab world today.

Mazhar loves to share how, when asked by Christian leaders in India what they could do to see Christianity more naturalized among Indians, Mahatma Gandhi responded, "I would suggest . . . that all of you Christians . . . must begin to live more like Jesus Christ . . . if you will come to us in the spirit of your Master, we cannot resist you."[2]

Such Christ-likeness Mazhar envisaged as being the outstanding characteristic of Christians living among those of another faith. As one Hindu intellectual during Gandhi's life said to India's Christians, "if you Christians would live like Jesus Christ, India would be at your feet tomorrow."[3]

Gandhi himself sought to live the Christ-like life by following Christ's Sermon on the Mount, making that the foundation of his practice. E. Stanley Jones wrote, "I bow to Mahatma Gandhi and I kneel at the feet of Christ. . . . A little man . . . has taught me more of the spirit of Christ than perhaps any other man in East or West."[4] Consequently, perhaps unknown to himself, Gandhi presented an Eastern face of Christ to India and helped Indians to visualize Christ walking down Eastern roads, dwelling among Eastern villagers in lowly poverty, simplicity, and love. Many Hindus believed Gandhi was the Eastern incarnation of Christ and others began to see the meaning of the cross because they had seen it in one of *their* sons.[5] Gandhi reflected the Easternness of Christ, and this Easternness had profound implications on the Indian context. One Christmas day, Rabindranath Tagore, the Nobel Prize–winning Bengali poet and friend of Gandhi, wrote this amazing prayer: "Great-souled Christ, on this blessed day of your birth, we who are not Christians bow before you. We love you and worship you, we non-Christians, for with Asia you are bound with the ties of blood."[6]

Another individual whose life Mazhar greatly appreciates, and whom Muslims respect and admire, is the late Charles de Foucauld (d. 1916), the Christian missionary-monk and mystic who served among the Tuareg Muslims in North Africa. Charles de Foucauld's goal was simply to offer a "Christlike" presence in their midst. About him, Muslim writer Ali Merad wrote, "he regarded the imitation of Jesus as his greatest happiness and, even more, as his true raison d'être. To imitate Jesus, to strive at all times to act as he himself would have done; to treat each person as 'not a man, but Jesus,' is, from the Muslim point of view, the most eloquent way to espouse the authenticity of the Gospel message."[7] As a result of his life display of Christ-likeness among

Muslims, when Foucauld died, the Tuareg chief, the amenukal Moussa ag Amastane, wrote in a moving letter to Foucauld's sister in France, "Charles the marabout [Islamic "holy man"] has died not only for you, he has died for us too. May God have mercy on him, and may we meet him in Paradise."[8]

In the spirit of Gandhi and Foucauld, Mazhar understands following Christ to mean "living like Christ, or being 'Christ-like,'" and he believes this requires taking the path of sacrifice and self-denial. This is the kind of Middle Eastern Christ Mazhar demonstrates to his Muslim friends.

Embracing Suffering and Sacrifice

Mazhar sees Muslims as the people he is called to serve by laying down his life alongside them day by day. He says, "All too often we only present part of what is entailed in following Christ to others. For there is great sacrifice often required too, and many will experience suffering." Again he looks to Gandhi as a model. Gandhi called his type of power "soul force" or "the power of suffering": taking suffering on oneself but never causing suffering. Normally, the Hindu doctrine of karma has little or no room for the cross. But with Gandhi's teaching that Hindus could joyously take on suffering for the sake of achieving righteous purposes, there came a new sensitivity to the cross.[9] In light of this shift, a Hindu intellectual once said, "What the missionaries have not been able to do in fifty years, Gandhi by his life, trial and incarceration has done, namely, he has turned the eyes of India toward the cross."[10]

The example of Gandhi's sacrificial approach made it easier for Indians to move from the thought that if one man could take suffering on himself in order to bring peace and reconciliation between Hinduism and Islam, then if there was one divine and holy enough, this one might take on himself the sin of the whole human race in order to bring peace and reconciliation between us and God.[11] When Gandhi died for the nation of India, his death pointed to the cross, illustrating on a national scale what we see in Christ on the cross. Upon his assassination, Said Hussain, a Muslim and India's ambassador to Egypt, said, "The savior of India has been crucified. He is gone; it means India will walk eternally in the shadow of his cross." In the Muslim city of Hyderabad, Gandhi's death was commemorated by a procession carrying his garlanded picture with a cross near it. The Indian people saw the connection.

While there is much more in the meaning of the cross than Gandhi's example and experience illustrated, by shedding much light on the understanding of the cross, his life raises the question of what the effect in the Middle East might be if those who bear Christ's name were really more like

Christ, catching and demonstrating his spirit and outlook in the midst of suffering and sacrifice.

Suffering has been part and parcel of the Mallouhis' lives. Christine Mallouhi says, "While we have enjoyed deep acceptance from people throughout the Middle East, 'normal life' has also involved harassment, loss of health, eviction from several adopted home countries, seeing my husband imprisoned three times, living under surveillance, dealing with informers, living in wars and in the midst of terrorist attacks, living amidst great danger at times and having to take many risks, in addition to the countless shifts and situations, the separations from our sons, etc." In a letter of response to someone who had written strongly criticizing their peaceable, generous, and sacrificial approach to Muslims, suggesting they were compromising their faith in Christ, Christine wrote the following, on behalf of herself and Mazhar—words that highlight the deep challenges they have faced over the years and how the experience has shaped them—toward exhibiting grace as opposed to breeding bitterness and judgmentalism.

> We have both left mother and father and our whole family and homelands. We sacrificed our family life and our children saw their grandfather just three times in their lives. There are many costs covered in these couple of sentences. These things were not forced on us by circumstances like refugees, it was part of the cost to follow Christ. We have painfully left our children more than once for an entire year while they were in school and had many family separations with children or one or both of us parents separated for months. At one time we were all separated from each other in different countries while Mazhar had disappeared while in prison. We didn't know if he was still alive. He had given himself up for dead. At one time during our children's teen years we were scattered on three continents. We suffered regular trauma and harassment from the Egyptian Muxhabaraat [secret police] including breaking into our home and scarring our children, spying on us and our home and our mail and phone, we have not been free to speak on the phone, write letters, speak our minds, visit certain people, to be together as a family. We paid a price to do so. We have crept around back streets in the dark trying to lose a tail in order to visit people and pray in their homes. We have gone outdoors on winter nights to huddle in the yard in order to whisper with each other about people and situations, fearing bugs in our house would put others in life threatening situations. We have been betrayed by other people wanting to harm us. Mazhar has faced many interrogations including psychological abuse, blind folded, handcuffed and standing for many hours and sleep deprivation, he has been imprisoned three times, once solitary confinement for 19 days in a small cell sleeping on the concrete floor with nothing else except a rat and where he permanently lost feeling in his thigh from lying on the floor, he

faced death sentences and an attempt on his life by a family member trying to cut his throat, he has been suddenly deported leaving our family stranded and in turmoil in a war zone during the Gulf War, for 25 years we consistently lost homes and friends in a number of countries through being evicted. Disruption to the children's school was a nightmare. Mazhar cannot enter the two countries where our children were born and consider home, so we can't go back for a family visit to heal wounds and re-gather the fun memories. There is not an area of our life where we have not suffered continual loss: possessions, physical health, mental health, friends. I have almost had faith beaten out of me by overwhelming difficult circumstances. Far from hiding the cost aspect of following Christ in our sharing with our Muslim brothers and sisters, many of those who follow Christ have stories similar to ours and at least one appears to have been martyred, other have been baptized in times of intense persecution being willing to die. I am not listing these to boast of afflictions. . . . God has been equal to every trial and brought us through and returned blessings of Himself for losses. . . . The result of our trials is to hear God's Spirit continually more clearly telling us not to judge, especially by appearances or by our own criteria for what faith should look like. . . . God seems to delight in working outside our boundaries to show his grace. I have written this and Mazhar has seen it and joins me. Christine, for both of us.

Mazhar's prison experience in Syria profoundly affected his understanding of Christ's sacrificial suffering: "Focusing on my misery I asked, 'Where is the victory out of suffering, the earthquake that opens the door?' [a reference to Peter's release from prison in the Book of Acts]." Mazhar at first interpreted his not being delivered as God having deserted him, and therefore he recounts

I got worse and became bitter. After seven or eight days, Christ visited me (as if he was physically present). He asked me, 'What are you experiencing that I didn't experience? I was also cut off from the world, darkness overcame me, I was alone, spit upon, falsely accused. . . . I love you enough to share with you my suffering.' I understood that when Christ was on the cross he was left with nothing to hang onto . . . no deliverance, no sense of the Father's presence. I learned that when we are in this situation with nothing to hang onto that's when we need to follow Christ and learn to say 'Father, into your hands I commit myself.' God wanted to transform this experience into a blessing by my embracing the bitter until its piercing brought drops of the sweetness of the fellowship of his suffering. We don't follow God because He makes our life comfortable and serves us, but we follow a God who is transforming us into His image. When Christ was on the cross he was still reaching out to others; God is a God who suffers for us and with us. I allowed God to teach me there in prison and began to focus on God's agony as He allowed Christ to suffer and die, and on the martyrs in history, as well as friends of mine, that suffered for various beliefs they held or principles they stood for. I thought of modern saints in pain and suffering of other kinds—the woman whose husband left her, others struggling with cancer, lonely widows—and as I picked up their burdens to help carry them, I learned that God was trusting me to share His pain with Him. The greater love we carry the greater pain we may bear, making the love still greater. As in the physical arena, bearing weight causes the body to grow and be strengthened, so in the spiritual realm bearing the weight of each others' burdens promotes spiritual growth and strengthens our faith. I felt as if I was released from my dismal surroundings and from my personal internal prison—feeling liberated . . . completely free from any fear. I drank deeply of the depths of the Father's love and suffering for us.

This prison experience deeply softened Mazhar's heart—a dramatic difference many people noticed—which led him to being much gentler and more loving to others. This has resulted in displaying a more "grace-oriented" attitude toward both those fellow Arabs who have hurt him and those foreigners who he thinks often do great damage in the Muslim context. This echoes the wonderful story associated with Temple Gairdner, the respected Anglican priest who served in Egypt in the early 1900s. An Egyptian recalls observing a Muslim sheik insulting and trying to shame Gairdner in public. Gairdner responded by putting his hands over his eyes for a moment and praying silently, and then spoke with great kindness to the sheik. Later the sheik said, "Till that moment I had not believed in your religion, but I believe in it now, because I saw a highborn Englishman take an insult from me in silence. There must be something within him to cause that."[12]

Once after Mazhar was refused entry upon arrival in an Arab country he deeply loved, the long return trip home to Beirut gave him time for reflection and he found himself struggling with his anger and resentment. "Sometimes it is very easy to give up and become bitter or hopeless," he says. "While traveling home I meditated on Paul's letter to the Philippians, and was reminded that the resurrection of Christ is not just a past historical event, but must be something that happens in our life daily. His suffering is our suffering and His resurrection is our resurrection."

Mazhar has had enough disappointments of all kinds for several lifetimes. Once when a financial deal went south, carrying with it all Mazhar's life savings, the person appointed to tell him that all of his money had been lost recalls Mazhar remaining very calm upon hearing the devastating news. Mazhar then warmly invited him over to eat, drink, and smoke a cigar as they mourned together the loss of his money. Reflecting on the various hardships he has undergone throughout life, Mazhar says, "There is something in brokenness, in crisis, that takes the spirit home to God and gives insight which we don't normally get in everyday life."

Loving Your Neighbor as Yourself

Having undergone banishment from his family, imprisonment, national eviction, and solitary confinement, the sacrifice of suffering has not only spiritually deepened Mazhar, it has also developed in him a profound sensitivity to the needs of others. He is known throughout North Africa and the Middle East as a big-hearted man. Taking very seriously Jesus's second-greatest commandment of "loving your neighbor as yourself," his relationships with people are fueled by an incredibly deep compassion and love for men and women in all stations of life—genuinely accepting them just as they are. Gentleness, kindness, open-heartedness, and joyfulness exude from him, and people are drawn to him like a magnet. Children love him. Strangers almost instantly bond with him because of the warmth and the depth of being he displays. He has the ability to make every person he comes across feel like they are the center of the universe.

Mazhar's refreshing, spontaneous relational manner enables him to connect with people everywhere he goes—showing an authentic compassion to even the stranger he meets on the street. He asks people about their deepest needs and problems, and is carefully attuned to crisis moments. When someone is in a crisis, Mazhar is lavish in his time and attention, and this results in his forming deep personal attachments. "One of the most impressive aspects about Mazhar is his concern for the well-being of others," said a Westerner living in Cairo. He went on to share that he had had a bout with cancer a few years ago; though not knowing him well, Mazhar found his telephone number and called on him several times to check on his heath. There are untold stories throughout the world of people he has helped through "dark times," giving mercy to those in need.

Mazhar has a renowned capacity for people and friendships, both Muslim and Christian, and works hard at staying in touch with them, regardless of where they live. He knows by heart the phone numbers of hundreds of friends around the world. As soon as he walks into a city, he begins calling friends. Without considering the cost, he phones people around the world regularly to check in and see how they are doing. If he hears someone he knows has had a problem, he will immediately be on the phone encouraging him or her and praying for them.

Everywhere Mazhar has lived, in the Middle East and in the West, he has formed a weekly meeting of men, drawn largely from the local intellectual and artistic communities. Many deep relationships have come about as a result of these get-togethers, as Mazhar loves to sit with the men and talk for hours. For Mazhar, heaven is sitting with friends around great food, drinking red wine, enjoying laughter, and smoking a *shisha* (Arab water pipe), enjoying stimulating conversation about politics, spirituality, philosophy, and literature.

Everywhere Mazhar has lived, large numbers of people have been attracted to him. When living in Fez, Morocco, a city of 1.3 million people, he was known to so many people there that he once received a letter addressed simply to "Mazhar Mallouhi, Fez." This disposition for loving people was evident early on, when he was a young student at Fuller Seminary in Southern California. For income he worked for a time at a gas station, and he was so popular with clients that they would drive miles out of the way just to purchase their gas there. The station's gas sales increased by 300–500 gallons a day due to Mazhar's presence.

Much of Mazhar's success in the Middle East relates to key Muslim leaders who have helped him because of friendship, not necessarily because they endorsed his ideas and faith in Christ. An Australian couple who visited the Mallouhis in Beirut recalls the respect people had for Mazhar everywhere they seemed to go. One day he drove them south to the city of Sidon, but the freeway was blocked due to repairs. Having trouble finding another road south, Mazhar asked a local policeman on traffic duty for directions. As he did so, the officer recognized him, greeting him warmly. However, the directions he had provided weren't clear, so after a long circle through side streets and a Palestinian refugee camp, they found themselves going back to Beirut past the same policeman. When the policeman saw Mazhar again, he jumped on his motorcycle, left his busy traffic post, and rode ahead of them, parting the traffic, to show them the way. Mazhar had indeed been to his home before, and had spent time with him.

Mazhar naturally brings people together. I recall a bookshop owner in downtown Beirut telling me that Mazhar is the "glue" that holds together their literary and bookselling community in that part of the city. Mazhar is deeply passionate about family values and brotherly love. Often, just after meeting someone, Mazhar will delve into deeply personal details of their life and belief system. Focusing on an issue they have been struggling with and are yet unable to resolve, Mazhar and his direct style are therefore refreshing to Muslims, as he knows from personal experience the issues with which they struggle. While Mazhar's approach would be considered abrupt in the West, his "cut to the chase" attitude is one that shows a genuine and sincere interest, even compassion, to the Arab stranger he encounters on the street.

Most important of all, Mazhar loves people regardless of their faith orientation. Being "people centered," he does not see "Muslims" or "Christians," but rather simply people made in God's image and journeying toward God to greater or lesser degrees. Once in North Africa, Mazhar recalls his friend Muhammad asking him, "Will you still be my friend when I reject your message [Mazhar's love of Christ]?" "Of course" was Mazhar's reply; but it did show a perception that many Muslims have of Christians that they are only "friends" for the agenda of conversion. Sometime later, Muhammad deeply hurt Mazhar. They were eventually able to sort things out and Muhammad experienced forgiveness from him. Sometime later, Muhammad actually defended Christian faith as being different due to its importance of love for others. He now describes himself as someone who is attempting to follow the way of Christ. Again, this experience recalls the comment of a Muslim leader about the Anglican priest in Egypt, Temple Gairdner, whom Muslims respected: "I felt he loved me for myself, not because I might become a Christian . . . and in this I found he was like Christ. And he loved our children and always played with them."[13] Today Mazhar, living in Beirut, endears himself to the range of religious traditions across Lebanon—from participating in Sufi groups, to meeting with Shia leaders, to partying with Catholic and Orthodox friends.

Many of Mazhar's relationships come about thanks to his tremendous sense of humor. His laughter is infectious and he loves to joke with others; it's his way of celebrating his love of God-given life. When driving and stopped at a traffic light, Mazhar more often than not will start conversations and humorous interchanges with either those in cars next to him or the traffic police. Once, when he managed a coffee shop in Morocco, he noticed the plainclothes policeman assigned to watch him was walking past, and he called out to him, saying, "Where do you think you're going? You are supposed to be here, keeping an eye on me."

Contrary to the Western approach of being primarily task-oriented (often followed by Western Christians in the Muslim World), Mazhar is instead people-oriented. He often sees the Western church as too preoccupied with programs, strategies, and internal ecclesiastical bureaucracy. Mazhar himself does not have a thought-out methodology but rather simply loves people for who they are and the joy of being with them, and therefore focuses on touching their hearts. Naturally the Mallouhis are deeply loved in return. Al-Jazeera television (the "Muslim CNN" of the Middle East) chose Christine as the subject for a special program titled "Friends of the Arab World," spending two days interviewing the Mallouhis in their Beirut home and filming their life.

Mazhar has observed that many Western Christians living in the Middle East actually avoid relationships with Muslims. He loves to recall the absurd story of a Westerner who came to Morocco as a missionary and who put verses of the Bible on small pieces of paper and then put them in tin cans and hid them in the fields, so that farmers when they ploughed would find the cans and discover "the treasure." Not only is this totally ridiculous and what Mazhar would regard as the antithesis of living out one's faith in Christ among others, but as if to add irony to injury, all those farmers are illiterate.

Mazhar exhibits a love for people with no ulterior agenda. He humorously tells the story of his first visit to the U.S. and of being invited to a Christian couple's home for dinner. While eating, he quickly realized that they were actually using the dinner to sell him Amway products. This shook him as it is totally contrary to the understanding and practice of hospitality in an Arab culture. It is sobering to have him observe that Christians often establish relationships with a hidden purpose behind them, as opposed to genuinely loving people just for who they are.

In this connection, the example of Charles de Foucauld is once again pertinent. Living among the Muslim Tuareg peoples in the southern Algerian desert, Foucauld sought to simply love them and demonstrate the life of Christ among them. Commenting on the effectiveness of Foucauld's approach, Muslim writer Ali Merad wrote, "When this European man or woman, when these Christians, gave up their advantages and chose to come and share the . . . lot of the Muslim population in the mountains or the desert, such a choice must have appeared to be the outcome of a conversion bearing the unmistakable mark of the divine. Hence the signs of respect, trust and affection with which the Tuareg surrounded their venerable neighbor [Foucauld], the 'Christian marabout' ['holy man']."[14]

Exhibiting The Middle Eastern Hospitality of Christ

Mazhar's commitment to Jesus's commandment and life illustration of "loving your neighbor as yourself" naturally translates into practicing a hospitality that makes even the reputation of Middle Eastern hospitality look meager. The famed Middle Eastern custom of elaborate and generous hospitality is known the world over. This is particularly true of the Bedouin, whose hospitality is deservedly famous, as anyone who has experienced it can witness. Nothing the Bedouin do for the guest is too good and nothing too bothersome or difficult. The Bedouin host does all in his ability to convey the honoring impression that entertaining his guest is the greatest happiness he has ever known.

"The guest is a guest of God" is a well-known Arab Muslim proverb that reflects the theological depth of their view of hospitality. Experienced Islamists and Arabists, such as the late twentieth-century Christian French scholar Louis Massignon, repeatedly address the spiritual importance of hospitality to Muslims. Their model is of the Old Testament patriarch, Abraham, and his experience; in welcoming the stranger, we are welcoming God among us. Another popular Arab proverb says, "God comes to us in the person of a guest." Massignon, in his lifetime study of Islam, termed this *l'hospitalitée sacrée*—"sacred hospitality." Hospitality pre-figured for him the stance of God himself toward human beings—the sacredness of the guest. Paradoxically, this Islamic code of hospitality enabled Christian missions to penetrate parts of the Muslim world considered today by some as the least receptive to Christian work (such as the Gulf countries of Oman, the UAE, and Kuwait), and establish the few historic Christian posts that still exist there today.

Hospitality is so fundamental to Islamic culture that even when Mazhar was jailed overnight in Cairo prior to being deported, the Muslim fundamentalists in his cell served as his hosts, sharing with him a blanket and food. Likewise, during the Gulf War of the early 1990s, while Christine was alone with their sons in Cairo following Mazhar's deportation, their Muslim friends did the shopping for her and would refuse to be reimbursed, releasing her from having to stand for hours in crowded lines. They would respond to her expressions of thanks by saying, "It's my pleasure to do this for my brother Mazhar."

Small wonder then that Egyptian Christian theologian, Dr. Ekram Lamie, would say, "Mazhar is the truest Arab I know; full of generosity, he is a master of hospitality." Likewise, a Tunisian Muslim leader describes Mazhar as "this short man with a huge smile, large hands of hospitality, and a heart of love, [who] has befriended and blessed countless people." Because of this openness, a steady stream of hundreds of people a week flowed through the Mallouhis' house in Cairo. Some come to party, some to pray. They include Muslim fundamentalist sheiks, Catholic priests and nuns, Baptist pastors, Coptic Orthodox, Communists, Jewish rabbis, Baha'is, and all kinds of Western expatriates. The Mallouhis opened their home to every person God brings along, including at times people they found in the street, whom they helped and fed. One family was a mother and her newly delivered child. The couple had miscalculated the delivery date and used all their money for the hospital bill. Christine recalls how once four Scandinavian men arrived at their house with backpacks. They were given their address in a campground in Spain and told this was a great place to stay in Morocco. Once Mazhar saw a young Australian lady at the airport in Cairo who had just arrived, flustered and clearly not comfortable by herself in this strange Arab city. Offering to help, he learned that she had booked a hotel, but being that it was late at night, he brought her home and she actually stayed for Christmas with the Mallouhi family. Even early on as a young single student at Fuller Seminary in the U.S., Mazhar would host dinners, cooking Middle Eastern food for thirty to forty people. People who have visited the Mallouhis, whether in Beirut, Tunis, Rabat, Fez, or Cairo, say that it seemed like they devoted all their time to them, lavishing attention on their guests.

Ironically, however, when Muslims read about Jesus in the Gospels, one of the first things they recognize is his exceptional practice of hospitality, his characteristic trait of welcoming all who came his way. Once in a desert oasis in the Gulf region, Mazhar thanked a man for his hospitality to them, to which the Muslim man replied, "Don't forget that as an Easterner, Christ was very hospitable. He took his obligation as a host seriously and fed the five thousand."

Embodying the Spirituality of Christ—
Living In the Presence of God

In reading the Gospels, Mazhar sees Christ as someone who naturally lived in and embodied the presence of God as he journeyed throughout Palestine. Interestingly, this is quite similar to a Muslim's understanding of prayer, for to a Muslim, prayer to God can take place anywhere—in the street, on the sidewalk, in a field, at a football match, and so on. The gathering for communal worship, something that is quite strongly emphasized in Christianity, is often immaterial to Muslim spirituality.

Mazhar's perception is that Christians often focus too much on what they do inside a building, as opposed to the natural living out of their lives in all contexts of life. In this sense, Mazhar embodies a unique display of spirituality in his following of Christ: one that is very akin to Brother Lawrence's "practicing the presence of God at all times." Mazhar takes a "God view" of life, and brings God into all of life quite spontaneously. He sees his faith in Christ as a way of living out his life, and desires to display to all the beauty of Christ. It is fascinating to watch him talking about the sweetness of Christ to those gathered around him in Arab cafés, as he puffs on a water pipe and fingers his prayer beads.

An avid walker, Mazhar prays while walking, and describes prayer as living in a continual listening disposition toward God. In this sense, he sees prayer as essentially attempting to participate in God's will—which more often than not he believes will involve him directly in the answering of the prayer request.

Sensory in orientation, Mazhar has become more of a mystic over the years. Hence in Islam he identifies and resonates most with Sufism and ties that into his own experience of hearing and listening to the voice of Jesus. Several times Mazhar has had mystical experiences or visions where he visually saw and physically felt the presence of Jesus near him. Today his spiritual interaction is largely with those focused on seeking harmony and who are interested in getting closer to Nabi Isa (Teacher Jesus), and experiencing him as someone whom they desire to have become more a part of their lives. In his embracing of greater and greater mystery throughout his own spiritual pilgrimage, he needs fewer answers to the more complex questions of life.

At the same time Mazhar is very proactive and completely natural with others in sharing about his own faith in Christ. He often takes the Gospels (Injil) with him to read in the café, just as Muslims read the Qur'an everywhere. People often ask him, "What are you reading?" Not infrequently, when he notices Muslims next to him reading over his shoulder out of curiosity, he lets them finish the page before turning it. Experientially oriented, he primarily shares with others from his own spiritual journey—believing that others will see Christ through us if we have truly experienced him. Mazhar loves to highlight, "The first disciples of Christ had a beautiful expression: 'Come and see.'" He truly relishes his walk with God, and as a result his love for God is infectious. He believes "when you see someone in love, it shows." According to Mazhar's observation, many Western Christians feel hesitant and unnatural in sharing their own spiritual journeys with others, let alone with Muslims, and therefore act artificially. He enjoys telling the humorous story of a young woman sharing about Christ who was so nervous talking with an elderly Muslim lady that she said, "My name is Jesus, and I want to tell you about Jessica." Paradoxically, there is no need at all in a Muslim context to feel uncomfortable sharing about one's spiritual journey, as "religious" speech is appreciated and respected, in contrast to the West where people are uptight when talking about religion.

Mazhar's natural way of sharing about Christ is illustrated in an experience with two well-known writers in Tunisia. One day, the Tunisian writer Hassan Ben Othman (who has criticized and written strongly against Muslim fundamentalists to the extent that he is called an "infidel" by some) and Mazhar were walking along with Hassan Ben Nasser (another respected Tunisian writer). Ben Othman said to him, "When I read one of your books, it made me think that you might be a 'missionary.'" Mazhar's natural and authentic response was, "Thank you for honoring me today. You have reminded me of my responsibility in life of sharing about our beautiful Lord." This open and natural approach is greatly respected by other Muslims. Once when Mazhar visited the office of his friend and Muslim writer Ahmed Swayden's wife, who serves as a director in the Ministry of Economics in Damascus, she called out to her friends on the floor and said, "Here is our missionary friend working in North Africa." As a Muslim, she was honored to have this type of "missionary friend."

Collaborating with Arab and Islamic Culture

Just as Jesus fully employed the Palestinian Jewish culture of his day to enhance his communication of the Kingdom of God, Mazhar also proactively seeks to use and benefit from today's Arab (Middle Eastern) and Islamic culture in sharing about Christ with his fellow Muslims. His eager collaboration with important aspects and values of his local culture actually facilitates an authentic natural display of what it means to be a follower of Christ.

Mazhar is often asked by foreigners, and sometimes Arab Christians, how he is able to be so publicly open about his faith in Christ within a Muslim context. In this regard, he benefits from *Islam's "command to witness to their faith."* When Mazhar is asked by Muslims if he is a "missionary" (due to his passion of sharing about "his Master" with them), he asks them in response, "Are you a missionary?" When a Muslim asks him what he means by that question, Mazhar says, "Well, you have a *shahada* don't you? [The *shahada* is the statement of belief that all Muslims recite out loud daily: "There is no God but God, and Muhammad is His Prophet."] Well, when you confess the *shahada* and tell others about it, does that make you a missionary? I too have a *shahada*, and I must talk about it with others. Does that make me a missionary?"

Another aspect of Arab culture that has opened many doors for Mazhar's work is the prominent *Arab emphasis on status and position.* Instead of chafing under it, he chooses to use it to gain an open and respected platform to introduce the Christ of the Middle East. As a result of the literary credibility he has obtained, for many years Mazhar has proactively built close friendships with respected leaders of Arab society, from prominent Muslim imams to key political and commercial leaders. Whenever he visits a new place it is his practice to make contact early on with the local Islamic leadership in that community. If a prominent sheik talks with and befriends Mazhar, this enables others in that local Arab community to feel much more secure and free to openly discuss with him issues of faith.

One of the strongest cultural mores in Arab society is to avoid, at whatever the cost, any possibility of being shamed, whether personally or publicly. At times this desire to avoid shame provides a natural door for Mazhar to encourage Islamic leaders to genuinely explore the teachings of Christ. Once when he led a group of Westerners through Al Azhar Mosque in Cairo, he asked one of the local sheiks to share with the visitors about the Islamic faith. As Mazhar translated the sheik's words from Arabic to English for the guests, it became clear, due to his inaccurate information about the New Testament, that the sheik had never read it. Mazhar stopped translating and said to the sheik in Arabic (which the visitors could not understand), "How can I explain to them that you, a religious leader in this prestigious mosque, have not studied, let alone opened, the New Testament (Injil). This is embarrassing to me as an Arab." The sheik then begged Mazhar not to let the guests know about his failure to do so, as not to be shamed in front of them, and then promised to read and study the New Testament if one were given to him, in order to know firsthand what it says before he ever lectures on it again.

Preserving *honor* in this way is one of the most prominent values within Arab culture. Mazhar therefore believes that one of the fundamental principles for Christians to follow is to respect and honor Muslims at all times. This is why he strongly believes that if Westerners desire to learn about Islam, they should do so from Muslims themselves, and not from Westerners, even those who have obtained a post-graduate degree in Islamics. Mazhar has taken many Christians to sheiks to learn about Islam. Conversely, he also works to gain the right for Muslims to learn firsthand about Christ from Christians. In visiting with sheiks, he often speaks to them about breaking down the walls that divide the two faiths by posing the question, "If I want to study about Islam, is it fair for me to study what a Buddhist believes about it? Or should I come to you and ask a Muslim sheik? We need to obtain our information firsthand and not accept others' interpretations of our faith."

Mazhar believes that *honesty and integrity* need to be the pillars upon which Christians build their relationships with Muslims. This mandates that Christians have no hidden agenda, for as the Arab proverb states, "You can't carry two watermelons in one hand." Mazhar himself lives with the assumption that he has nothing to hide and believes that all should be out in the open. Once when a government informant visited Mazhar's house (at his invitation), he purposely left the man alone in the room to give him a chance to investigate. It was his way of letting the man know that he had nothing to hide.

This emphasis of Mazhar's on the need for honesty and the need to demonstrate complete integrity is illustrated in the special counsel he gave to an American desiring to obtain a visa for Syria, Mazhar's native country. Syria refused to grant visas to anyone who had been to Israel and this individual had been there ten years ago. Many Westerners who had been to Israel found ways to fudge on the visa application, but this individual's conscience did not allow him to do so. He then spoke to Mazhar about the situation, and Mazhar advised him to go to the Syrian consulate and ask to speak to the consul in person and then to tell him that he really wanted to visit his country, but there was a question on the visa application that troubled him: "Have you ever been to occupied Palestine?" Then Mazhar suggested he ask the consul, "Is this a political question about my attitude toward the Palestinian issue or do you just want to know if I have ever been in the geographical territory of Palestine? I am not a Zionist, but I don't want to mislead you about my visit there some years ago." He went and did this just as Mazhar had recommended and the Syrian consul instructed him to come back after lunch. Upon his return, the consul shared with him that he should reject his application, but that because he had told the truth, he was going to grant him the visa. Mazhar's American acquaintance then went to the clerk, who requested him to submit the application, but not to answer the question about visiting occupied Palestine. He did as instructed, signed the application and submitted it, noticing that the clerk then put a check in the box that he had not visited occupied Palestine. He was then promptly given a visa. Interestingly, the person immediately ahead of him in line was refused a visa because the Syrian consul was convinced he had gone to Israel.

Presenting the Incomparable Beauty of the Eastern Christ

The primary focus of Mazhar's life and writing is to display a positive and culturally relevant Jesus to Arab Muslims, as opposed to presenting Christianity. He is not at all interested in comparing "this religious system versus that system." He is passionate about "his Master" and his faith in Christ is contagious. Hearing Mazhar say with deep affection, "How I love my Lord," as he often does, ignites a desire to deepen one's own journey with Christ.

Focused on Jesus, and not on religion, Mazhar says, "Christ came to bring the Kingdom of God in the human heart—not to establish another religion. His message is very simple actually. However, as they say, when the Christian faith moved to the Greeks, they made it into a philosophy. When it went to the Romans, they made it into an institution. And when it went all the way West, it was turned into an enterprise, a business."

Mazhar shares his belief that Christians have often presented a Christ completely covered over by their Christianity. However, Christianity and Jesus are not the same, he emphasizes. Mazhar shares the following analogy about religion getting in the way of seeing and experiencing Christ: "Religion can often end up being like the man who sells bottles of water near a fresh running stream—the people who buy the bottled water have no idea about the close proximity of the stream. And even the person selling the bottled water often does everything possible to keep people from seeing the nearby stream, because then his own business is finished."

Virginia Cobb's comments on what followers of Christ have to share with their Muslim friends are profound.

> Our message is a *person we've experienced*, not a doctrine, system, religion, book, church, ethic. Christ is extremely attractive to Muslims. They have the highest respect for him and yearn to know more about him. We can present the person Jesus and his teachings as our supreme and only emphasis, the only thing we have to add to the foundation of reverence for God and moral emphasis already found in Islam. Our faith in him is that once we lead a person to him, he will be in direct contact with that person, transform and guide in all else. . . . We must emphasize Christ as a living person, and leave all else in a secondary position.[15]

Christians are often inaccurately called a "People of the Book." Instead, we should be "People of the Person," Mazhar suggests. The Christian faith has nothing to do with knowing a creed, or living a set of moral laws, or believing certain doctrines, but rather everything to do with knowing a person. A problem many Christians have often had is that they try to present Christianity as a better religion than any other, yet it isn't necessarily so. (Let's remember that Jesus himself wasn't a Christian.) As Mazhar demonstrates, people are not typically interested in Christianity for all kinds of abstract reasons; they are fascinated with Jesus as he really was and is. The Jesus who is presented in Gospels is what naturally attracts people. Yet it is often difficult to see *that* Jesus for all the religious and cultural baggage surrounding him.

This echoes what the late Anglican Bishop Stephen Neill wrote when addressing Christian witness among Muslims, "The [follower of Christ] has no other message for the Muslim than Jesus Christ himself. He asks no more of the Muslim than that he will look at Jesus Christ, as he is presented in the Gospels, patiently, sincerely and without prejudice. . . . The Muslim thinks that he already knows about Jesus all that it is possible to know; why should he suppose that he still have anything to learn? . . . But, if he can be persuaded to look at Jesus, strange things may happen."[16]

Hence, Mazhar is always talking about Jesus and sharing with both Muslims and Christians about the beauty, fullness of life, and joy that he has found in Christ. His passion is to see all people, regardless of faith tradition, walk in the footsteps of Christ, living the way he lived, and following his teachings. "When Christ said, 'I am the way'. . . he was saying, 'my way is the way to live your life; a way that leads to God,'" reflects Mazhar. When asked about his primary motivation for sharing with others about Christ, he responds with this story: "Let's say I have a friend who has a son who has been separated from him for many years. And every time I am with my friend (the father) he talks about how much he loves his son, misses him, and longs to be with him. Then one day as I am walking through the city I see his son. Now let me ask you, What kind of friend am I to the father if I don't go to the son and tell him how much I know his father longs for him?" In regard to his Muslim brothers and sisters, he always starts where they are, not where Christ is, and gently leads them toward Christ. Often it is references to Isa al Masih (Jesus) in the Qur'an that compel Muslims to seek out more information about Jesus. As very few suitable publications about Christ's life for Muslims in Arabic existed in the secular market (even though Christ is such an important figure in the Qur'an), Mazhar, through his publishing association, Al Kalima, published a very readable biography on the life of Christ titled *The Master: A Life of Jesus*.

An illustration of Mazhar's approach to sharing about Christ with his fellow Muslims comes from Vincent Donovan, a Catholic priest who worked among the Masai peoples in Kenya. Addressing the Masai, he writes in his excellent book, *Christianity Rediscovered*,[17] "Everyone knows how devout you Masai are, the faith you have, your beautiful worship of God. You have known God and he has loved you." Similarly, Mazhar believes God has created this world and is already present and working within his creation. The role of followers of Christ is not to take God with us, but to discover "the God who is already present" and proclaim him as the God who is the Father of the Lord Jesus. God has always gone ahead of us, and is both already there and being experienced. No one should attempt to bring in an opposing God, who is bigger and better, but instead share how the existing God is bigger and better than is recognized, and can be experienced more fully through Jesus Christ.

In this sense, we Westerners who seek to follow Christ are called to make every effort to be sure we are following and presenting the Christ of the Gospels. The challenge for those who call themselves followers of Christ is to not let our existing preconceptions (or those which we have perhaps been taught—albeit if in the church) get in the way of seeing who Jesus really is. In C. S. Lewis's book, *The Magician's Nephew* (in the Chronicles of Narnia), one of the characters says, "For what you see and hear depends a good deal on where you are standing." Often religion (such as institutional Christianity) can get in the way, like a folding screen, in front of Jesus, where Christianity covers up the living Christ. Yet, as Mazhar's life and message highlights, if anything is true about the Christian faith, it is true because of Christ, not because of Christianity, which has grown up around him over the centuries. The challenge is to work toward making sure we are following the Christ of the Gospels. And really the only way to know who the real Jesus is, whether one be a Christian or Muslim, is to be immersed directly in the Gospels—for the central message of the Gospels is not primarily the teaching of Jesus, but Jesus himself.

This requires going on a lifelong quest, spending our lives searching for Jesus—for a summary of the Christian life of faith is essentially about a continual encountering of God in deeper and closer ways through Christ. In this regard, we will never get to the point of knowing or understanding all there is to know or understand about Jesus. The spiritual life is "a meeting of Jesus for the first time"—over and over again. I love the way the late English writer Malcolm Muggeridge put it: "Jesus, for me, has been a long process of discovery—a process that is by no means over, and never can be. Like an infinitely precious and rewarding human relationship which goes on developing and constantly reveals new depths and possibilities of intimacy." At Jesus's trial, surely Peter was deeply right when he insisted of Jesus, "I don't know the man." For even after all those years of following Jesus, he still really didn't know who he was. And neither do we. For Christ will always be beyond our full grasp.

Kahlil Gibran, the famous Arab Lebanese writer of Christian background, spent the last years of his life writing what became his longest book, titled *Jesus, Son of Man.*

In regard to how Jesus breaks our stereotypes, Gibran writes, "No other man ever walked the way He walked. Was it a breath born in my garden that moved to the east? Or was it a storm that would shake all things to their foundations?" As C. S. Lewis, one of Mazhar's favorite Western writers, asked, "'What are we to make of Jesus Christ?' This is a question which has, in a sense, a frantically comic side. For the real question is not what are we to make of Christ, but what is He to make of us?"

In planting Jesus as a Middle Easterner in today's Arab Islamic society, Mazhar makes the way of knowing Jesus something more natural and legitimate for Muslims. As Mahatma Gandhi enabled Indians to visualize Christ walking down their Indian roads, so Mazhar returns Christ to his cultural origins, walking naturally down the roads of the Middle East.

Opening a Middle Eastern Book: Returning the Christian Scriptures to their Middle Eastern Origin

7

God walks in the Holy Scriptures seeking people.

—ST. AMBROSE

I think it is very unlikely that the Bible will return as a book unless it returns as a sacred book.

—C. S. LEWIS

I RECALL HEARING AN ARAB MUSLIM living in the West say, after reading the Christian Scriptures for the first time, "It reads like a letter written from home." In this regard, Mazhar's most important literature projects focus on re-presenting the Christian Scriptures as the ancient Middle Eastern writings that they are, returning them to their authentic cultural origin for today. Many Muslims see the Bible as a culturally Western religious book. However, as Mazhar points out, "The Bible is not a Western book, but rather a collection of sixty-six books actually rooted in Middle Eastern culture more ancient than that underlying the Qur'an." His vision is to introduce a natural and authentic home for the Christian Scriptures in the heart of the Muslim world, where they are accepted as a normal part of Arab society. Mazhar therefore spends most of his time and energy working to present the Christian Scriptures in ways that Muslims can understand and respect.

This distinctive emphasis is best illustrated in Mazhar's re-presentations of the Gospels of Luke and John, and the Old Testament book of Genesis. He writes in the introduction to one of these publications, "In order to bring the Bible back to its original roots, where it should be, we decided to attempt to re-read it with a different approach and from a different angle." In this regard, Mazhar works in close cooperation with Muslim Arabs and actively seeks cooperation and counsel from influential Muslims, including well-known literary figures, as he works to produce publications that re-present the Scriptures in a way that addresses their felt needs, and to shatter stereotypes, overcome prejudices, and illuminate and resolve typical Muslims misunderstanding of the text. As mentioned in chapter 3, Muslims were the ones who first challenged Mazhar to publish the Christian Scriptures in a presentation that is oriented to them in order that they might more easily understand the Bible. With the feedback he receives from hundreds of Muslims on these biblical texts, he then develops commentaries to address the issues raised. These publications are titled *An Eastern Reading of the Gospel of Luke*, *A Sufi Reading of the Gospel of John*, and *Genesis: The Origin of the World and Humanity*.[1] Each of these publications includes the biblical text and a Muslim-focused commentary that effectively explains the Scriptures and presents Christ as the Middle Easterner that he was. The commentary acts as an interpreter to explain the text to the Muslim reader in a way that makes it understandable by helping to remove their theological misconceptions and barriers. Sensitive and difficult terms such as "Son of God"[2] and "the Trinity"[3] and questions like "Why are there four Gospels?" he explains so average Muslim Arab readers can understand them within their own cultural context.

In these publications, Mazhar effectively addresses the issues that would be in the forefront of the Arab Muslim mind. For example, in *An Eastern Reading of the Gospel of Luke*, Mazhar draws a parallel between the Roman occupation of Palestine during Christ's life and the modern day occupation of much of Palestine by an equally aggressive army. The *Genesis* publication shares how the book contains the spiritual roots of all three of the Middle East's religions—Islam, Christianity, and Judaism—and then focuses on helping readers see how Christ was a fulfillment of God's covenant with Abraham, whom Muslims view as their historical father. The theme throughout the *Genesis* publication is of God breaking into darkness and chaos and bringing light and life.

The publication titled *A Sufi Reading of the Gospel of John* is oriented toward Sufi Muslims (Sufism is the mystical segment of Islam that emphasizes the personal experience of God as opposed to religious dogmatism and ritual). As Adib Sa'ab, one of the leading Lebanese intellectuals, comments in his extensive review of this *John* publication, "Mazhar Mallouhi's work in his 'Sufi' commentary of the Gospel of John . . . is the first work to open the door of comparison between the Gospel text and Islamic Sufi heritage. . . . [It is] a source of rich inspiration and enlightenment, not only in a practical sense, but also philosophically and theologically, especially in the field of religious language and religious symbolism." Throughout the preparation of this publication, Mazhar received much support and assistance from Sufi religious leaders and scholars. In Sufi communities the seeker after God puts him or herself in submission to a spiritual guide who leads them along the path of light. Mazhar's *John* publication thus presents Jesus as the ultimate mystic and spiritual guide who shines the light on the path toward experiencing God and his love, and who deserves our loyalty. Throughout the publication, well-loved Sufi masters' writings about Christ are entwined with Jesus's own declarations about himself.

In his excellent review, Nizam Mardini, the well-known Muslim writer and journalist, highlights the effectiveness of Mazhar's approach in *A Sufi Reading of the Gospel of John*:

> The essence of the Sufi approach is illuminated by the spirit of the Lord Christ and his teachings. Indeed, the Sufis continued to deliberate upon this truth secretly amongst themselves, until it was divulged by Hussain bin Mansour al-Hallaj [the Sufi mystic and martyr—AD 858–922], a deed which cost him his life. . . . The text of *John* [the Gospel of John] extensively employs the term "Son of God," which has led to much speculation. Therefore Mazhar has worked to clarify this expression . . . that has led to so many misunderstandings between Christians and Muslims. . . . The concept of discipleship in the Gospel of John takes on a special dimension, as it is linked with one of the disciples of Christ who had a special relationship with him. . . . The death of Christ was the necessary result of his struggle with the Jews, as the Gospel of John portrays. Yet even though his death was very brutal, this was not a defeat in itself, since he allowed God's love to be accessible to all.

Remarkably, Nizam Mardini closes his review of the *Luke* publication with these words: "The Muslim Arabs are confused about the real significance of following Jesus Christ. His followers ask for one thing: to believe that his words about himself come from the Word of God, which puts us into permanent and uninterrupted contact with God. Following Jesus' footsteps means to get engaged in a spiritual relationship with him, learn from him . . . and accept his other followers as members of the same family."

Mazhar also includes Muslims' contributions of articles and introductions in these publications. In his introduction to *An Eastern Reading of the Gospel of Luke,* Dr. Muhammad Fadhel Jamali, the late prime minister of Iraq, writes, "We Muslims know less about the Christian faith than Christians know about Islam. Therefore, I encourage you as a Muslim to read this book to understand what they truly believe." Another introductory section in the *Luke* publication is by Dr. Hashim al Aoui Alqasmi, the president of the Department of History at the University of Fez, Morocco. Renowned Muslim Arab writers and scholars, Dr. Radwan al-Sayyid, professor of Islamic studies at the Lebanese University and an advisor to both the late prime minister of

Lebanon, Rafik Hariri, and the current Lebanese prime minister, Siniara; and Dr. Muhammad Yasser Sharaf, a scholar of Sufi thought and mysticism and an advisor to the Royal Court, United Arab Emirates (Abu Dhabi), wrote lengthy introductions for *A Sufi Reading of the Gospel of John*. Muhammad Said al-Ashmawi, the former security advisor to the high court in Egypt, wrote endorsements for both the *Luke* and *John* publications. Mazhar's "Easternized" publications of Scriptures have thus been endorsed by Arab Muslim leaders ranging from a former prime minister to current government cabinet and parliament ministers to journalists to Islamic university deans and professors.

Not only is their content exclusively oriented to Muslims, but also equally important is their external packaging and the way they are distributed. The Western proverb "You cannot tell a book by its cover" is contrary to Arab thinking. To a Muslim, God's holy word needs to be presented in an honorable fashion that conveys great reverence and importance. The appearance of the book itself commands respect for the message. Hence these Eastern presentations of the Scriptures are truly works of art, in beautifully detailed hardbound volumes, printed with ornate Arabic calligraphy (in the artistic Islamic style done by a renowned Syrian calligrapher), and on par with the quality that Arab readers expect in editions of the Qur'an. This quality presentation helps to overcome the prejudice many have of even touching a Bible, creating a sense of reverence and openness to it. Once when a Christian in Syria brought a box of these publications home, as he was unloading them from the car, a Muslim lady walking by noticed the covers, and came over immediately, asking in great excitement, "Oh, is that the Injil [Gospels]?" The external presentation attracted her to it and made it acceptable to her. Another Muslim woman, who was known to strongly believe the traditional Muslim view that Christians had corrupted the Bible, exclaimed after reading the *Luke* publication, "This is exactly what I have needed. It is the Injil with a Muslim feel to it. It was written by a Muslim, you know." The response of many Muslims to these publications is "this is like one of our books." Often, Muslims receive them by kissing them and holding them to their foreheads. Once when Mazhar was walking down the street in Beirut, a Muslim man in his mid-forties stopped him, kissed him on the head, and thanked him for producing the *John* publication. One Muslim university professor, upon reading the word "Injil" in the title, gasped at its beauty and literally received it as a holy book with outstretched hands on bended knee. Because Muslims see the Arabic language as both the language of God ("God's chosen medium for the Qur'an") and the cornerstone of Arab identity, in these "Eastern Readings" Mazhar deliberately uses the literary language of Arabic, *al-fusha* (as opposed to more simplified Arabic colloquials), that educated Arabs have historically employed for formal Arabic reading and writing. In this regard, there is a Muslim expression: "Arabic has always refused to become Christian."[4]

By presenting the Scriptures as culturally Middle Eastern, Mazhar has gained unprecedented access and acceptance for the biblical books. At Arab book fairs in North Africa, a region with very few local Christians, *An Eastern Reading of the Gospel of Luke* has been a consistent best seller. In various educational institutions, such as in some Arab Muslim universities, it has even become a required textbook. Through the principles of respect and reciprocity, Mazhar has found an amazing openness to these publications of the Scriptures. As one Taliban leader said after reading the *Luke* publication, "I wish all the Taliban would read this." In 2004, the annual *Arab Publishers Journal* listed *A Sufi Reading of the Gospel of John* as one of the most significant publications of the year. Upon the release of *John*, a special personalized gift edition was given to ministers of parliament in Lebanon, Syria, and the Arabian Gulf. At an international book fair in Baghdad, where thousands of these *Eastern Readings* publications where distributed, the organizing director wrote, "This is a drop in the bucket. I need twenty-five thousand more to meet the need. People here are literally fighting over each other to get these books . . . two Muslim men were having a tug of war over our last copy of the *Genesis* commentary, each declaring how long they have been searching for a book like this and why 'I' should have it." Upon being given a copy of the *John* publication, a Muslim member of parliament in an Arab country exclaimed, "This is what my people need—a Bible that we can actually read. We have thought that the Bible was a book from the West and so we were a little nervous about reading it, but the way this is done is perfect. It makes me feel at home before I even read it. I will finish it in two days." When a Muslim professor of religious history at the Islamic University of Zeitouna in North Africa finished reading *An Eastern Reading of the Gospel of Luke*, he commented enthusiastically, "This is the first time we have seen that Christ has Middle Eastern roots related to our culture. We had formerly received Christianity through the Western colonialization view. I want everyone in our Department of Islamic Studies to read this."

Ironically, the only criticism Mazhar has received from these re-presentations of the Scriptures is from some Christians themselves who feel that these publications, both by their "unchristian" appearance and open and respectful content, compromise their Christian faith. Paradoxically, after reading these publications Muslims are even found to be defending Christians and their beliefs. A humorous example of this comes from Oman in the Gulf. A Muslim Omani man, after reading through *An Eastern Reading of the Gospel of Luke*, told his Muslim colleagues at work when he heard them insulting Christians for their belief in "three gods" [the standard Muslim understanding of the Trinity] that this was a misunderstanding on their part, and he explained the Trinity to them afresh. Wide media attention has been given to these publications in the Arab press, speaking positively about their unique role in helping to build bridges between Muslims and Christians. When *Annahar*, a respected international Arab newspaper, ran a substantial article on both *An Eastern Reading of the Gospel of Luke* and Mazhar's philosophical approach in the publication, Ghassan Tueni, the former minister of culture and ambassador to the United Nations for Lebanon, went out personally to purchase a copy. [5] He then extensively drew upon the publication in a published lecture he gave not long after, quoting from it throughout, highlighting it as a bridge-building model for Christians to share with Muslims in these times of increased tension between the two religions.

Many Arab Christians find these publications serve as a natural and beautiful gift for their Muslim friends. One Maronite Catholic priest reserves a portion of his monthly income to purchase the *Luke* reading to give to his Muslim acquaintances. The patriarch of one of the largest historic Orthodox Churches in the Middle East personally distributes these publications and refers to their existence as "realizing one of his long dreams. . . . They are exactly what we need in the Middle East . . . a bridge using a language the audience outside the perimeter of the Church can understand, clearing up misunderstandings about our faith. As Christians, your publications 'whiten our faces' [giving them something proud to present to their Muslim neighbors]."

Coupled with the Middle Eastern presentation of the Scriptures is Mazhar's strong belief that their distribution should be exclusively through legal sales channels, as opposed to smuggling or free mass distribution of any sort. Therefore Al Kalima's main publishing partnership is with one of the largest and most respected secular Arab publishing houses in the Middle East, Dar al Jil, headquartered in Beirut and owned by Maronite Catholics. This enables Mazhar's books to be sold legally and openly through normal secular or Islamic outlets in twenty-three Arab countries and in Pakistan and Iran—from supermarkets in the Gulf States, to book fairs in North Africa and Iran, from Arabic Muslim bookstores in Egypt and bookstalls in front of mosques in Iraq to street bookstands in countries like Libya, Yemen, and the Sudan. Amazingly, the *Luke* publication has been the bestselling title of the large Dar El Jil publishing house at book fairs throughout the Middle East and North Africa. All these publications have been approved by government censors for sale in the mainstream market and therefore do not bear the stigma of smuggled contraband that much Western or Protestant Arab Christian–produced literature does. Upon seeing the *Luke* publication on sale at a government book fair, one follower of Christ from a Muslim background observed, "For years I have had friends asking me for [legal, non-contraband] Bibles. At last

I have something worthy and honorable to give them." Over the years, Mazhar has seen the very negative effects of smuggling. Smuggling he views as blocking all possibilities for the Bible to be taken seriously and naturally by Muslims or for the Bible to be endorsed officially as a legal book, something his sales and distribution approach has proved is very possible. Even though Mazhar has government permission to import these publications, shipments sometimes get held up due to other Christians smuggling literature who have been caught. Mazhar acknowledges that all of this requires a long-term distribution perspective.

As Mazhar does not want Muslims to incorrectly label the Scriptures as "Christian" books, and as they are not culturally "Christian" in orientation or appearance, he does not distribute them through Christian bookstores or churches. This approach has made the Scriptures widely available and officially acceptable in most of the countries considered "closed" to the Bible. At the same time, the greatest local financial support for these publications comes from Muslim readers themselves, as the proceeds from the sales are reinvested to underwrite reprinting and further publications. Numerous Arab charities also use these publications by putting them on the shelves of community and school libraries, and the public shelves of mosques and jails. *An Eastern Reading of the Gospel of Luke* has been made available to every public library in the West Bank and Gaza, and even to libraries in Palestinian refugee camps.

Through these publications, Mazhar is also attempting to broaden Muslims' understanding of the inspiration of Scripture. He elaborates,

> We address the question of authorship in Genesis as this is intertwined with how one understands inspiration . . . in attempting to clarify this, it leads toward them accepting the idea of God's Word becoming enfleshed in humans and human processes, and thereby opening the way for seeing how God became enfleshed in Christ. If Muslims see the Bible, or the Gospels for that matter, according to their idea of inspiration taken from the way they see the Qur'an, this does not leave room for God to send his Word in human form. To a Muslim, the "mother book" of the Qur'an already existed in the Heavens and God sent it down to Muhammad to record it down word for word, with Muhammad being a vehicle of dictation. This understanding of inspiration does not allow the human instrument to interact with or give a home to the Word of God. However, when Muslims begin to understand that God reveals His truth to humanity by putting his Word in human channels and through human processes, where there is genuine interaction with human instruments, then the idea of the incarnation of Christ fits a pattern from the beginning.

In these commentaries on the biblical texts, Mazhar does not avoid textual criticism, something which is not allowed in Islam with regard to the Qur'an.

In the Introduction to *Genesis: The Origin of the World and Humanity* it says: "As writers, we draw upon centuries of learning and upon our modern education in the classroom and in life so that we can offer a well informed reading of Genesis that is relevant to the new century. We do not shrink from the challenge of scholarly examination of our Scriptures, in which we seek divine inspiration and wisdom. In this commentary and articles, we try to appreciate both Jewish and Muslim understandings of the stories in Genesis. We present the Christian viewpoint alongside others, allowing the reader to access where truth lies." On this approach, Mazhar comments, "This is a model for Muslims who have questions about the Qur'an but cannot ask them publicly. We are showing we have nothing to be afraid of in modern literary scholarship. Some Muslims ask us, 'Why can't we study the Qur'an in this way too?'" Some Muslims of course are doing this, albeit largely outside Islamic countries. One of the first responses Mazhar received from the *Genesis* publication was from a Muslim professor in Syria who purchased it at a book fair in Damascus. He wrote, "I have been looking for a commentary that dealt with the textual issues. I couldn't find anyone who would discuss it at this level with me. They just wanted to talk about Jesus, but I needed answers to these questions." As a result of being able to look at these issues through the lens of modern scholarship, he now considers himself a Muslim follower of Christ.

Once in the Arabian Gulf as Mazhar was walking in a street during the late evening, a young man walked out of the mosque's evening prayers who, as Mazhar describes, "had the light of God on his face." Mazhar approached him, introducing himself as a writer, and asked the man if he could be of assistance by reading *An Eastern Reading of the Gospel of Luke* to let him know if he was communicating the message of this Gospel effectively. The next day the young man came to Mazhar, whom he believed to be Muslim, and said, "God told me last night that you are the spiritual guide I need." Over the next several days, the young man and Mazhar discussed the publication together during many sessions, and he not only became a follower of Christ but also led his entire community to do likewise.

There are numerous and often remarkable stories of Muslims recounting how upon reading these publications they understood the message of Christ for the first time. One Arab sheik recalls a reading in the Qur'an that says, "If you have questions then go to the previous scripture" [translated from the Arabic]. Having many questions, he felt pulled to do what that passage said. However, he wondered how this might ever be possible as his religious tradition also taught that all "previous scriptures" had been changed, and therefore were corrupted. Years passed and then at the age of seventy he came across the book that he thought he had given up hope of ever seeing. With great excitement he purchased *An Eastern Reading of the Gospel of Luke*. He began to read it both at home and while at work in the small shop he owns. When at home he would put it on the "holy book" stand (a wooden stand for the Qur'an) next to his Qur'an in the living room. One day as he entered the room he was astonished to see a bright light radiating from the Luke publication. His family did not believe him when he shared this occurrence with them, thinking that he was just getting old and senile; it happened a second time late one night. However, the third time the light appeared happened to be when his large family was all gathered together in the living room. Together they decided to find out, according to their interpretation of this experience, why "God was honoring this book. Did it have something to do with the prophet Isa [Jesus] which the book was about?" With considerable effort, he contacted a Christian pastor who wrote a column in the local newspaper. The pastor went to visit the sheik at his shop and found him reading what looked to him to be the Qur'an, only to be astonished to learn from the sheik that it was actually *An Eastern Reading of the Gospel of Luke.* He likewise went and purchased the publication and the two began to meet together to discuss the teachings of Christ. As a result, the sheik and all his extended family of over seventy persons became followers of Christ. The message of Jesus continued to spread through family alliances, and eventually over 1,500 people spread over several countries now consider themselves Muslim followers of Christ.

Fundamental to Mazhar's Eastern re-presentations of the Scriptures is his strong belief that many Arab Muslims can more easily understand the Bible than Western Christians, as they are already steeped in the Middle Eastern culture in which it was written. In this sense it naturally comes to life for them. Consequently their fresh interpretations can shed new light for those who are not from the Middle East.

Below are a few examples from Mazhar of how Middle Easterners bring the Scriptures to life:

- In the story of Adam and Eve's disobedience in the Garden of Eden, Mazhar sees them as feeling shame as opposed to sin ("shaming one's father is the worst experience a Middle Easterner can face"). He points out that this echoes the Old Testament prophet Isaiah when he talks about the Messiah taking our shame.
- Within the Old Testament story of Lot, as Lot struggles with offering his daughters to the men of Sodom, Mazhar sees Lot as caught between two primary Middle Eastern values—preserving his honor and providing hospitality. Hence, in his *Genesis* commentary on this story, Mazhar addresses whether hospitality or honor is preeminent in Middle Eastern culture.

- Westerners often see the story of Joseph as his brothers being jealous that his father, Jacob, gave him a "coat of many colors." However, Mazhar points out that this action on the part of his father is very close to those practices of the Bedouins today, and therefore the colorful coat was not the issue per se, but rather the fact that it symbolized that he was to be eventually appointed as the leader of the tribe.
- In Psalm 42 we read, "As the deer pants for streams of water, so my soul pants for you, O God." Mazhar explains that the desert Bedouins discover water by finding and following a thirsty deer who leads them to it.
- Proverbs 25:22 reads, "If your enemy is hungry give him food to eat; if he is thirsty, give him water to drink. In doing this, you will heap *burning coals on his head.*" To the Western ear this sounds like a way in which one might return the harm an enemy has done to you. However, "returning the harm the enemy has done to you" does not agree with the teaching of Christ who said, "Love your enemies, do good to those who hate you, bless those who curse you, pray for those who ill treat you." (Luke 6:27–28). Mazhar points out that the picture of "heaping burning coals" comes from the Bedouin or village life where families depend on a fire for cooking and warmth. If a woman's fire went out, it would take effort and time to re-start the fire, so the family would be left without food and warmth. The woman, or a child, would go to a neighbor requesting burning coals. In a spirit of generous hospitality the neighbor heaps burning coals from their hearth onto a pottery platter which is carried on the head back to the needy home. Heaping burning coals on the head is therefore an expression of blessing your neighbor and giving them life and light.
- The announcement of Christ's birth is more fully understood when knowing the traditional Arab customs. Mazhar describes this scene in the words below, which are taken from *An Eastern Reading of the Gospel of Luke.*

> Occupied Palestine: in Nazareth, a village in Galilee, according to custom a group congregated outside the house of a young couple. The time had come for their first baby to be born and their friends impatiently awaited the news. The local musicians arrived at the scene, toying with their instruments. Would they be used today? If the child was a boy, according to custom they would break into joyous song and there would be dancing and rejoicing. Every woman longed for her first child to be a son. At last the beaming midwife appeared at the door and cried out, "A son has been born to them!" The crowd broke into wild shouts and the musicians joyfully played with abandon. Great pride and joy came to

this family and the whole village rejoiced with them. This is how the birth of our Lord Jesus Christ (Sayidna al Messiah, His peace be upon us) should have taken place, but his mother, the Virgin Mary (peace be upon her), missed this celebration because political circumstances forced her to be homeless at the time of her delivery. Far from home and family, without a proper roof over her head, or her family women to help her at the birth of this first special child, the young village girl must have yearned for the joyful traditional celebrations of Nazareth. But God the Generous One knows the longings of every heart and in the wonderful story of the birth of our Lord Jesus Christ (His peace be upon us) he shows us how he cares for us individually and becomes involved in the details of our lives. While God was bringing to pass the greatest moment in world history, he remembered his servant, a young bewildered girl, and reached out to her, fulfilling one of the longings of her heart. God sent his own birth announcer and own orchestra to celebrate the birth of his beloved one. Shepherds arrived and excitedly told Joseph (Sayid Yussef, God is pleased by him) and his mother Mary (peace be upon her) the amazing story of angels that filled the night sky, singing praises to God, announcing the birth of this special firstborn son. God sent his own birth messengers announcing to the world this "good news of great joy to all people for a son has been born".

- In Jesus's parable of the prodigal son (or "the Lost Son" as Mazhar prefers to title it), we see the emphasis in *An Eastern Reading of the Gospel of Luke* of how the Father disregards the fact that his son *shamed* him due to his unconditional overwhelming love:

> The son's desperate circumstances cause him to remember the loving father he has turned away from. He returns in humble repentance, pleading for his father's mercy and forgiveness. He does not ask to be received back as a family servant, living under the same roof and sharing the benefits of the family, only as a hired daily laborer. But the father has been watching the road for his loved lost son to return. He runs to meet him on the road; an elderly man will not usually lose his dignity by doing the unusual actions of hitching up his robe to expose his legs and running in the street. But the father gave up all thoughts of self to bring his son under his protection and take the insults and stones of the community on himself. His son has disgraced the community and broken the Law, and indignant people would want him stoned according to the letter of the Law. "If a man has a rebellious son and will not listen to his father or mother . . . they shall bring him to the elders . . . and all the fellow citizens shall stone him to death" (The Noble Law, Deuteronomy 21:18). The father does not even wait for his son's confession, but in joy freely receives him back with full honors. God loves his sons and longs for them to be found.

• When the Apostle Paul's Epistle to the Galatians says, "Carry each other's burdens, and in this way you will fulfill the law of Christ" (Gal. 6:2), Mazhar explains that he is referring to the Middle Eastern custom of how, when a person is carrying a load on his back down the street and it becomes too heavy, he will cry out, "Brothers, help me." Then someone will take over for a short period.

In the *Luke*, *John*, and *Genesis* reading publications, Mazhar used existing Arabic translations of the Bible (the standard Van Dyck translation for *Luke*, and a translation done by the Jesuits for *Genesis* and *John*). Mazhar does not endorse the few highly contextualized "Islamicized" translations of the Bible that exist, which are in a Qur'anic format that use the Qur'an's language and phraseology, as well as its rhymed prose style. The intention of the various Christian groups that have made translations of this sort has been to improve their readability for Muslims. However, Mazhar's belief is that their attempt to imitate the Qur'an as much as possible in structure and style is acting dishonestly to the Muslim reader, as it is a misrepresentation of the way the Christian Scriptures have historically been formatted, shaped, packaged, and communicated, and therefore, they can be seen by the Muslim reader as an attempt to mislead or deceive. Interestingly, these Islamicized Arabic translations of the Bible have never taken root in Muslim society and some are banned, as one such publication popularly referred to as the *Sira*; just two years after its publication, it was condemned by the Muslim World League and the Islamic Research Academy in Egypt asked the then grand imam of Al Azhar to have it banned.[6] These publications have effectively been shut out of the Arab world.

Seeing these Islamized Christian Scriptures as not keeping integrity with both Muslims and the original Scriptural text, Mazhar does however readily acknowledge that the existing translations of the Bible in Arabic have all been done by Christians for the minority Arab Christian population. Laden with ancient Church terminology, these translations can often confuse Muslim readers, as it is extremely difficult for an Arab Christian to understand the Muslim worldview sufficiently well to clearly convey the meaning of Scripture to a Muslim reader.

In this regard, with the encouragement of numerous Muslim academics, Al Kalima has embarked on its most significant project to date: to retranslate the four Gospels and the Book of Acts, using the approach of dynamic equivalence, into modern literary Arabic for the Muslim reader. To be titled *An Eastern Reading of the Gospels and Acts*, the translation is being done in close cooperation with Muslim scholars, and it will be the first Arabic translation of the Scriptures initiated and guided by Muslim followers of Christ. While maintaining the integrity of the original text, the new translation will use words and explanations that are understandable to Arabic-speaking Muslims, incorporating not only language, but culture, to touch the minds and hearts of Arab Muslim readers.

Mazhar and Al Kalima have conducted an initial linguistic survey of the Gospels among 1,500 Muslim readers with no exposure to the Bible from a cross-segment of society from various Arab countries. The readers were given Scripture portions of the five primary existing translations and questioned on comprehension, literary style, and their impressions. Like the Eastern readings of *Luke* and *John* already in circulation, this new translation publication will also contain an introduction and explanatory articles that will address the most significant issues that have been highlighted through the feedback they have received from Muslim readers. Questions Muslims often ask will be dealt with, such as "Why are there four Gospels? Doesn't this prove that they are falsified and can't be trusted?" One of the reasons Mazhar is including the Book of Acts is that it will help Muslims understand the story of the early followers of Christ and how they faced fierce persecution from Jews and Gentiles, a story still going on in some places of the Muslim world today. While the translation work is in progress, drafts are tested on a continual basis among eager Muslim readers.

Re-presenting the Scriptures as the Middle Eastern books that they are may be Mazhar's most lasting contribution to Arab Muslims, enabling the Scriptures to find their way into the homes of millions of Arabs in a naturalized way, and touching lives for generations to come.

Once upon a Time . . . Telling Eastern Stories of Faith to Muslim Audiences

8

How can a word open the hearts
That are sealed with the locks of gold?
What should I do?
I possess nothing but words.
So let the wandering winds carry my words
And let me impress them on paper,
The testimony of a visionary man,
In the hope that the thirsty heart of a great man
Will find these words refreshing
And spread them among the people.

—SALAH 'ABD AL-SABUR (TAKEN FROM
THE TRAGEDY OF AL-HALLAJ)

SINCE ANCIENT TIMES Middle Easterners have seen stories as having a redemptive nature. This is clearly displayed in the classic *Thousand and One Nights*, a veritable cornucopia of storytelling. This group of Eastern tales was passed down by word of mouth for hundreds of years by bazaar storytellers, until the collection took its present book form in Cairo in the fifteenth century. The title of this Eastern classic refers to the situation the beautiful Scheherazade finds herself in as the new wife of Shahriar, the emperor of Persia. Shahriar, disillusioned by an unfaithful wife, vowed that he would marry a new wife every day and have her executed the next morning. However, the wise and beautiful Scheherazade, on the night of her marriage, decides to save not only herself but also the young women of Persia, by beginning to tell Shahriar a tale which so fascinated him that he would postpone her execution planned for the following day for one more night so that he could learn the end of the story. Scheherazade cunningly tells him stories for one thousand and one nights, by which time Shahriar is convinced of her goodness and allows her to live as his wife. In a very literal sense, stories spared Scheherazade's life. It is from her nightly stories that we get some of the most famous Middle Eastern tales known to the West, such as *Sinbad the Sailor*, *Aladdin*, and *Ali Baba and the Forty Thieves*. In addition to being entertaining, all these stories teach moral lessons, and often have striking parallels to biblical stories.

There is an Eastern story of a spiritual master whose disciples complained that while they loved to listen to his parables and stories, they longed for something deeper. However, to all their complaints he would always simply reply, "You have yet to understand, my friends, that the shortest distance between a human being and truth is a story." Story, with its concrete images, as opposed to abstract concepts, is very often the shortest distance to truth. Known for his parables on faith, Søren Kierkegaard, the nineteenth-century Danish philosopher and follower of Christ, pointed out long ago that "an illusion can never be destroyed directly, and only by indirect means can it be radically removed . . . one must approach from behind the person who is under an illusion." This is why the prophet Nathan in the Old Testament approached the murderer King David with a little story about sheep.

While the West tends to be more analytical in its approach to communicating and approaching faith, many cultures instead communicate truth and wisdom by telling stories. Stories are especially powerful in the Eastern tradition and therefore culturally they are one of the most effective mediums through which to address issues of faith. As a Middle Easterner, Jesus himself was a master of the short story, using the form to communicate the truths of the Kingdom of God to peoples' hearts. In fact, Matthew says that "he said nothing to them without a parable" (Matt. 13:34). Jesus doesn't sound like St. Paul, or Thomas à Kempis, or Martin Luther when we hear him teaching in the Gospels. "Once upon a time" is what he says. Once upon a time someone went out to plant some seeds. Once upon a time somebody found a great treasure in a field. Once upon a time someone lost a precious coin. Once upon a time a man decided to hold a great feast to which everybody was invited and which nobody wanted to attend. The Gospels are full of such stories Jesus tells.

When Jesus spoke in parables he made use of a literary genre which had a long tradition in both the Semitic milieu and the Greek and Roman world. Many of the images used in Jesus's parables are also found in the writings of Hillel, Shammai and other great rabbis. Even the Old Testament, a group of ancient Middle Eastern books, is primarily a collection of stories about the interaction between humanity and God and vice versa.

The Arab heart has cherished storytelling for centuries, with the *hakawati* or storyteller retelling the many Arabic fables or folktales and thereby keeping them alive. The Middle East has both a long and rich literary history, dating back to the late sixth century, just prior to the development of the Qur'an, which was to have the greatest lasting influence on Arabic literature. However, attempting to emphasize the linguistic beauty of classical Arabic, a large proportion of Arabic literature before the twentieth century is in the form of poetry, with comparatively little fictional prose being written.

In the nineteenth century a revival took place in Arabic literature, referred to as *al-Nahda* or the Renaissance. While the literary resurgence was associated in its early days primarily with Egypt, by the early twentieth century it had spread to the other countries in the region. Authors from Syria, Egypt, Lebanon, and North Africa began to create original works of fiction. This modern literary and cultural renewal led to the development of the twentieth century's greatest Arab writers known the world over, writers such as Abdul Rahman Munif from Saudi Arabia, Naguib Mahfouz (1988 winner of the Nobel Prize), Taha Hussein and Tawfiq al-Hakim from Egypt, Khalil Gibran, Tawfiq Awwad, and Amin Maalouf from Lebanon, as well as famous poets such as Adonis and Nizar Qabbani. Many of the novels and much of the poetry written in the Middle East during the twentieth century addresses politics and conflict in the region and consequently some of the writers, due to the changing political scene, faced censorship and even imprisonment at times.

Stories of Faith for Muslim Audiences

Storytelling is central to what Mazhar Mallouhi does among Muslims, using stories with his audiences to travel the distance between truth and a person's heart. As a Middle Eastern communicator, he thinks and talks in stories, and enjoys entertaining his listeners with story after story. However, much more than entertainment is taking place, as Mazhar is using the stories to share spiritual truths, indirectly illustrating divine principles. Mazhar is not interested in debate or apologetics, for he believes that a simple story will communicate more than hours of reasoning and discussion. Mazhar is deeply versed in the full range of Arabic literature, in addition to his own stories, and his speech is full of quotes from the greatest Arab poets and writers. An acquaintance of Mazhar's living in the Gulf States relates an experience of Mazhar once visiting his Muslim friends, fellow Gulf Arabs, "He spoke poetry to them of the love of God. Five years later, these people were still talking about this."

Soon after his decision to follow Christ and his teachings, the young Mazhar found that the most natural way for him to communicate his new faith to his fellow Muslims was to write novels with a spiritual theme in the mode of a Leo Tolstoy or Fyodor Dostoevsky, Russian writers who had greatly influenced him. Some of his readers and admirers, such as Hamad Bennani, a former journalist with the Arab League who now runs a literary center in Tunis, upon first reading Mazhar's novel titled *Lost in the City* therefore considered him a "petit Dostoevsky."

Mazhar has no patience with Christians who want to make polemical war with Muslims, and his seven novels written over the course of forty years clearly demonstrate his belief that the pen is mightier than the sword. His first novel, *The Traveler*, a modern day Arab prodigal story, has sold more than one hundred thousand copies. According to a study conducted by the Arab League, each Arabic language book sold in the Arab world typically is read by twenty to fifty persons. This would mean that a minimum of over 1.5 million Arab readers have read this title alone. Muslim writer and editor of *Noor el Haq* magazine, Jalal Mahmoud Turk, upon reading Mazhar's *The Long Night,* wrote, "I devoured this book in the last three days. . . . The author has . . . a powerful and charming style of Arabic writing."

Prestigious Arab literary journals and daily newspapers frequently mention Mazhar's books. In 2004 the popular Lebanese youth magazine, *Salaam* (Peace), which features style, jewelry, and socialite happenings, began serializing Mazhar's novel *Lost in the City*. Various television programs focus on his literary output as well. He was recently interviewed for thirty minutes on *Good Morning Lebanon* (Television Lebanon) about his writing.

In the spring of 2006 Mazhar was invited to be the guest speaker at the prestigious Tunisian Writers' Union, during the Tunis International Book Fair. The Arab poet and professor of literature at the University of Tunis, Dr. Muhammad al-Ghazzi, in his introductory speech titled "Mazhar Mallouhi, the Prolific Writer: Man of Letters and Son of Many Cultures," presented Mazhar and his novels in this way:

> His works of fiction and his intellectual works . . . point toward a body of values which are at the heart of every effort that strives for longevity and permanence. . . . These values are in fact the values upon which the great monotheistic religions are founded, the values which are the wellspring of all enduring works of fiction . . . the values which lie at the heart of all Mazhar Mallouhi's writings . . . his works spring from these values, and return to them in a strum of the eternal oud (Arabic lute). The writings of this man summarize the give and take between the messages of Christianity and Islam . . . [in his words] are the voices echoing back and forth that belong to many ages and many places, which are in reality the voices of Christ, John the Baptist and Plato, as well as the voices of Lord Byron, Gibran Khalil Gibran, and Pasternak. . . . Mazhar Mallouhi dons the mask of the prophets, in that he de-

pends upon their language, makes use of their symbols, and quotes their maxims and metaphors. . . . The novels of Mazhar Mallouhi . . . work toward the reconstruction of a fallen world, a world hell-bent toward degeneracy, death and annihilation. . . . There is a secret unity that ties together all of his works, raising the same questions and centered on the same notions which recur in spite of the different ways of presenting them. . . . Mallouhi calls for a necessary alliance between Muslims and Christians . . . he has many talents and he belongs to many nations . . . he belongs to many complementary cultures that come together to make a harmonious whole . . . calling for a dialogue that joins cultures and civilizations, so that the world might become more beautiful and splendid.[1]

Mazhar's novels are written in an Eastern tradition, focusing on Arab characters in the genre of Arab melodrama, which is very popular in the Middle East. From the beginning, his books were not accepted in Christian publishing houses or bookstores, as they were seen, according to publisher Hugh Thomas, as both too "spicy" and too "pro-Muslim." His novels are oriented to Muslim Arabs and have among their objectives honoring Arab culture while building bridges to Christians. As most Muslims have little exposure to Christianity in any form, through his novels Mazhar seeks to give Muslim Arabs exposure to the person and teachings of Christ in a context they can relate to, focusing on Muslim sensibilities, such as the struggle for freedom on the societal and individual levels. As the poet and academic Dr. Muhammad al-Ghazzi says, "The concern for the individual in the works of Mazhar Mallouhi is not separate from a concern for what is corporate and shared, because the author brings the two together in a harmonious joined whole: the external world and the world of the self becoming like two mirrors facing one another, each one reflecting the contents of the other so that images multiply other images, and symbols also multiply each other with the text becoming a kind of labyrinth."

Some have said that Mazhar writes novels that he wished were at his disposal during his own personal journey, thereby helping those on a similar path. Jalel El Mokh, a Muslim Tunisian writer, sees Mazhar's fiction as mixing philosophical and spiritual ideas together with his own personal journey, and as therefore being to some extent autobiographical. "They are very deep and yet tremendously accessible," El Mokh says. Zahara Hamani, a Muslim professor of Arabic Literature, considers Mazhar a skilled communicator: "As I read his novels I sense that they are really very much a part of his own story." Hamani believes that through them, "Mazhar is trying to help people find God. In the books, there is also a search for values in a decadent and corrupt society, with suffering being a major theme." Mazhar's own process of writing is that he actually "writes" the book in his mind over the course of years and then when it comes time to put it onto paper, he sits down and writes it very quickly during an intense short period—almost "living" the book's plot while putting it into words.

Muslim Tunisian book wholesaler, Babay, says that Mazhar's novels are popular because they are "highly readable." However, he says, "Mazhar puts in the 'red pepper,' which is Christ." Mazhar's novels contain a strong theme of the importance of Christ, and actually a significant number of Scriptural quotations are interwoven throughout. When asked about this in an interview for *Assahafa* (a Tunisian government newspaper), Mazhar replied, "I strongly believe in freedom of expression and I have deep Christian thought in my books because I want Muslims to understand what Christians believe—that Christian faith is a religion of love—thereby breaking down the wall of hostility between the two. . . . My message is a war against ignorance of Christianity, for Christianity is an integral part of Arab history. Arab literature owes a lot to Christian writers throughout its history."[2]

Mazhar's novels weave the teachings of Christ into accounts of struggle and redemption. His novels all deal with realistic characters that grapple with life-and-death choices. Of Mazhar's seven novels, four have ended up as best-sellers. His first and best-selling novel to date, written as a young man in Beirut in 1963 when he was a new follower of Christ, is titled *The Traveler*. It is a story of a modern day prodigal, a young man whose physical journey from Beirut to Egypt to Morocco mirrors his spiritual journey, focusing on his own sense of lostness, emptiness, and despair, which led to a suicidal state, and then to his transformation and discovery of new life through the person of Christ—only to find new challenges as he suffers for his new faith. In his novel *Lost in the City*, written in 1967, Mazhar's main character is a young woman, Muna. Orphaned as a young girl, she is forced into prostitution and ends up a victim of society. The depth of suffering she experiences causes her to question God's existence and love. She discovers the character of God as she is introduced to Christ, which helps her overcome her destructive desires for revenge, enabling her to find personal liberation in the power of forgiveness.

The Long Night, published in 1989, is a story about the human struggle for freedom set within the context of young Syrian intellectuals in a fresh revolutionary fight against the long night of French colonialism in the mid-twentieth century. Once having obtained that "independence," the novel's protagonist, Ru'uf, experiences disillusionment as their struggle for freedom ends with a new long night under a self-focused and corrupt Arab regime. However, Ru'uf, in his struggle for liberation, ultimately discovers and experiences true freedom through faith in Christ and in following his teachings.

Commenting on *The Long Night*, poet Dr. Muhammad al-Ghazzi writes, "In [this] novel freedom in the most general sense becomes the focus . . . of the book, with the author reflecting whether freedom is not a kind of individual rebellion from all that is imposed, or if in fact freedom at the end of the day is a kind of victory of the person over the self before it is the victory over another, and indeed an eternal rebellion against the self, which could be phrased . . . 'as a continual ascent towards the absolute.' . . . This novel is in reality a kind of baring of the Arab reality and perhaps even human reality, which demonstrates with a profound dramatic sense the depths of human souls as they interact with the reality that surrounds them." Bashir Jumkar, in his review of *The Long Night* in the newspaper of the Socialist Union of Morocco, writes, "*The Long Night* . . . brings the historical and the general together with the personal and the particular (the self). It questions modern Arab history raising issues such as: . . . What does freedom mean if it is confronted by persecution and terrorism? These are questions posed by the novel . . . while opening the door for us Arabs to enter our lonely little room in order to reflect upon our own historical disaster (the Palestinian defeat of 1948), and to ask ourselves what exactly is the Arab reality that we belong to. . . . In the times of despair the protagonist of Mallouhi's . . . novel tears off his warrior's garment, and when he discovers reality around him he finds himself back at his point of departure, with the only difference that this time he stands by the nearest monastery or mosque praying and repenting. . . . The present question poses itself on the generation of despair . . . and is still kept suspended in the long Arab night that was and that still is."[3]

Mazhar's novel *Moment of Death*, first published in 1991, is an exploration into the reality of the suffering of humanity, particularly as experienced by many in the Arab world. Quoting much Arab literature and poetry, and therefore deeply philosophical, the book is stylistically different than his other novels. It is written as a series of reflections held by the only character in the story, beginning with his life and the problem he faces, leading to contemplation on the question of why suffering exists, to the conclusion that the main reason for suffering has to do with the heart of humanity—that the problem exists with and in us. This leads the character to consider Christ and the example he sets of a man dying to himself in order to recreate our human nature. The novel addresses the ultimate question of humanity's choice to live in paradise or make its own hell. The character contemplates the various attempts throughout history to create an ideal society and why they failed, and therefore focuses on the need for each to be given a new nature. The core message of the novel pivots around the account of the arrest and crucifixion of Christ, and the reason that the crowd chose to have the criminal Barabbas released, and Christ crucified. Mazhar points out that they selected Barabbas because he was one of them, and therefore mirrored their nature, where Christ, on the other hand, called for them to die to themselves in order to find true life. Unlike those in Mazhar's other novels, this character does not make the decision to follow Christ, and instead the question is left hanging: Who will he choose, Christ or Barabbas? The book ends with an epilogue of H. G. Wells's powerful short story, "Country of the Blind."

The Significance of Storytelling

As an "Arab Muslim follower of Christ," Mazhar, out of his love for his Muslim brothers and sisters, shares stories which relate truth that addresses their areas of struggle. Many have expressed that their lives have been changed by reading one of Mazhar's novels.

A professor living in Tunisia wrote,

> I have given away more than seventy copies of Mazhar's novels to Tunisian friends [all are Muslim, some even are Islamic fundamentalists] and have had a very favorable response. Most people I have given these books to read them within one to two weeks, as the stories are gripping, and [they] have spoken highly of the style and the content. One person, on beginning to read *The Long Night*, remarked, "This book is about me. This is my life he is talking about." . . . I once gave this same novel to a *hijab*-ed [head-covered] woman in my class and she came back a week later wanting to talk about it, with six pages of notes. . . . *The Long Night* seems to have spoken directly to her deepest spiritual needs and desires. Another friend, a Da'wa member (a Muslim "missionary"), has read all of Mazhar's novels and responded positively to each of them. After reading *A Moment of Death*, he said, "We need a million copies of this in Tunisia, so every Tunisian can read it."

A young Muslim woman studying law wrote to Mazhar, "After reading *Lost in the City*, I understand for the first time the true meaning of Christ. God was in Christ becoming part of humanity as a person, a part of us, living our pains and joys in order for his life to help us know God. Christ came to lift us up to God . . . not just a historical event but Christ in us in daily life today."

After visiting Iraq in 2003, a book distributor from Lebanon wrote to Mazhar, "My last memory from Baghdad is the one-room home of the gate-keeper where he and his twenty-year-old daughter were taking shelter from the hot sun. Not sleeping—but reading two of Mazhar's great novels. You could tell that they had already bitten into *Lost in the City* and *The Traveler*. They couldn't put them down until they had read them from cover to cover. This is also something that happened to a dear friend of ours, who's been working for the National Security [in Iraq] for many years. He loved the way [in the novels] that following Christ . . . is not just something connected with Church."

Mazhar was sent the following account by someone living in the Middle East:

> I gave our friend, a twenty-six-year-old Muslim woman, an autographed copy of *Lost in the City*. Coming from a traditionally strict Islamic family, she told us that she started reading the book as soon as she got home. Her bedroom is her only refuge from her disciplinary father. She stayed up the whole night reading and continued all the next day at work. Finishing the book that same day, she was so moved by it that she gave it to a friend right away. When I asked her about the book, she said she loved it and went on, through tears, to recount to me the hardships the central character in the book went through. She said she realized how others are in far worse circumstances than she, and therefore she decided to work on being less negative about life.

Another person wrote from Iraq: "When I entered one home I saw three members of the family lying on the couch or floor reading. When I looked a bit closer, I realized that they all had gotten ahold of three different novels of Mazhar's. So into the books were they that they did not seem to notice anything that was going on around them. Novels speak like nothing else!"

An Australian medical group, when visiting a hospital in Nazareth, mentioned their personal connection with Mazhar and a local Palestinian woman exclaimed, "Ten years ago I read a book by Mazhar Mallouhi which changed my life." She was so excited she ran to show them the book. What emerged was a very beaten up, curled, and stained copy of *The Traveler*, with no binding and loose pages everywhere. She said innumerable people had read the book.

Parables and Analogies

In addition to being a story-oriented culture which produces novels of depth, the Middle East is also very parable- or analogy-based. Frequently, the response to a question will be given in the form of a parable or analogy. Again, this is something that comes very naturally for Mazhar. The following is a "sampler" of his parables and analogies which are focused on the life of faith and questions that surface from Muslims in the interaction between Christianity and Islam.

On Religion

Concerning personal faith vs. religious obedience: Once there was a Bedouin (desert dweller) that wandered into a city in Saudi Arabia. As he walked the city streets, in the window of a shop he saw a black box with moving pictures on it (a television). The television screen was at that time showing the tremendous beauty and variety of life below the ocean's surface. The Bedouin, who had never seen the underwater world, stood in wonder and amazement. Desiring to show his fellow Bedouins in the desert this phenomenon, he bought a television, and together with the detailed instruction book, headed back to the desert. After following all the directions in the instruction book, he gathered everyone to his tent and told them about what they would see. However, when he pushed the ON button, nothing happened. They waited one day, two days, but the images never came onto the screen. Why? Because there is no electricity, or power, in the desert. Religion can be like following a detailed instruction book—it can mean nothing without personal faith, the "power" behind it. The book doesn't give life.

On Islam and the Qur'an

On reading the Qur'an: When Mazhar is asked, "Do you read the Qur'an?" he responds, "Yes. But when one feels like they are drowning, do you reach for a book on how to swim, or a hand? The prophets it seems to me gave me a book, whether it is the Qur'an or the Christian Scriptures, but Jesus gave me a hand."

On fasting during Ramadan: When asked if he is fasting during the Islamic month of Ramadan, Mazhar responds, "This is a very personal thing between me and God. Do you fast for people or for God?" "For God" the person will respond. "Then why are you asking me?" "Well," the man might say, "In Ramadan we fast, we don't drink, and we don't have intercourse with women." Then Mazhar will ask him, "Before and after Ramadan do you do these things?" "Of course!" is the quick response. Then Mazhar will share a story about a man whose neighbor loves a woman and asks her to marry him and she agrees on one condition. The condition is that for one month a year she will be faithful and the rest of the year she will go with whomever she wants. "Do you respect a man who marries a woman like this?" he will ask. "Of course not" is the reply. Mazhar will then share with the person how one can all too easily let the month of Ramadan be the only time when we seriously focus on living for God, instead of seeking to live and obey God at all times.

On the sinful nature: One friend of Mazhar's recalls being with him at a meal Mazhar hosted with other Muslims. Some of those at the table were trying to argue that humanity is not sinful, regardless of the illustrations given of recent crimes that had taken place in the region. Mazhar simply got up from the table and said he would be bringing pork for the main course. They said they weren't allowed to eat pork because it was unclean. Mazhar said that the pork was fine as it had been rinsed off with water. They responded that this wasn't enough. Mazhar then explained that he had washed it with soap so it definitely was clean. This time they responded, "No, the problem is that it's dirty from the inside, it is unclean." Mazhar smiled with a wink and said, "You're right, and in a similar sense so are we." They finally agreed when it was explained in a way they could understand.

What do you think of Muhammad? When asked this, Mazhar will often say, "When you are citing a reference for a job you don't list someone you don't know, but rather someone you are familiar with. I don't know Muhammad well enough and therefore I am not in a position to evaluate him. If you want to know about Muhammad I will take you to a sheik. However, while I cannot give you a reference for the person I do not know well, I can give you a reference for the person I do know well. I know Christ well and I can tell you about him."

On Christian Faith and the Bible

The Gospel has been corrupted: When sharing from the Christian Scriptures, Mazhar is frequently told by fellow Muslims that the Bible has been changed and corrupted. Mazhar will respond, "Friend, you may be right. You have to help me understand all this better. How has the Bible been changed? How do you know that it's been changed?" Then he will tell a story about a forged Egyptian pound note. "In order to tell it is counterfeit, you have to compare it to an original. So if you say the Bible has been changed, are you saying that you have the original? If so, please get it and help me understand it better."

On the New Testament: When a fellow Muslim says to Mazhar that Christ's followers manipulated the content of the New Testament, making it corrupt, he will share the following analogy. "If I am working in a bank and embezzling, do I leave any evidence in the books that will condemn me? If I do so then I am really stupid. If someone changed the Scriptures they will change it for their own benefit." Mazhar then will open the book of Romans and read the list of those who St. Paul says will not enter the Kingdom of God. "Remove all these things!" he will say. "For this list is my own human nature without the work of God in me. I want to do all these things, so take them out."

On the Gospels (Injil): When Mazhar asked his fellow Muslims, "Why don't you read the Gospel?" they most often respond, "Because it has been corrupted." Then Mazhar will ask them, "What is the percentage of the corruption? 80 percent, 60 percent, 15 percent? Even if it is 99 percent, do you want to miss this one word of God?"

On the validity of the Christian Scriptures: When someone accuses Mazhar of basing his belief on a "corrupted book," the Gospels, and that the original is lost, Mazhar may respond, "If you and I have a business deal and we went to an attorney and write up a contract and I then later accuse you of changing the contract, in the court what will the judge say? He will request to see the original contract. Can you imagine saying to him, 'It is lost.' Of course not. We can still read the ancient manuscripts of the Egyptians, Persians, even the people of Ugarit and Gilgamesh. Do you think that God cannot keep the record of his own word?"

On the use of "Son of God": When Muslims ask Mazhar why Christians use the terminology of "Son of God" for Jesus (which they see as blasphemous—yet they do believe in the Virgin Birth), Mazhar will agree with them that this is a problem, a concept that is most confusing. Then he will ask them, "Perhaps you can help me in understanding this? Suppose you work in city hall at the birth registrar and Mary comes in with the baby Jesus to register him. You fill in under the category Mother: Mary. What will you write in the place for Father?"

On Muslims teaching about the Christian faith: When Mazhar sees Muslim sheiks teaching other Muslims incorrectly about Christian faith, Mazhar will ask, "By what authority are you teaching about Christianity?" The sheik will respond, "By the authority of the Holy Qur'an and Hadith [the tradition of what Muhammad is supposed to have said and done]." Mazhar will then ask him, "What do you think of a Chinese professor teaching Palestinian history according to his knowledge of Israeli history? We always make enemies of the things we are unfamiliar with. This is unfair and creates divisions in society. When we discuss something it should be from a base of knowledge, not of unfamiliarity or ignorance. If we teach about Christian faith it should be based on our firsthand experience of it, and by studying their Scriptures."

On the Islamic view of God (Allah): When asked about his view of Allah from the Qur'an, Mazhar will answer, "Every religion has something to teach us of the creator God. However, let me ask you, 'What do you think about a very good and nice person who has a family on a little farm, and yet one day, after writing a manual on how to run the farm, walked away from it and his family, and to this day no one knows where he went?" The person will often say, "He is not a person of compassion, and there is something missing in the relationship between himself and his family and farm." Mazhar will then share about his experience of understanding how God interacts in the world through Christ and became part of humanity, not leaving us to ourselves.

On Christ: Often Muslims will say, "We believe in Christ." Then Mazhar may respond, "What will you think if you introduce yourself to me as a professor of Italian literature and your name is Sonia, but when I write a history of your neighborhood I describe you as a seamstress named Zahra. When I run into you in the marketplace, how would you feel when I describe you in this way? Either we need to accept the way Christ introduces himself or not."

On the Life Journey toward God

On the inevitability of suffering: Mazhar will often share the analogies, "If you want to pick the flowers the thorns will pierce you. If you are putting out a fire, sometimes the flames burn your fingers."

On prejudice: Once when Mazhar was buying an item in a shop in Egypt, a rather rigid middle-aged man was listening to an Islamic fundamentalist sermon over a loudspeaker. Soon in walked a foreign woman who came to offer her condolences on the recent death of the man's father. The man, Mazhar observed, reacted coldly, quoting the Qur'an in a way that put a wall between them. He then sat and ignored her. Consequently, the woman left. Mazhar was very upset with the man who offended her when she was offering him compassion. After a while Mazhar said to him, "How many children do you have?" The man replied, "Three. Fatima, Ali, and Muhammad." Mazhar responded, "Suppose you invited me to your house to stay three months. I know Egyptians are very hospitable. However, as soon as I walked in I said that I didn't like Fatima and ordered you to throw her out of the house if you wanted me to stay. How would you feel as a father and a host?" The man replied, "I would consider you rude and impolite and abusing my hospitality." Mazhar agreed and said, "You are right. Who gave this foreign woman compassion to walk here to you to offer her condolences? She is a child of God. Can't you see we are all guests of God and how we treat each other, we treat God? If you hurt any child of God's you hurt God."

On how prayer can become ritualistic: Mazhar will ask, "If you are in Mecca, where do you face? [Muslims always pray facing Mecca, their holy city.] Wherever we look we are surrounded by God's presence."

On God's love for us: "The Muslim Berber women in North Africa use tattoos for beautification. This reminds me of a beautiful picture of God's love. Can the nursing women forget her child once he or she moves away? To help guarantee that their child is always at the forefront of their minds, the Berber woman tattoos the symbol of her child who is away from her on her hand, thereby saying, 'I will never forget you as I have engraved you in the palm of my hand.' And throughout the day, as she works, she is reminded of the loved one she longs for."

The Truth of Story

While there is no question that stories compel interest, the hearts of stories point to the truth about you and me and our personal stories. Therefore the stories Mazhar tells are really about each of us. Once upon a time is therefore our time. In Mazhar's stories, or whoever's stories, it is not just a lesson that people see, but it is themselves that that they see and God that they see. In this sense the storyteller, be it Mazhar, Jesus, or ourselves, is her- or himself a story.

Storytelling matters enormously because it is a story, of course, which stands at the heart of our faith in Christ and which perhaps more than anything else speaks to our hearts and illumines our own lives. This is the primary story above all others that we have in us. It is ultimately God's story. Each of our individual stories is in countless ways different from what it would have been without God's illumination in our lives. As followers of Christ, it is impossible to imagine how any of our stories would have turned out without God's story, for it is essentially a love story, of a God who through Christ showed us, Christians and Muslims, his love for us. The greatest way we can honor God's story is by living with our hearts open to it, as it is told through the stories of us all. Therefore, perhaps the most important words for us all, let alone for Christians in their interaction with Muslims, are "Once upon a time. . . ."

Questions to a Muslim Christian Pilgrim: An Interview with Mazhar Mallouhi

9

ℒ

NOW THAT YOU HAVE READ THE STORY of Mazhar's life and of his testimony to Christ, perhaps you are wondering what it would be like to meet this man. The following interview is one I conducted with Mazhar at his home in Beirut. My intention was to ask him the kinds of questions I thought readers might want to ask him if they were sitting in front of him after having read the contents of this book that has focused both on his life and approach to Islam, and on a larger scale, on his faith in Christ. The questions seek to elicit his views on Christology, Islam, various theological issues, the Scriptures, the Church, obstacles for Muslims, how religion colors society, and his spiritual journey.

Author: What attracted you to Christ?
Mallouhi: His kind human qualities: compassion and care—even his tears. I grew up learning the Qur'an, literally with a stick over my head, picturing an angry God, ready to throw me in hell for any mistake. In the Gospels I read about a Christ who was loving, and who identified with me as a human.

Author: How is Jesus generally seen through Muslim eyes?
Mallouhi: Muslims see themselves as honoring Jesus more than Christians [do], and he is very highly regarded by them. For example, they do not believe Muhammad performed miracles, but accounts of Christ's many miracles are found in the Qur'an. From more of a folk standpoint, Muslims often go to Christian shrines for help in answered prayer. While they do not see him as God or the Son of God, they do see Christ as the coming judge of the world. However, since the Crusades there has been a reaction against elevating Christ. For example, today you will find Musa mosques [mosques named after Moses] but it is rare to find Isa mosques [mosques named after Jesus].

Author: When you were seriously thinking about whether to follow Christ, what parts of the Christian faith were stumbling blocks to you? Another aspect of what I want to ask is, since you have been a follower of Christ, what elements of Christian faith have been difficult for you to believe in, how have you dealt with these, and for those you overcame, what helped you to do so?

Mallouhi: Obviously, coming from a Muslim background, the "the son-ship of Christ" was a major hurdle. Can anyone fully understand this? Additionally, the crucifixion of Christ was difficult to comprehend and accept, as it demonstrates "the good being defeated by the evil." The above became clearer as I walked with God. As I followed Christ these were obstacles I had difficulty accepting. And it took many years.

Another obstacle for me was the emphasis Christians place on a tribal God: the God of Israel. While reading the Scriptures, I found that my connections with Christians actually confirmed the idea that this was "their" God. I still have a problem with Christians pushing this tribal God mentality. I don't believe God is like this. The idea that God will move all of human history for Israel's benefit is a huge problem for the whole Muslim world. I cannot accept this and do not believe it is truth. I have reconciled with God on this, but not with Christians who hold this view.

Author: Has your vision of Allah changed, and if so how?

Mallouhi: Before I lived in a hell and the world was a dark place—and I was in a mental state of suffering. I believed God was angry with me and with everything else. I felt Allah gave me a book [Qur'an] and left. So I lived in fear, afraid of God. All the other religions I read about gave me the same idea of God. I admit I loved Nietzsche's writings deeply—that God had died—Nietzsche lived in similar circumstances; he said this angry god has to die. I hated the world, my friends, family, and myself.

And Christ changed my understanding of God. I love the story of the woman caught in adultery, as this totally changed my thinking about God. Dostoevsky planted the understanding for this in my mind. Christ did not look at her to accuse her, but looked at the ground so as not to shame her. He participated in her shame. The experience of God through Christ gave me joy and peace—it covered me—the whole world changed for me. God is not an angry God, but a loving Father, suffering with his son on the cross and suffering with me in this world.

Author: Let's look at some key theological issues for Christians. How about the Trinity? As you may know, there has in the last several decades been a renewed Trinitarian emphasis in the church. How important is the Trinity to you? How do you understand it? Do you think someone needs to believe in this, knowing that this is a very difficult thing for a Muslim to accept?

Mallouhi: I don't understand it, but I live with my Master, with my Father, and God's Spirit, and that is the reality to me. And whatever form Christian theologians want to put on it is up to them; however having a "form" for this is not a necessity for me. Western Christians, for example, sometimes argue that the "Allah" that Muslims use is not the real God. This is very sad, because God has all the names of the world. He doesn't have only one name. Everything is his.

So while I don't understand the Trinity, I find myself growing into it. I love my Master, my Father, and feel that the Holy Spirit leads me.

Author: What does the Holy Spirit mean to you?
Mallouhi: God's Spirit inspires me to seek God and read the Scriptures in a different way. God's Holy Spirit is not something magical, but you need to surrender yourself to him. When I pray I ask the Spirit of God to "take me" and then I experience God in a different way. The Holy Spirit shows me God and Christ through the act of submission everyday.

Author: How do you view the traditions of the Church? Are they important to you?
Mallouhi: Going to church to me is often like "going to the dentist." It is a difficult experience. It is also often culturally very foreign to me. The one time I felt I truly had a positive worship experience in a Christian Church service was in a very small Anglican gathering in Rabat, Morocco. There were only a few of us present, but the liturgy, the cantor response, and the celebration of Holy Communion all together led me to worship God. In church services I find that I am more often than not an observer of what is happening at the front, and it is often entertainment. In the mosque I am a participator in worship.

I do like small fellowship groups, which I see as a celebration around food and the study of the Bible and journey toward God together. It is also a celebration of life together with others. Christians often make it very difficult for Muslims who decide to follow Christ because they say, or imply, that true fellowship with God depends on going to church and/or attending certain Christian meetings. A Muslim of course can pray anywhere, and doesn't require a special place or get-together.

Author: What is your view of the sacraments of Holy Communion and baptism? Is Christian baptism necessary?
Mallouhi: As I just shared, the one memorable experience of Holy Communion in a church that I have had was in a small Anglican gathering in Morocco where there was one line of people facing the priest with cantor/response

liturgy. As far as Holy Communion is concerned, sharing a meal with others who follow Christ is what I find as my "holy communion." Sharing the bread is very significant in Arab culture. When you meet a Middle Easterner who likes you, he will want you to share his bread, to be part of his family. The root is in the Old Testament, such as the stories of Melchizedek and Abraham, Abraham and the three strangers, and Jacob and Esau. For us Arabs, this is still our tradition. My father and grandfather did not go to lawyers for agreements. They broke bread. When tribes fight, in order to seal their reconciliation, they break bread together. It is sad that the Church has lost this meaning; we have lost the sense of responsibility for each other. It has become instead a church liturgical tradition.

I see baptism in a way like the Islamic *shahada* [a creedal act]. And therefore I take this very seriously. Baptism is an important testimony for following Christ and showing dependence on him. It is often a big struggle for a Muslim to be baptized because it is seen as a decisive break from their tradition and an entrance into a new community.

Author: Would you encourage baptism for someone from a Muslim background?
Mallouhi: It depends on the person concerned. Someone from a Muslim background usually takes a high view of baptism. It is very important for them. In a sense it is the equivalent of when a Western Christian becomes a Muslim and has to go to the mosque and say the *shahada*. So I usually encourage baptism. Of course it is not necessary, as millions of people follow my Lord without having been baptized.

This highlights a challenge within Western Christianity. Often Western culture has become more influential in religion than spiritual things. Why do I say I see myself as "a Muslim who follows Christ"? This is something I am very proud of. You see, traditionally, if I am born a Christian, I am a Christian. If I am born a Muslim, I am a Muslim. Often when a Western person becomes a Muslim, he or she will take the Muslim culture and this ends up becoming more important than his or her spiritual journey—more externally focused than internally focused.

When we lived in Cairo in the late 1970s, a whole community of Westerners became Muslim. And when I would visit them, the women would sit in another part of the room from the men, and when the men demanded service from them, they would jump. It was so completely other than their own culture. It seemed ridiculous. What they adopted were the traditions of Islam as opposed to the spiritual and mystical elements of the faith.

And as a Muslim who became a follower of Christ, people tried to teach me about Christian culture and tradition. I know many people from a Muslim background that have left their culture and have become increasingly like

Western Christians. In fact, I know individuals like this that have left their own country, like Jordan, or Lebanon, to have their children in the U.S. so that they could deliver a "Christian baby." The focus is on the external, the physical, not the spiritual. I can speak a Western "Christian" language, go to that kind of church, and use their terminology, but Christ may not have really touched my heart. And this frequently followed path is what we are trying to break in our work and publications—that it is instead about following our beautiful Lord who loves all traditions and cultures. This is the problem with some large Arab evangelical churches. They bring young followers of Christ from a Muslim background into Christianity, more than to Christ. And this is tragic.

Author: Following from this, I want to ask you about the creeds that resulted from the early Church councils—the Apostles' Creed, the Nicene Creed, and even the Athanasian Creed. How important are these to you?

Mallouhi: These creeds have not been very important to me. What is of importance to me is that I am related to my Lord each day and that he is related to me. I remember hearing of an Anglican bishop on a cruise around the world. He came to a small island and saw three fishermen. And he started talking to them about God and they said that they also fear God. He then asked them how they pray. They said, "We lift our eyes toward heaven and say 'we are three and you are three and we thank you,' and we rejoice in this." The Anglican bishop corrected them and instead taught them the Lord's Prayer, and then went on his journey. On the return journey he stopped at the island and asked them how they were doing in prayer. They said, "We couldn't remember the prayer you taught us very well, so we stopped praying. Can you teach it to us again?" And the bishop recognized the mistake he had made and encouraged them to go back to their own prayer.

Sometimes these traditions can get in the way, instead of being an inward spiritual reflection of our true selves. It must come from me. It must be something that touches me and touches God at the same time.

At times I encourage followers of Christ from Muslim backgrounds to write their own *shahada*. I recall the experience a friend of ours had. He had his PhD from Al Azhar [the intellectual and spiritual heart of Sunni Islam—in Cairo, Egypt], and he became a follower of Christ. We encouraged him to pray, without giving him any instruction to follow or anything written down on how to go about prayer. After three months he came to us and said, "When I pray I feel I am lost. I feel I am not honoring God in my prayer. I have no structure. This doesn't work for me. In the past I used to wake up early in the morning and recite the Qur'an and pray five times a day. Now I feel I am cheating God. I feel I am not doing anything for God while I pray. I am not using my body [a Muslim bows prostrate on the ground] and I am not using my mind [in the sense of using beautifully thought-out prayers to honor God]." So we recommended he use the Arabic-language Book of Common Prayer [Anglican] and he found it very helpful—even though it is full of Christian terminology. Muslim worship is participatory; in the mosque one repeats what the sheik is saying—one is not just sitting and observing. And the Anglican prayer book encourages this participatory worship as well.

Author: How have your views of the Qur'an and the Bible developed during your faith journey?
Mallouhi: The Qur'an was presented to me as the Word of God, but seemed to have no connection to my daily life. At one stage I rejected it completely, but then came to see the light it does share about God. But I cannot accept, as most Muslims do, that it is the full revelation of God. When I hear it recited it moves me deeply; the language is beautiful and high. Arabic is a sacred language to Muslims, so the Qur'an still has an emotional and spiritual effect on me.

Concerning the Bible, it often seems to me that Christians worship the book more than the author. Personally, I see the world as "a book of the presence of God." If a rock doesn't excite me, nothing else will. The Bible and the Qur'an both talk about God. To me the critical difference is Christ. If you take Christ from the Bible it is to me just a book. Christ is the Gospel. Previously the Bible was just a historical book to me, not the word of God. However, because of my experience with God on the Golan Heights, in 1959, the spiritual light in the Bible became very real to me, and I saw Christ through it.

Author: What are the "key texts" for you in the Bible?
Mallouhi: In the New Testament, I have to first say the Sermon on the Mount, which is the key text in my spiritual journey. I also relish the Gospels, especially Jesus's parables. The two specific parables that have spoken to me over and over again are the parables of the lost sheep and of the waiting father [prodigal son]. The Gospel of John, due to its mystical nature, has a special attraction to me.

In the Old Testament I enjoy many of the Psalms, and the prophets, such as Isaiah, as well as the book of Job. Of course, the Old Testament is a foundation to prepare for reading the New Testament. However, I believe that the Old Testament needs selective reading. With all the injustices Israel has done and is doing to Palestinian Arabs, Arabs often have difficulty reading it, as it is "a history of the people of Israel." When I hear the Psalms read, for example in church, and when it says "The God of Israel," I find this a stumbling block for me, because this presents a tribal God. It is limiting God. The Old Testament is also difficult for Muslims too. For example, when they begin reading it they soon come to the story of Lot getting drunk and having sex with his daughters. For this to be in a "holy book" is *haram* [forbidden] for a Muslim.

Author: How do you handle the Old Testament? Do you think God told Joshua to go and massacre others, even down to their last animal?
Mallouhi: I cannot reconcile God ordering massacres in the Old Testament. I struggled with this for many years when I read the Bible like the way I understood the Qur'an and took it at face value. It was a discussion I had with Father Elias Chacour [the Melchite Catholic Palestinian archbishop of Galilee, nominated for the Nobel Prize for Peace several times] that helped me to reconcile this tension. I asked Abuna [Father] Chacour to help me to understand the very controversial facts reported in the name of God in the Bible. And he shared how often these are either certain interpretations of what God said, or what individuals wanted him to say to approve of their actions. Father Chacour shared about how Israel was no exception and did the same thing many of the pagan nations surrounding them did in registering war and peace, love and hatred in the name of their deities. He helped me understand how those in power kidnapped God and moral values for their own personal benefit and intentions . . . and how those few whom the Byzantine theology calls "fools in God" . . . the prophets and righteous, kept protesting and never resolved to silence in order to protect God's compassion and God's love for all human beings. Father Chacour helped me to read the Bible in between the lines, where you can feel and touch God's fingers. On the big picture we struggle against the prevailing mentality and the cultural colors of a certain nation of a certain people at a certain time. All is under God's control but not all is God's will and work.

It is amazing to see what Aisha, the wife of Muhammad, said to him once [found in the Hadith]: "I don't see God doing anything except your will." [Mallouhi quotes it first in Arabic and then English.] What she is saying to him is that "whatever you want to do, you rationalize it by saying you are doing God's will." She was criticizing Muhammad's use of God to validate his actions. And we of course do the same thing in how we use God.

For me, understanding that the Bible was written over various time periods and cultural settings requires that I interpret through the lens of the progressive revelation of the character of God, which is most fully disclosed in the Gospels.

Author: Do you continue to consider that Muhammad was a prophet? Did Allah use him to bring any new revelation?

Mallouhi: I do have a respect for Muhammad. But I think Muhammad changed when he moved from Mecca to Medina and when the Jews and Christians began to be against him. He had their sympathy when he was in Mecca. It is difficult to evaluate him. He called his people to worship God against pagan worship. He reintroduced the Abrahamic faith into a pagan area. This is in line with all the prophets. I compare him with Solomon, the great king and teacher of the people of Israel in the Old Testament, who ended his life doing the opposite of what he initially preached and demonstrated. The problem with Islam is that it stopped where Muhammad began. He began a revolution 1,400 years ago, but today they codified him.

The Sufi mystical movement in Islam gives credit to Muhammad for its view of a God of love and compassion. But this is outside the classic Islamic understanding. Personally, I see his greatest fault as leaving us with a mixed message about Christ.

Author: How do you feel about religion?

Mallouhi: It is very sad for me to walk in the street and see people dressed like a Muslim sheik, a Christian priest, a Christian nun, or a veiled Muslim woman. There is something in this that makes me uncomfortable. Religion so often seems to separate us from other human beings. I don't like it. I try to avoid any language that would make the other person feel they are not part of my life—any language that divides us, as opposed to uniting us. Some Christians here in Lebanon ask, "Are you a believer?" They are in effect trying to see if you believe like them—and "believer" is the word they use. And it results in dividing people, i.e. "I am a believer and you are not." Everyone here "believes in something!"

I prefer to say I am someone "who fears God," or "who is in love with God," rather than use any labels. We see in the New Testament that a religious institution crucified my Lord. Do we still crucify him? Through religion, I think we often do.

Personally, I have not been part of an official religious institution. But rather I have focused on serving and working together with others interested in spiritual matters. I feel we often limit our Lord, putting him in a box, building a structure around God. And then too often we lose the power in it or can't experience the spirit of it. I am fed more often than not by those outside the church. I do, however, love fellowship with followers of Christ, and wherever I have lived I have started such groups—people meeting together to talk about Christ and grow together in our understanding of God. This is what "church" is to me.

I am really not against religious institutional structures. And I do not believe in undermining the church. But somehow we end up following the tradition of the institution instead of following the life-giving spirit of Jesus.

Author: From your perspective, in what ways have we in the West acquired a distorted view of Christian faith?
Mallouhi: First of all, in the West there is a "missing Father." When I go to the U.S. and I am around Christians and listen to their talk, and when I drive in the country and I see the church signs, and when I watch Christian media, it bothers me because it is always talking about "Jesus," often with no reference to God—only Jesus. Even when quoting the Scriptures, there is no reference to the Father. So Jesus has become in a way like a product that is marketed—like McDonald's or Starbucks—you drive in the street and you will see "Jesus" signs and then Starbucks, as if Jesus became a marketing product. And this really hurts me very much. The church no longer appears to be a place to worship God, it instead became a place of production—a marketing of Jesus—not the place where people can come to see and fear God.

And the Heavenly Father is not there in our conversation. When our Lord taught us how to pray he said, "Our Father, who art in heaven, hallowed be thy Name." We are not God-focused enough. We too often are not seeing the Father through Christ. We stop with Christ. I believe that many Catholics have gone too far with Mary. But in a sense we have just come down one step—to Christ—where they may have come down another step. And yet all of my worship and all I am seeing about God in Christ is that he takes me to the heart of the Father. Christ said "I came that they may know you [the Father]." His entire ministry was directed to the Father. "I am in the Father and the Father is in me." And Western Christians are often using the word "Jesus, Jesus, Jesus. . . . Jesus told me, and I told Jesus." In a sense the word "Jesus" can no longer have much meaning . . . because it is now emptied of its unique power . . . as it is used incorrectly. We are too Christocentric. Often it seems when Christians talk with Muslims they put Jesus in the place of God the Father. Yet, we read that Jesus continually focuses us on God and gives glory to him. Christ came to bring us to the Father, to make the Father known, to give glory to the Father, and to show us how to give glory to the Father. Yet we often talk about Christ alone. I find Christians even praying to Jesus in the name of Jesus.

Secondly, I often observe that in the West there is a surplus of information about Christ, but that he is not really present. I can go to a Christian bookshop in the West and can see how much material there is about Christ, but it is not him—he has become a resource of marketing for making money, for having conferences, for activities of every kind. It reminds me of the story of the hemorrhaging lady and Jesus. You know our culture in the Middle East is that everyone wants to be around a famous person . . . and at that time when Jesus was walking in Palestine everyone was around him . . . but this sick woman felt that if she touched him she would be healed. And she came behind him, not in the front, and with the crowd around him, everyone was touching him—like today with all the conferences and media, all about him, but not really him. But this woman came, broken, and touched his garment, and he asked, "Who touched me?" And the disciples in effect responded, "Are you crazy? How can you ask that? Everyone here is touching you." But he only felt the touch of that woman. And I feel the same thing is happening today. In the midst of all the activities and products around the name of Jesus, we are not allowing this woman to touch my Lord. There is too much information and too many materials and products and seminars about him, but it is not him. Also, I find that Western Christians often talk about Christ irreverently, as if he is their "buddy."

Thirdly, I would say they often worship the book more than the author. People are always talking about the "Bible, Bible, Bible." I am reminded of the story related to my own Arab culture . . . about our tradition, which is very conservative, where we aren't even allowed to sit with our fiancée before we have the first engagement ceremony. There was a young man really attracted to a girl . . . he pursued her . . . but she rejected him all his life until she herself became twenty-eight years of age, which was considered "too old" not to be married in our culture. At twenty-eight, no one had asked to marry her. But this man was still following her and so she felt this was her last opportunity to marry. So she told him he could send his parents to visit her family. His parents sat with her family, asked for her hand, and they agreed to the arrangements, and then they had the first ceremony. He was now allowed to come and sit with her. And the first day he came he started reading the first love letter he had written to her, which talked all about her—how she dressed, about her friends, where she went school, day after day . . . these letters really were the history of her life. After he did this for several weeks, she looked at him and said, "You are an idiot. You are reading your love letters to me, and yet I am sitting now beside you. Aren't you going to take the opportunity to discover who I really am?" And I see my Lord asking us, "Is it enough for you to read love letters from me?" When I was in prison in Syria, not having a Bible with me, I was challenged when thinking about my friend, Hassan Ben Othman, a writer. When I read his writings I can feel his presence beside me; I can smell him. What about my Lord? As a tourist, I wanted to see the Great Wall of China. And I read everything about the Great Wall, and I have the guidebook that speaks of it. When I go to China and walk on the Great Wall, do I keep reading the guidebook, or do I look around and experience the wall? We are limited in experiencing God just in this book, the Bible. What about the entire creation? The whole world became a book for me, not just this book we call the Bible. I love the word of God, but I also experience and see God in all that is around me.

Fourthly, I find that the Church in the West often claims an exclusive ownership of the truth. You know, the Church, especially the evangelical wing of it, acts as if it owns the truth. Speaking personally here, I do not want to own the truth, but rather that the truth owns me. If the truth is Christ himself, then I can never own him. But I want him to own me. And that's my struggle in life. If the good in me doesn't attract the good in the other, there is a problem with me. We say in an Arab proverb, "With the eye that looks at me I look at you." I think of all we are missing. Say I go to your home for a party that you are hosting, and I play with your kids. This will bring much joy to your heart. I feel the same as I walk in the street, I joke with this person, I love this person . . . this brings joy to my Lord. How in the world can I say, "I love you, God" when I hate his creation, I hate his children? I have my sons, whom I love dearly. But if somehow they become rebellious . . . they are still my sons. And if someone somewhere met my rebellious sons and loved them, and decided to help them and look after them, I owe that person a big debt in my life.

It is a problem for me to see a preacher in a Western church or in the Christian media say "God loves you and so do I." How can he love me when he has never met me, never smelled me, never touched me? Loving others has lost its meaning. It's a commitment, a decision, and it's work. And how can I love God and hate the Jews, or the Muslims, or the Hindus, for they are all created by him. This is a specific struggle for me in regard to the conservative wing of the Christian Church.

Author: Have Christians been a strong influence in your life, and if so, what was it specifically about them?
Mallouhi: Generally speaking, they have not been a very positive influence. As you well know, there is a deep animosity between Muslims and Christians. Both sides are profoundly hurt and there is a lot of mistrust. And my experience is that Christians tend to focus on their "Christian world," a subculture. They have "hijacked God" into their community.

Of course, some individual Christians have had a very positive influence on me. But I would have to say that their attitude is outside the typical Christian circle. In the early phase of my journey with Christ, Hugh Thomas, an Englishman, appreciated my Arab Islamic tradition and modeled to me how to be a follower of Christ. And some priests and monks have influenced me with their view of God.

My experience of Christians is that many are dogmatic about their belief that they will be in heaven because they affirm a certain doctrine or theology (i.e. a creed), but in their lives are not showing the mercy and compassion of God to others. Additionally, I have found that many Christians draw lines for God to act according to their specific wishes.

Author: Don't you think that often Christians, especially evangelicals, would say, "I love those people so much that I am giving them the truth?"
Mallouhi: But this is the exact same thing a Muslim would say. So it comes back to loving others and what that means. Truth without love ends up as fundamentalism. And love without truth can end up without any substance, as liberalism is in its worst form. So how do we balance this? Can we see the character of Christ demonstrated in how we love people? How did he do this? By accepting them as they are and by giving himself to them.

Author: What have you brought with you from Islam that enriches your practice of following Christ?
Mallouhi: Certainly the greatest thing I learned in the traditional school of Islam, and continue to learn, was to have a tremendous reverence for God. Also, they bred in me a holy respect for the Scriptures that teach us of God. Islam also has emphasized to me the benefit of using one's body in prayer—such as prostrating.

From the mystical practice of Islam (Sufis) I have learned to exalt God with the way we live our lives, the way of contemplative prayer and meditation, and the importance of silence.

I should say that when I am in a mosque, I feel I am in a "house of God." Sacred places that exalt God's majesty and honor him are very important for Muslims in their worship of God. I of course don't have the same sense in a church that is built more like "city hall." I do, though, love to meditate in the great European cathedrals.

I also use the Muslim prayer beads and recite the character of God with them. These beads are a helpful devotional and meditational tool.

In Arab culture the deliberate intention (al-niyya) to do anything is very important. In Islam, particularly for prayer, a worshipper must take time to dedicate his intent to offer God prayer. The prayer is not valid if a person does not dedicate their intent beforehand. You cannot just rush into the house of God unprepared. So for me this is important in my spiritual life. When I pray I do this and focus on God, entering into his presence before I pray or meditate or whatever.

Author: Are there any aspects of the practice of Islam that you feel you must leave behind?

Mallouhi: Really only two things: the *shahada* [the Islamic creed—"There is no God but God and Muhammad is his Prophet"] and the pilgrimage to Mecca. Often I encourage Muslim followers of Jesus to write their own *shahada*.

Author: What would you say are some of your own difficulties with "traditional Islam"?

Mallouhi: Traditional Islam groans at those who are more intellectually oriented. The development of the traditional Islamic faith and belief pretty much stopped after the fourth caliph. After the fourth "school," progressive thinking stopped—the *ijtihaad*. And we Arab thinkers are tired of this lack of developing thought. We became slaves for the Qur'an. There is a sense that the Muslim is the victim of the Qur'an. And progressive Islamic thought is often banned, such as Nawal El Saadawi's book, and Nasr Abu Zaid's book banned by Khomeini. So when talking about this traditional school of thought, we are tired of it. The intellectuals want new thinking, a new way. Traditional Islam has not been allowed to think. William Blake describes this beautifully when he wrote about "the night and day being the only thing we could see." Traditional Islam tries to put all my brain into a little box, limiting what we are allowed to think. The Sufis (mystical Islam) opened the gate to give new expression to how we may love God. One can dance to God, and sing to him, experiencing God's presence in an open-minded way—for the truth.

Author: While Protestant Christianity in the Middle East is largely a Western expression of Christian faith, the historic Churches in this region, which date back to Pentecost, are genuinely culturally Eastern. What do you perhaps find in these historic Eastern Churches that gives you inspiration and encouragement? Also, what influence have these Eastern Churches had in your life?

Mallouhi: I must repent for some things in my life. When I came into the Protestant community in Lebanon, as a new follower of Christ, I was first asked to drop all my relationships with Muslims, as the Christians viewed them as infidels. I was encouraged to be negative toward Muslims and attack Islamic belief. Furthermore I was encouraged to also attack the Catholic and the Orthodox Churches because the Protestants believed they were not true "believers." Later on, I began to read Catholic and Orthodox writers and they opened for me a new way of thinking of God, and seeing his beauty, and I repented, asking God to forgive me for accepting the view I had been taught to adopt. And from then on I began to work toward building relationships with Catholics and Orthodox, and now their scholars

assist us in our publications. We have even used the Catholic Arabic translation for two of our publications, *Genesis: The Origin of Humanity* and *A
Sufi Reading of the Gospel of John.*

***Author: In regard to the genuine Middle Eastern culture of these historic
churches, in your view, if a Muslim wanted to become a part of a Christian
church, would it be better for them, say in Egypt, to go to the Coptic Orthodox
church, as opposed to a Protestant Christian community?***
Mallouhi: I think a Muslim feels more comfortable in a Coptic Orthodox
church. They would be more at home there than in a Protestant church. Muslims love tradition, and the Copts (the ancient Egyptians) have a lot of tradition, as do the other historic Middle Eastern churches. While the other
Protestant churches speak Arabic, they are filled with Western terminology
and Western thinking. And also the Muslim man finds it difficult culturally to
sit together with a woman in a worship setting, as the men and women are
separated in a mosque. And the Coptic Orthodox church keeps this gender
separation in its worship as well. There are many more similarities between
the religious cultures of Islam and the Coptic Orthodox church, than with the
Protestants. Furthermore, there is the issue of identity, which is of supreme
importance to an Arab. In Egypt for example, the Copts take great pride in
being very Egyptian. I recall how the wife of a well-known pastor from a large
Protestant church in Egypt saw our friend's wife (who came from a Muslim
background) wearing a head covering. And she automatically remarked,
"What happened? Have you gone back to Islam?" This would not happen in
a Coptic Orthodox church because many women there still wear head cover-
ings as part of their Middle Eastern tradition.

***Author: What would you say are some of the problems a Muslim might have in
relating to the historic Middle Eastern churches?***
Mallouhi: One problem is that Christians are (as minorities groups often are)
quite insecure and therefore remain somewhat reserved and even hidden away.
For example, in the U.S. you have large Turkish and Armenian communities
that are part of your society, but you would be hard-pressed to find a Turkish
or Armenian bookshop. They are insecure and "hiding" somewhere. This is
the same for Christians in the Middle East. Often you will see a Christian
bookshop in a remote or out-of-the-way area, not in a public place. So as
Muslims we have no access to see Christians and learn about their faith. The
problem is not with the Muslim. The problem is with the Christian—who
very often feel Muslims do not desire Christ. In fact, many Christians in the
Middle East don't want to share Christ with the Muslims because they feel
they don't deserve him.

For example, I met a military general, an Arab Christian, at the book fair here in Lebanon. He was looking at my books. He had read my publication titled *An Eastern Reading of the Gospel of Luke*, and I started talking with him. He said to me, "I know what you are trying to do. You are trying to present my Christ to the Muslims, but they do not deserve him." So often the problem here in this region is that the church "hijacks" my Lord and puts him in their private box. Father Samir Khalil (a Jesuit priest and Islamic scholar in Beirut) said that when he saw how a Muslim friend of his received our publication titled *A Sufi Reading of the Gospel of John,* for the first time he realized that we can't reach out to our Muslim brothers and sisters without this kind of approach. And as a result of the effectiveness of these publications, Christians like him have become much more open to a new approach toward bridging Christ to the Muslim community. The Catholics here have now written a beautiful review of our new Muslim-oriented publication of John's Gospel.

Author: What about icons and statues in the historic churches? Is this a problem for Muslims who do not use any imagery in their worship?
Mallouhi: Yes, this is a big problem. Here in Lebanon, for example, you can drive in the mountains and see statues of Mary, the Mother of God, as opposed to just Mary, the Mother of Christ. But Mary, the Mother of God (the Father)! Muslims view this as pagan worship. Some Catholic Christians say to me, "you don't really respect Mary." And I respond by saying, "look, I think I respect and appreciate her more than you. When she said to the servant at the wedding about Jesus's requests, 'Do whatever he tells you to do,' this is what I try to do, whatever Jesus tells us to do." However, I of course do not want to argue with them.

Concerning icons, the greatest difficulty for a Muslim is when an icon depicts Christ. This is not acceptable to Muslims, as no images are allowed of God's prophets. However, personally, I can see how icons may get in the way of approaching God the Father. Many in our Middle Eastern culture often have a view of God as angry, and therefore not really approachable. So other indirect avenues to approach him are created.

Author: What is your view of Christian pilgrimages and shrines?
Mallouhi: The emphasis on shrines looks to me, as someone from a Muslim culture, like paganism. I believe real pilgrimage should take place in the human soul. The Muslim mystic and martyr Hallaj said something along the line that "while people have a place to go on pilgrimage, I go inside myself." And that "while they sacrifice a lamb, I give myself completely to God." Sometimes I think that these shrines are buffers for people who desire to

meet with God, but who see him as a harsh God, and therefore are afraid to get too close to him.

Author: Has becoming a follower of Christ changed any of your moral or ethical principles?

Mallouhi: More and more I am learning that I am a guest of God in this world and how I treat everything is how I treat God. I believe we are born to love and tolerate the other, and to not be prejudiced to the other. But the way our specific environment influences us is what makes all the difference in how we see the other. I recall the experience of a good friend of ours. He moved to the U.S. and his little daughter, six or seven years old, went to school. He asked her if there were any "African Americans" in the school. She didn't understand what he meant by that. But she was always talking about her friend Andrew. One day when he went to pick her up from school she was standing there with Andrew, an African American, holding his hand. This is so lovely!

Growing up in my hometown, I sucked the milk of my mother, which was anti-Christian and anti-Jew. And one of the reasons I joined the Syrian army was with the idea of being part of pushing the Israelis out of the land and into the sea. But when I experienced the love of God to me and to others, I had to transfer it, to demonstrate it. I can't love the head and hate the body. So I started building relationships with people. And my entire view of life changed. Not just of the Jews, but of everyone in the world. For whatever I do to others is like doing it to God. As an expression of God's love I need to demonstrate his character, to the flowers, on the streets, and so on. Everything in my daily life has to do with God.

When we were living in Morocco I had a close friend who was a rabbi. We would have coffee together several times a week. We invited him to our home and we had a beautiful relationship with him although he would not come to our home. To show you how important human touch is in life and how beautiful it is to break the barriers that exist between us, I will tell about an experience I had. One time I walked into a bank in Israel. As I walked in, everyone stared at me as I am an Arab, as if waiting to see where I might drop the bomb! This was an Israeli-only bank, and no Palestinians used it (as an Arab I looked Palestinian). As I looked around, I noticed a lady that looked like a Moroccan. I went straight over to her and asked her if she was a Moroccan Jew. She said yes and I asked her if she knew my good rabbi friend in Morocco. She said he was her cousin! Everyone was still watching me. Immediately the atmosphere changed in the bank. And she welcomed me and I went to get my wife, and we ate and drank together. The entire atmosphere changed because of a little touch.

Who is our enemy? It is the person we don't know. It is always those unknown to us who are our enemies. When we moved to Morocco in 1979, living in Fez, the Ayatollah in Iran had just come to power, so fundamentalist Islam became quite a strong influence in the Muslim world. And I discovered that a certain Muslim sheik living only about 200 meters from us was extremely fundamentalist and militant. He would often attack his own government as being too secular, and of course he would attack the West (his mosque was actually closed down at times by the Moroccan authorities due to his extremism). So I had to make a decision as to whether we should move out of that neighborhood or work to build a relationship with him. I went to him and met him, introducing myself as his neighbor and as a follower of Christ from Syria. He didn't even ask me to sit down, which in our Arab culture is a real insult. He told me straight away that God will only accept the faith of Islam and that I am going to hell. I responded by saying, I am sorry you feel this way, as I sure hope I don't see you in hell. However, his attitude changed because of the way we lived among them. And they reported back to him on how we were helping our neighbors. For example, I would take anyone that needed to go to the hospital after midnight, and helped people in that community in many different ways. People started talking to him about me, about the kindness I showed to the community, and he started coming to my home. Now let me ask you this question: After two years of a relationship together do you think he would speak negatively against Christianity? Of course not. Genuine relationships with the other are what count. And interestingly, one of his followers became a disciple of Christ as a result of all this.

Another example related to this is that a woman used to come to do aerobics with my wife in our house. She belonged to the Muslim Sisterhood, so of course I would leave the home during this time. She was very hesitant to learn about our faith in Christ or to read our Scriptures. Then one day she came and expressed interest in doing so. We asked her what made her change her mind. She said she went to that sheik and asked him if she was allowed to read the Gospels. And he said, "Yes, because I know fine Christian people here, so it is acceptable."

I was sitting recently in LAX airport [Los Angeles], reading an Arabic newspaper. A rabbi passed by me, giving me a dirty look. He went a good distance away from me and sat down. I said to myself, he is another human brother, a child of Abraham, what should I do? Should I send him to hell in my mind, or should I encourage him, and touch his life? To show you how deep we sow hatred among each other, as I thought about going over and talking to him, I found myself wondering if other Syrians might be in the airport and see me talking to a rabbi (this is of course a fearful paranoia), and view me as someone giving intelligence to the Mossad [Israeli intelligence]. I gathered my courage and went over to him. I greeted him, and he hesitated a little. I told him I am from Syria [which does not accept the existence of Israel] and asked him if he minded if I sat down and talked to him. He said "please sit down." I explained to him that every time I see a Jew or Palestinian I feel a pain in my side due to all the tensions between them. And then I told him that he appears to be someone who fears God. And I quoted what Micah, the Jewish prophet says, "What does God require of us. To do justice, to love mercy and to walk humbly with God." I shared with him that I needed him to help me know how to cope with this tremendous conflict between the Jews and the Palestinians. I discovered in my conversation with him that he was such a beautiful person. He encouraged me not just to pray, but to act, getting our hands dirty in this world for God. But it required humbling myself, walking over my pride, my tradition, my prejudice, and everything I had been taught growing up, in order to touch this child of God. And it was a discovery of beauty.

So this is how God is changing me—toward seeing the beauty in the other. And it results in genuinely reaching out to the other.

Author: There is a sense that the raison d'être in your writing and life's work is to help Muslims see who Christ is. Therefore, I am assuming you desire Muslims to become like you, followers of Christ? And if so, why and what is it they would be gaining in your view?

Mallouhi: This is what I have been devoted to all my life. Let's say my son was estranged from me, and he is in another country, and you ran into him. And as my friend you know how much I love him and desire a relationship with him. Wouldn't you, as my friend, try and be a bridge to reconcile him to me? This is exactly what I feel about my Muslim brothers and sisters. Muslims believe they are the children of God, but while they have a lot of information about the Father, they often don't experience him personally in their lives. And my spiritual journey has led me to believe that the Father (God) longs to embrace his children and have full communion with them. So this is my desire.

Once I was trying to explain this to a lawyer friend of mine, a Muslim, in Fez, Morocco. I took him for a drive and said, "Mustafa, I need your help." He responded, "What help do you need?" I said, "I have a friend of mine who is a father, but his son doesn't really know him. The son's knowledge of the father is abstract and cloudy—there is little clarity. And my friend the father is really crying in his heart, and dying to take his son to his chest, so he can know him fully. And I need your help, Mustafa, how should I handle this?" As he knows most of my friends, his immediate response was, "Who is it you are talking about?" Later I told him it was he. This is what I have experienced in my own life. I know how much the Father wants his sons and daughters to embrace him and experience his love.

Author: Have you met Muslims who have surprised you in their knowledge of God and in their experience of God to such a degree that you have wondered if knowing about Christ would really add anything to their spiritual lives?

Mallouhi: I have met many Muslims who I believe are farther spiritually than me, and a million miles closer to God, loving God and devoted to God with complete sincerity. You know, Christians talk a lot about Christ and needing to see him introduced among those of other faiths, but I am reminded of what my Lord said, "In the last days they will come and say, 'By your name we did that, in your name we have done this.'" And he will say, "Go away, I don't know you." This is shocking. And the ones who have done the right thing often don't even know his name.

But as a Muslim, not ever hearing about Christ in the way Christians speak of him, I can look at the Great Creator and live in a clear conscience, devoting my life to God and to his children. Wouldn't this be the person that my Lord spoke of who gave a glass of water by my name. This is not about doctrine and belief; this is about just a little touch of loving, reflecting God's character. And this of course is a challenge for us.

Author: So if you have met Muslims that you would say are "millions of miles closer to God" than you, then why would you think it beneficial to share about Christ with them?

Mallouhi: In Arabic grammar a sentence is described as "the beginning (the subject) and the news (predicate)." God is the beginning and Christ is the news about God. Christ is the demonstration of God's character. There are many of us talking about God, and while God created us in his image, as Christians and Muslims we often create him in our own image. This is our problem. The difference Christ makes for me is that through his life and teachings I am able to see the heart of the Father. The benefit of Christ is that we see the beauty of God through him. Without Christ, something of the picture of God is missing for me. This is how I feel. So I walk with Christ, I share his journey, and I try to offer the beauty of my Lord.

We are part of several groups of Muslim mystics, Sufis; sometimes we meet in our home, other times in theirs. But we walk together this spiritual journey toward God.

Author: Why don't many more Muslims come to faith in Christ? Do you ever see this happening in larger numbers? Certainly, some Western Christian groups say this is taking place, and at the least this is their vision.

Mallouhi: You should see how much Christ is admired by Arab Muslims (read the wealth of literature on this, such as the symbol of the cross/sacrifice for humanity). The issue is that the West presents Christ as the enemy of Muslims.

The linking by Christians of the present state of Israel and all its injustice to Christianity is the main obstacle. God is in this way presented by Western Christians, albeit indirectly, as still a tribal God who hates the Arabs. Muslims of course don't see the justice of God in this. Naturally, social and political events are linked with Christianity. The Gospel has not been presented to Muslims in a way that comes to them as genuine "Good News."

The human tendency is to pick up on the negative things. The Muslim media picks up any negative comments from the Christian world about Islam. For example, if you go to Bahrain, in the Gulf, you will hear some of the elderly local Muslims speak negatively about Samuel Zwemer, the famous American Protestant missionary, who served in the Gulf region in the early 1900s. Although he is a great hero to Western Protestant Christians, there was something in his attitude that did not link with his message to them and his life's efforts given to them. It is very sad that the spirit of Christ was not evident to some Muslims. So it requires generations of sowing the true spirit of Christ. This is why we are translating the Gospels into an Arabic language that Muslims can understand [instead of the current translation of the Arabic Bible that uses Christian cultural terminology]. It is why we are honoring their culture by publishing our presentations of the Scriptures for them in a beautiful way [as all Muslim sacred texts are published, out of respect for God]. We do all this to help them see that the Gospels belong to them, and are not from some strange culture [i.e. Western]. This is why we have Muslims helping us translate the Gospels, and why we ask leading Muslim scholars to write some of the introductions for our publications. In this sense we are all learning from each other.

The evangelical wing of the Church loves sensational stories. Personally, I have never physically seen large numbers of Muslims follow Christ, although they have been reported to me. I have seen individuals and small groups of Muslims become followers of Christ. I have been asked to go to another Arab country to visit a group of intellectual Shia sheiks that have starting following Christ after reading our publication, *A Sufi Reading of the Gospel of John*. And they are still very much in their local Muslim religious context. I have heard of another situation where many have become Christ followers in another Middle Eastern country due to another publication we did, titled *An Eastern Reading of the Gospel of Luke*. But I am not yet sure of all that will surface from this.

Author: How important is the issue of identity to a Muslim? And more specifically, as it relates to someone from a Muslim background who decides to follow Christ?

Mallouhi: Identity is very important in the tradition of Arab culture. For example, the Berber in Morocco's desert will always refer to themselves as to which tribe they are a part of—and they will share with you about their tribe's history, accomplishments, etc. The Old Testament (which is Middle Eastern literature) is always talking about identity; who they are, which tribe they belong to, the genealogies, etc. Even when it comes to the New Testament, we see how important it was to Christ followers at that time that Christ had the proper genealogy. In Western culture, this is not that important. But for us it is very important. Not just who you are, but it is really more about who you belong to.

For example, my family in Syria has a genealogical tree that traces our heritage back to Muhammad, the Prophet. I personally am not sure how accurate this is. But this demonstrates the profound need to have a sense of belonging.

This is illustrated in seeing some of the Iraqis that are returning to Iraq now [post–Saddam Hussein]. They may be professors from Oxford or Cambridge, but in Iraq now they dress like the Bedouin, and sit like the Bedouin, because that is where they belong.

This is a big struggle for those Muslims who become followers of Christ because we sense that we lose our identity. And this is why many in this situation end up having mental and emotional problems. I know of this happening a number of times.

And Islamic culture of course comes out of the ancient existing Middle Eastern culture in which the Bible was formed. If you walk today in the old city of Muscat, Oman, you will feel that you are seeing the Old Testament opened up before you. The way people act, their hospitality, it is just like Abraham and his culture in the Bible, or when you see the shepherds and the way they lead the sheep, etc. All of it reflects the Old Testament culture.

Our culture, as Arabs, is very dear to us. One of our own struggles as Arabs relates to our children. They are becoming Western and are losing their own culture—so we almost feel like they don't belong to us anymore. This is very serious to us and we are threatened by it and struggle with it. This is why you will often see an Arab from Detroit coming to Yemen, Syria, or Lebanon to choose a bride for their son, because it relates to their sense of belonging. It is a desire to keep their tradition, and this is very deep. This is who we are, our identity, and in a sense it is all we have.

And in our culture, the way the street corner looks, or the architecture of the mosque (which reminds us of God), the sound of the call of prayer from the minaret (that reminds us of God's existence and leads us to respond to the prayer), all this is deeply in us, in our blood. I love Tchaikovsky, Beethoven,

Rimsky-Korsakov, Handel, and all these excellent composers. But when I hear a Bedouin in the desert playing with a small and simple local instrument, my hair literally stands up and I want to dance. This is in me—it is my blood—all my being.

It is very hard for the Western person to understand this. Especially for the American, as they move a lot. They don't have a deep sense of belonging—of roots. If you come to my city in Syria, for example, many people moved from my city to Damascus to work. But every one of them has a house back in their home city. They view themselves as belonging there. Contrast this with Americans who can move from California to Ohio to Florida, and never really settle in a place—that sense of belonging is lost.

So when I become a follower of Christ, do I lose my sense of identity? Or do I instead have my identity enriched? My Lord said, "I did not come to demolish the law, but instead to fulfill (enrich) it." He takes me further, not to demolish our Arab duty, where we have hospitality, and kindness, and so on, but he enriches it, taking us farther and deeper into our culture—enhancing it.

When my Lord talks about the "Kingdom of God," what does that mean? He himself is the Kingdom. When I have my Lord fully in my life, this is the "Kingdom of God." It is not related to how I look, or what shoes I wear, or whether I am barefoot, or wear Western clothes, like jeans, Christian jewelry, like a cross, or whatever. . . . This is not the question. The question relates to my heart.

When I came to my Lord, the one thing my family and even my entire home community couldn't understand was the change in my life. Usually when I was in the military when I returned home I was completely drunk. They had never seen me not drunk. But when I came to know my Lord I would go sit with my old uncle, or cousin, or whoever, and cut their nails, wash their feet, etc. This is extremely honorable to do in our society. Everything was new in my life and they couldn't grasp this. This is why they struggled with how to handle me. On one side they saw me as betraying them, and on the other side they saw a new human being.

So what I am trying to say regarding identity is that it is critical for one to keep oneself in one's culture. And when one follows Christ, one's own culture and identity should be enriched. Light should be brought to that culture. This is why it is so important for me to stay and live within my Muslim cultural community.

Author: So how would you describe yourself now?
Mallouhi: I am following my master, Christ, as a Muslim mystic. Islam for me is a full civilization, and all of my being has grown up in this atmosphere. Of course there are things in our history and culture that I don't like or agree

with. But equally there are many things I love and admire. So I find Christ helping me enrich my culture.

So I consider myself a mystic who follows Christ in an Islamic society. I find myself very at home and accepted in a Sufi group that I meet with, and we are actually working together to see the light of God through Christ.

Author: So would it be correct to say that a major element of your own spiritual journey has been the search for your own identity? I recall that at the beginning of your journey with Christ you were ostracized by your own Muslim community and put into a Christian society in which you didn't fit.

Mallouhi: In my journey with Christ, at first I entered a Christian community, and they were automatically suspicious of me—they didn't really believe I was a Muslim who had become a follower of Christ. I was the only student at the Bible school who came from a Muslim background. I was also the only student who paid for himself so that they wouldn't think I was among them for financial benefits. I used to eat only one meal every twenty-four hours, as I was saving money to pay for the school fees. Even in the midst of all this, they would still watch me constantly, with great suspicion. They were full of mistrust due to all the historical baggage, from the tension caused by the Christian Crusades to the persecution Christians themselves experienced from Muslims. This suspicion of Muslims was a part of their Christian tradition and culture. It had little to do with Christian faith.

And the same can be said of Islam. I was at first persecuted by my own community not because of Islam, but because of our tradition and culture. This tradition and culture is so important for us—with the tradition in effect becoming our religion.

So for Christians, their Church culture, or tradition, has nothing to do with actually being a Christ follower. And for Muslims, their own tradition or culture often has nothing really to do with Islam.

Actually, I strongly believe that in many ways, Muhammad (and the resulting development of Islam) was the victim of the church at that time, a victim of Christianity. If only the church had embraced Muhammad in the beginning, and tried to work with him early on, and genuinely exhibit to him the light of Christ. All that he falsely quoted and taught about Christians and Jews he actually obtained from Christians and Jews at that time. Muhammad got this false teaching about their own faith from them. And we all too often continue doing the same thing today. What kind of Christ are we presenting to the Muslims? At times it can seem like Christ is the enemy of the people. What is the "good news" for them? What is the "good news" for the Palestinians? The "God of Christians" often seems to be supporting the idea that Palestinians need to leave their homes where they have been for hundreds of years, to give it to the Jew who is coming from the Ukraine or New York, because some Western Christians with influence believe that for Christ to return this must happen. How could a Muslim accept a Christ like that?

Author: Would you say that you are more at peace now about your identity than you have ever been?
Mallouhi: I believe I have reconciled with myself beautifully and I am at peace. I used to be angry with many Christians in the past for the hurt I was caused, as I was struggling with what they were trying to make me become. I find myself at peace as a mystic who follows Christ with the tradition of Islam.

Author: Let's address the issue of eternal destiny, as both Christians and Muslims often emphasize this. Do you believe in a hell?
Mallouhi: I experienced a mental hell myself before knowing my Lord. I was in hell. And that is why I have paid a high price in my life (as has my family), suffering various forms of persecution, being put in jail, etc., to see people come to know my Lord. Because I know what life can be like outside of knowing him.

It is very hard for me to picture God, whom I love, and whom I know loves humanity, his creation, sending anyone to an eternal hell. God is just. And if he treats evil with evil then what difference is there between him and us. Ibn Bassam, a Sufi mystic, all his life prayed, asking God to make his body the size of hell and send him there in the place of the world. I see my Lord Christ having done that for humanity.

Author: What about Heaven?
Mallouhi: I believe in the afterlife with God. But I feel I am experiencing heaven today in my life. I remember speaking at a theological seminary in the U.S., and I was asked by someone there, "What signs do you see regarding Christ's Second Coming?" I responded by sharing that my Lord and I have been walking together since I came to know him in 1959, and that I am not going to miss any minute in my life not enjoying him. I am not waiting for the end; I am relishing the time with him now. I am not interested in being a part of a "planning committee," but I want to be on the "welcoming committee."

Author: What would you say was the purpose in Christ's coming and death?
Mallouhi: I believe it was to bring reconciliation between humanity and God. And everyone accepted fully by God is accepted because of this. Someone may not know about Christ, but the unconditional acceptance we have from God is because of Christ's death and resurrection.

Author: What role does creation, nature, even animals, play in your spiritual life?

Mallouhi: I see God in nature. When I sit in nature it is a meditation in the presence of God. It is like a spiritual symphony to me—with all of God's creation reflecting him. I find myself increasingly valuing animal life, and all of nature, as I see God in it all. For example, there are many donkeys in Middle Eastern countries. And I would find it very difficult to see someone abusing a donkey. Not only would if affect me, but I would most probably interfere.

Author: Do you see a role for Christians in preserving the environment?

Mallouhi: Absolutely! If I come to your home to stay for one month, at your invitation, how should I treat your place? Your garden, your children? If I am honorable I should treat you nicely, keeping your house clean, not throwing my dirty washing on the floor, not damaging the flowers in your garden, playing with and loving your children, etc. All of it is an expression of my appreciation to you.

And in life I feel I am the guest here of the Almighty God, and how I treat everything should be an expression of my appreciation for him—from nature, to animals, to humans—all that is in his world. My desire is to beautify God's home, leaving it better and more beautiful than when I arrived here. When Christ comes back, we want to be able to say, "Look at what we have done with your place." Actually this issue is really the most important. For whatever you create, you love. And this is God's creation and he loves it. So we need to value it and work to make it even more beautiful.

Author: How involved have you been in politics?

Mallouhi: Everything is political in this region, from your piece of bread, to the potatoes, to the onions, to the garlic you buy. People are constantly talking politics about everything, such as even the price of bread or garlic. So one cannot escape the subject.

In the past, I was involved in a political party in Syria. I was a member of the Baath Party, which originated in Syria through a Christian intellectual named Michel Aflaq and was strong force in Iraq, and of course rules Syria today. The goal was to unite the entire Arab world in a movement that was called Arab Nationalism. I actually joined the party when I was fourteen years old.

When Assad came to power in Syria, most of my friends fled to Iraq. I was in Beirut at the time. The ex-president of Syria came to Beirut, where I was, and I ended up being associated in the eyes of the Syrian government with these political dissidents. Hence I ended up blacklisted in my home country.

But in 1970 I withdrew from the Baath Party. Too often politics in this region cannot handle any opposition. They do not know how to handle differing views. One who is opposite to your thinking is viewed as the enemy. The beauty of differing viewpoints and philosophies can't be seen. What makes a painting beautiful is the variety of colors in it. Every color enhances the other, creating a beautiful work. When one removes the other colors, it becomes bland and ugly. And I began to see my party and my friends in the Baath party doing this—even putting people in jail—so I withdrew, as I could not see the other person as my enemy.

Since then I have not been directly involved in politics. I don't think one should seek to "cancel" the other out. In politics, one often has to fight and do this. For example, George W. Bush's fight with Saddam Hussein—this was not my fight. I have instead been called to work toward bringing light to the world and touching people's lives with love.

Personally, I am now interested in politics only inasmuch as my desire to be aware of what is going on in my society. So I read and talk with many others about politics. I have some strong opinions, of course, but am not politically active in an official sense. Of course, I am part of my society. When Rafik Hariri died [the former prime minister of Lebanon who was assassinated in March 2005], I walked in his funeral with my Muslim friends. And I went to his tomb and lit a candle with my family and friends. I am part of this society. When it suffers, I suffer.

I do feel that the Islamists, the Muslim fundamentalists, are the victims of the Arab dictatorships in the Arab world. If you throw only rubbish in a corner of your garden, you will eventually see mushrooms coming up. This fundamentalist reaction has come about due to the unjust societies they live in. The Muslims feel they have lost everything. Their societies have tried nationalism, socialism, etc. in the last fifty years and nothing worked for them. So the only place they can go is to God. And this is the root of Islamic fundamentalism. Of course, there has been bad teaching as well, which has had a negative influence.

Author: How much significance does politics in the Middle East have in relation to issues of faith, and specifically as it relates to Christ?

Mallouhi: Politics plays a huge role in the Arab World in relation to Christ. One of the first statements President Bush made after 9/11 was that the actions of the U.S. were a "crusade." This was of course in the Arab newspapers on the front pages, and continues to be. So all these military actions of the West are seen as being done in the "name of Christ." This affects the reputation of Christ and hence the testimony of Christians in the Muslim world.

And of course, Arab Protestants and Evangelicals here in the Middle East are viewed as associated with the West. It is the same feeling an average American has when driving through a small town in Ohio and seeing a mosque. There is a feeling that Muslims have come and "invaded" their society. If I am a Pakistani driving down a street in my country and I see a sign for the Anglican Church, and I remember what the English did in my country under colonialism, what does that church represent to me?

Author: How do you pray? Do you use any practices that come from Islam to help you in this?
Mallouhi: In my early Christian life, I used to give my Lord a kind of shopping list. Now I have learned that when I pray I have to be a part of the answer. I cannot tell someone that I will pray for him or her and not do anything to help his or her situation. When Jesus said to his disciples to pray for harvesters, they ended up being a part of the answer.

Mostly I just sit quietly and allow God's Spirit to take me into his presence. I don't use Islamic prayer postures, but I do like to just fall on my face in private, prostrate, and in quiet reverence. But I most often like to pray while walking. I hear God's voice by giving myself to him and meditating on the Scriptures.

I also use imaginative meditation in the Scriptures. I am the Lost Sheep and Christ comes looking for me to carry me home. Other examples of themes I meditate on are the Door, Light of the World, The Way, The Truth, etc.

As I shared before, I do use the Muslim prayer beads and recite the character of God with them, meditating and reveling in his names.

Author: What is your view on prayer? What is happening when we pray?
Mallouhi: I do not believe I am manipulating God or getting him to do the things I am requesting. To me, prayer is the action that helps me to know God's will and participate in it. Prayer is the place where I discover the passion of God's heart. Through prayer God shares with me his burden for people in need or in pain, so that I may go out and act on it. Prayer changes me, not God. In essence, what I am trying to say is that in prayer I am working to align myself with God's will.

Author: What is happening when a Muslim prays five times a day?
Mallouhi: My experience with Muslims is that they fear and love God, and yet that often formal prayer can end up being obedient to a duty, as opposed to an act of worship. Certainly, the Muslim mystics, the Sufis, focus on depth in prayer resulting in true worship. And this is why I am personally not keen

on the spiritual dimension becoming too tied to tradition, for it can become empty so very easily. To see the picture in Saudi Arabia of people being hit with a stick to force them to pray is completely tragic.

I recall the example of Rabia al Adawia, a mystic in the first Islamic century. She carried a burning torch and a bucket of water in the streets of Basra. And she was asked why she was carrying a burning torch and a bucket of water. She responded by saying that she wanted to burn heaven and put out the fire in hell, because she wanted people to worship Almighty God not because they fear hell or want the reward of heaven. For in destroying heaven and hell, God is the only end—the only reward. She thought of God as so beautiful that he deserves worship for no reason other than who he is.

I love the story of the dervish, the Muslim mystic, who went on pilgrimage to Mecca, having only the clothes on his back. And he lived as a dervish beggar, living off of what people gave him. He saw a barber cutting a rich man's hair and he asked the barber if he would be so kind as to cut his hair too. The barber left the rich man and came and cut his hair. The dervish was so touched by the barber's action, that he decided that whatever he collected that day, he would come back and give it to the barber. And that day a rich man gave him a bag of gold coins. As the day drew to a close, he went back to the barber and gave him everything he collected, even the bag of gold coins. And the barber asked him, "What kind of holy person are you? For you are giving me a reward for the service of love!" Do we say the same to God: "What kind of God are you? Who gives us a reward for our service of love to him?" Do we believe that God should reward us for what we do for him? Do we expect a reward for serving him?

Author: Share with us a little more about your own spirituality. How do you grow and what inspires you spiritually?
Mallouhi: I am primarily inspired by meeting people, getting to know them, fellowshipping with them, and sharing our spiritual journey together. The key for me personally is to meet people who are spiritually hungry, and searching, and then walk together with them on the journey to grow toward God.

The main way in which I grow is by seeing my Lord growing in the other. When I see Christ grow in others, it gives me growth, and challenges me.

In my own devotional life, I often take a theme and meditate on it. For example, when my Lord says, "I am the good shepherd," I will meditate for weeks about this parable. What does it mean when he says, "I am the good shepherd and my sheep know my voice and follow me"? I am sure you have seen in Cairo sheep following the shepherd, amidst all the noises in the city. And sometimes he is actually leading them to the slaughter, but they continue to follow him. Why do they follow him and recognize his voice? I meditate on this. How can I recognize his voice in the midst of this world? It is because of the relationship I must have with the Shepherd. So this relates to commitment to him. This is how I meditate on the Scriptures.

I often find Christians confused on knowing the will of God. It can actually sound quite silly to hear some of them speak about this. For example, when I married my wife, the first day she told me what kind of coffee she likes. So it would be crazy if every day I woke up and asked her, "How do you like your coffee? Two sugars? Milk?" Christians often act this way, asking over and over again, "God, what should I do?" When you are walking with God, you can understand him and hear his voice. The problem with the Christian world, especially in the West, is that we put a wall between God and us. Our experience with God is often secondhand. It comes from reading or hearing about someone else's experience with God. We too often don't have the direct personal experience for ourselves—like that Samaritan woman at the well, who after being with Jesus, ran back to the village and said "I have found him."

It is like a person from a small community who went as a tourist to the Amazon. When he returned, his entire community gathered around him and said, "Tell us, what did you see?" He struggled with how he should answer. How could he describe the beauty of the Amazon? How could he share about the colorful flowers opening at night? And the spectacular birds? All the beautiful sounds? How could he share about it and do it justice? He tried to tell them a little. And everyone in the community was impressed. They made maps of the Amazon to hang on their wall, and even a few in the community obtained their PhD on the Amazon. But no one in the community had been there.

Christians are often like this. We almost have "formulas" on how to go about the Christian life. But they miss the source. One of the mystic Sufis went to the mountain and told his disciples that he would see them after two weeks. He wanted to be alone with God. After two weeks he came down and they all gathered around him and asked, "What did you see?" How could he describe the spectacular mountains, the gorgeous flowers up there, and all the beauty of God? He was speechless. He said, "What I saw is beyond imagination." So he shared that he had decided to bring a flower back for each of them to show them. And he had gathered many flowers in his robe. However, on the way down from the mountain, he decided to leave his robe behind and came back with nothing. He instead decided to encourage them all to take the journey themselves.

So many of the well-known Christian teachers today (especially those in the media, whether it be on TV or via their books) are to me like the person selling bottled water on the bank of the river, and making a lot of money doing this. All of his success is based on not letting people see the river. And I am reminded of Christ when he said that if I don't leave you, you will not receive the Holy Spirit.

Author: How often do you read the Bible? Do you have a systematic way of doing so?

Mallouhi: I usually read it some everyday. However, the Scriptures are always a part of my life, my entire being. I don't regulate God by saying from "this time until this time" I will read the Scriptures. And I don't have a systematic way of reading the Bible either. It is much more of a natural part of my life. I found that life in the spiritual dimension, for me, is one of a liberating relationship with God, as opposed to a discipline.

Author: Let's move on to the topic of writing. Many know you as a writer, from both your various novels and non-fiction works. What are you writing these days and what do you still desire to write?

Mallouhi: For the last several years my passion has been to do a new translation for Muslims of the four Gospels and the Book of Acts [Acts of the Apostles]. The current Arabic translations of the Scriptures are full of Christian terminology that a Muslim can't understand. My burden is to see my Lord become an extension of their own skin [Muslims], so they can own him too. I am reminded of a good friend of ours from Tunisia who had obtained his PhD in comparative religion. All during his study he always saw Christ as a Westerner. However, after reading our publication titled *An Eastern Reading of the Gospel of Luke*, he telephoned to tell us that for the first time he now recognized Christ as a Middle Easterner, and not a Westerner.

Christian translations of the Arabic Scriptures tend to focus on using different Arabic—"Christian expressions, words, and ways of saying things," in order to distinguish between themselves and Muslims. Our passion is to do a new translation that focuses on the commonalities between the two in Arabic. So I see the major project of my life being this new Arabic translation of the Gospels and also the Book of Acts, which will be understandable to Muslims. Additionally there will be introductory articles written for a Muslim readership for each of the four Gospels and the Book of Acts. And many Muslims are now working with us on this project. We have hundreds of Arab Muslims reading the Gospels and the Book of Acts in the current available Arabic translations to discover what they find difficult to understand in the language. This then shapes the new translation we are working on of these Scripture texts.

Author: Why are you translating the Book of Acts as well?
Mallouhi: Because it is like the "Hadith" [the traditions around Muhammad's life and reported other sayings of his] in the Muslim mindset; the traditions and practice that developed after Christ's resurrection.

Author: You have often spoken to me of Tolstoy's and Dostoevsky's writings and the influence they have had on you. You obviously put value in literature, and in novels specifically. Do you see yourself writing another novel?
Mallouhi: Yes, there is still one book I would like to write. I would title it *The Infidel Christian*. What I mean by the use of that title is this: if a Muslim sees a Christian walking down the street they see that person as an "infidel." This is not because of that Christian's belief (which a Muslim would not know much about), but because of what Muslims are told about them and may have even observed themselves—that they believe in pagan worship, that they eat unclean food, such as pork, that they get drunk with alcohol, etc. So what I mean to do in writing this book is to change the way Muslims think about Christians, showing that this way of thinking is generally incorrect. I may actually write it in a dialogue format, responding to an individual who is searching.

Author: Who are your favorite authors/writers? Both Arab and others?
Mallouhi: I love Amin Maalouf, who is from a Christian Lebanese background. I know his father. He is a remarkably gifted writer. In *Leo the African*, when Mallouf writes of the pilgrimage, the spiritual journey, to Mecca, I have never read any Muslim writer describe it with such beauty. When he wrote *Samarkand*, writing about the poet Omar Khayyam, you would think Mallouf actually had spent his whole life there in that time period. A tremendously talented writer. He writes in French and it is translated into Arabic [and English].

I also like Abdul Rahman Munif, Naguib Mahfouz (Egyptian novelist and Nobel Prize winner), and Taha Hussein. In poetry I love the Iraqi poet Bakr Shakir al Sayyab.

Regarding non-Arab writers, I love Fyodor Dostoevsky, Leo Tolstoy, Ernest Hemingway, John Steinbeck, and Jack London. Of course, I read these authors in Arabic. One book that had a life-changing effect on me was titled *The Twenty-fifth Hour*, written by a Romanian writer named C. Virgil Gheorghiu. I also love the work of Nikos Kazantzakis.

Regarding Christian writers, my favorites are E. Stanley Jones, Thomas Merton, Henri Nouwen, Anthony de Mello, and Charles de Foucauld. Actually, Anthony de Mello's book, *The Song of the Bird*, had a great influence on me and continues to be a real challenge to me. I keep it by my bedside. I also like C. S. Lewis's writings.

Author: What is your driving passion for this last phase of your life?
Mallouhi: My passion is to see the Scriptures put in the hands of Muslims in a form they can understand. You may ask me "why?" My answer would be that if your father wrote you a love letter, wouldn't you like to read it?

In order for Christ to be naturalized among Muslims, I see it as critical that the Scriptures be re-presented in a manner that they can fully understand and accept.

Mazhar Mallouhi's
Primary Works to Date

Appendix

Novels

The Traveler—first published in 1963 (30 reprints) by Arabic Literature Mission (ALM), and now published by Dar al Jil (Beirut, Lebanon)

The Fugitive—first published in 1964 by Arabic Literature Mission

Lost in the City—first published in 1967 by Arabic Literature Mission, and now published by Dar al Jil (Beirut, Lebanon)

The Long Night—first published in 1989 by Dar al Jil (Beirut, Lebanon)

Moment of Death—first published in 1991 by Dar al Jil (Beirut, Lebanon)

Middle Eastern and Muslim-focused Presentations of the Scriptures

An Eastern Reading of the Gospel of Luke—first published in 1998 by Dar al Jil (Beirut, Lebanon)

Genesis: The Origin of the World and Humanity—first published in 2001 by Dar al Jil (Beirut, Lebanon)

A Sufi Reading of the Gospel of John—first published in 2004 by Dar al Jil (Beirut, Lebanon)

A New Translation of the Gospels and the Book of Acts—translated into modern literary Arabic for the Muslim reader; not yet published at the time of writing.

Notes

Introduction

1. E. Stanley Jones, *The Christ of the Indian Road* (London: Hodder & Stoughton, 1925), 51.
2. Jones, *Indian Road*, 13.
3. Jones, *Indian Road*, 33.
4. Jones, *Indian Road*, 183.
5. Jones, *Indian Road*, 28.
6. Jones, *Indian Road*, 92.
7. Jones, *Indian Road*, 53.
8. E. Stanley Jones, *Gandhi: Portrayal of a Friend* (Nashville: Abingdon Press, 1993), 8.
9. Jones, *Indian Road*, 77–78.
10. *Wisdom of the Sadhu: Teachings of Sundar Singh* (Farmington, Pa.: Plough Publishing House, 2000).
11. The Arab League estimates that every book in the Arab world is read by twenty to fifty people.
12. Kenneth Cragg, *Troubled by Truth: Life-Studies in Inter-Faith Concern* (Durham: The Pentland Press Ltd., 1992), vii.
13. Fouad Ajami, *The Vanished Imam: Musa al Sadr and the Shia of Lebanan* (Ithaca, N.Y.: Cornell University Press, 1986).
14. Interestingly, Mazhar Mallouhi briefly met Musa al Sadr in Cairo, shortly before he disappeared in Libya.
15. Fouad Ajami, *The Dream Palace of the Arabs* (New York: Vintage Books, 1998).
16. John Esposito's book *Islam: The Straight Path* is an exceptionally good overview that introduces the faith, belief, and practice of Islam from its earliest origins to its present-day resurgence.

Chapter 1

1. Abdullah Turkmani, from an interview with the author in Tunis, Tunisia, May 2004.
2. Muhammad al-Sayyid al-Julaynd, *Orientalism and Evangelism: A Concise Historical Reading* (Cairo: Dar Qiba', 1999), 8.
3. Heather Sharkey, *Arabic Antimissionary Treatises: Muslim Responses to Christian Evangelism in the Modern Middle East* (International Bulletin of Missionary Research, Vol. 28, No. 3, July 2004).

4. Sharkey, *Antimissionary Treatises*; Richard P. Mitchell, *The Society of Muslim Brothers* (London: Oxford University Press, 1969; reissued with a foreword by John O. Voll in 1993).

5. Robert Truett Gilliam, *A Muslim Response to Protestant Missionaries: The Case of Al Manar* (Master of Arts thesis for the Center of Arab and Middle East Studies, American University of Beirut-Lebanon, March 15, 2000).

6. David Dean Commins, *Islamic Reform: Politics and Social Change in Late Ottoman Syria* (New York: Oxford University Press, 1990), 31.

7. Sharkey, *Antimissionary Treatises*

8. Mustafa Khalidi and Umar Farrukh, *Evangelism and Imperialism in the Arab World*, 2nd ed. (Beirut: n.p., 1957), 36.

9. E. Stanley Jones, *Gandhi: Portrayal of a Friend* (Nashville: Abingdon Press, 1993), 82–83.

10. E. Stanley Jones, *The Christ of the Indian Road* (London: Hodder & Stoughton, 1925), 51.

11. Jones, *Indian Road*, 86.

12. Jones, *Indian Road*, 101.

13. Jones, *Indian Road*, 76.

14. Syrian intelligence finally caught up with Khalil Brieze in 1975, sentencing him to twenty years in prison, where he was tortured. He left prison partially paralyzed.

Chapter 2

1. Christine Mallouhi, *Waging Peace on Islam* (Downers Grove, Ill.: InterVarsity Press, 2000), 322.

2. Fouad Ajami, *The Dream Palace of the Arabs* (New York: Vintage Books, 1998), 119.

3. Ajami, *Dream Palace*, 117.

4. Ajami, *Dream Palace*, 79–80.

5. See chapter 8 for more information on Mazhar's novels.

6. Saladin Ben Ohbed, from an interview with the author in Tunis, Tunisia, May 2004.

7. Mallouhi, *Waging Peace on Islam*, 19.

8. Mallouhi, *Waging Peace on Islam*, 23.

Chapter 3

1. Augustine, *Confessions*, bk. 10, chap. 27.

2. Latif Lakhdar, *MERIA Journal*, March 2005.

3. "Africanism and Universality," an exhibition and congress marking the 1,650th Anniversary of St. Augustine's birth. Held in December 2004 at Carthage's Acropolium.

4. He had obtained an Australian passport by marrying Christine, an Australian.

5. Taken from a letter from Senator Charles H. Percy to His Excellency Hafez al-Assad, president of the Syrian Arab Republic, May 5, 1995.

6. Christine Mallouhi, *Waging Peace on Islam* (Downers Grove, Ill.: InterVarsity Press, 2000), 258.

Chapter 4

1. Ziauddin Sardar and Merryl Wyn Davies, *Why Do People Hate America?* (London: Faber and Faber, 2002), 10–11.

2. Mazhar Mallouhi looks at the looming shadow of the Saud rulers of Arabia, who he believes contribute to a lot of the terrorism by propagating fanaticism, and financing strident schools and mosques, as well as oppressing the local population in the name of religion.

3. Virginia Cobb, "Methods for Work among Muslims" (paper given at the Teheran Conference, 1969).

4. Christine Mallouhi's excellent book titled *Waging Peace on Islam* (Downers Grove, Ill.: InterVarsity Press, 2000) advocates a non-confrontational approach to Muslims, reflecting Mazhar's natural orientation toward Islam.

5. E. Stanley Jones, *The Christ of the Indian Road* (London: Hodder & Stoughton, 1925), 148.

6. C. F. Andrews, *What I Owe to Christ* (Nashville: Abingdon Press, 1932), 223–24.

7. E. Stanley Jones, *Gandhi: Portrayal of a Friend* (Nashville: Abingdon Press, 1993), 62.

8. Marie Louise Gude, *Louis Massignon: The Crucible of Compassion* (Notre Dame, Ind.: University of Notre Dame Press, 1996), 193–94.

9. Cobb, "Methods for Work among Muslims."

10. An address by the former archbishop of Canterbury, Lord Carey, at Beit Al-Qur'an in Bahrain, on November 3, 2001.

11. Lord Carey, address at Beit Al-Qur'an.

12. Kenneth Cragg, *Muslims and Christians—Face to Face* (Oxford: ONEWORLD, 1997), 14.

13. Kenneth Cragg, "Lost in Translation," a lecture given at Trinity College, Bristol, U.K., on October 11, 2005.

14. Cobb, "Methods for Work among Muslims."

15. Found in the Gospel of Luke (19:1–10).

16. Ali Merad, *Christian Hermit in an Islamic World: A Muslim's View of Charles de Foucauld* (Mahwah, N.J.: Paulist Press, 1999), 88.

17. E. Stanley Jones, *The Christ of the Indian Road*, 23.

18. Jones, *Indian Road*, 148.

19. Khalil Gibran, *The Prophet* (London: Penguin Books, 1992), 73.

20. Carl R. Raswan, *Black Tents of Arabia: My Life Among the Bedouins* (Ruminator Books, 1998 reprint edition), xiv–xv.

21. Lord Carey, address at Beit Al-Qur'an.

22. *London Times*, 17 January 2002, a joint article by Dr. George Carey, the Archbishop of Canterbury, and Zaki Badawi, the principal of the Muslim College in London.

23. Gude, *Crucible of Compassion*, 20.

24. Merad, *Christian Hermit*, 3–4.

25. Robert Ellsberg, *Charles De Foucauld* (Maryknoll, N.Y.: Orbis Books, 1999),17–18.

26. Cobb, "Methods for Work among Muslims."

Chapter 5

1. Riah Abu El-Assal, *Caught in Between* (London: SPCK, 1999), 126–7.

2. Samir Khalif, Protestant Orientalism: Evangelical Christianity and Cultural Imperialism (unpublished paper).

3. T. O. Beidelman, *Colonial Evangelism* (Bloomington, Ind.: Indiana University Press, 1982), 4.

4. Muhammad al Talibi, *Iyal Allah: Afkar Jadeedah fi 'Aaqat Al Muslim binafsihi wa bilakhareen* (Tunis: Dar Saras lilnashr, 1992), 158.

5. Rachid Ridaof *Al Manar Journal,* quoted in Robert Truett Gilliam, "A Muslim Response to Protestant Missionaries: The Case of Al Manar" (Master of Arts thesis, Center of Arab and Middle East Studies, American University of Beirut-Lebanon, March 15, 2000).

6. Name has been changed at the specific request of the individual or due to a special sensitivity.

7. Ali Merad, *Christian Hermit in an Islamic World: A Muslim's View of Charles de Foucauld* (New York: Paulist Press, 1999), 41–42.

8. Virginia Cobb, "Methods for Work among Muslims" (paper given at the Teheran Conference, 1969).

9. Cobb, "Methods for Work among Muslims."

10. E. Stanley Jones, *The Christ of the Indian Road* (London: Hodder & Stoughton, 1925), 33.

11. Cobb, "Methods for Work among Muslims."

12. Name has been changed at the specific request of the individual or due to a special sensitivity.

13. Herbert E. Hoefer, *Churchless Christianity* (Pasadena, Calif.: William Carey Library, 2001).

14. Amin Maalouf, *On Identity* (London: The Harvill Press, 2000), 3–5, 129.

15. Interestingly, in the twentieth century, the Christian Arabs (the historic indigenous churches) played a critical role in shaping the secular Arab cultural identity. As a Lebanese Christian historian, Professor Kamal Salibi says, "It is the Christian Arabs who keep the Arab world 'Arab' rather than 'Muslim'" (as quoted by William Dalrymple in *Lost Flock*, an article in *The Guardian*, October 30, 2001).

16. Maalouf, *On Identity*, 19.

17. Paul Tillich, *On the Boundary* (New York: Charles Scribner's Sons, 1966), 13, 68–9, 91–3, 97.

18. Taken from the statement of Tertullian, the early church theologian from Carthage, North Africa: "Anima naturaliter Christiana," the soul is naturally Christian.

Chapter 6

1. Christine Mallouhi, *Waging Peace on Islam* (Downers Grove, Ill.: InterVarsity Press: 2000), 322.

2. Mallouhi, *Waging Peace*, 118–19.

3. Mallouhi, *Waging Peace*, 145.

4. E. Stanley Jones, *Gandhi: Portrayal of a Friend* (Nashville: Abingdon Press, 1993), 83.

5. Jones, *Gandhi*, 77–78.

6. Jones, *Gandhi*, 143.

7. Ali Merad, *Christian Hermit in an Islamic World: A Muslim's View of Charles de Foucauld* (New York: Paulist Press, 1999), 21.

8. Merad, *Christian Hermit*, 7.

9. E. Stanley Jones, *The Christ of the Indian Road* (London: Hodder & Stoughton, 1925), 91–92.

10. Jones, *Indian Road*, 92.

11. Jones, *Indian Road*, 98.

12. Jones, *Indian Road*, 136.

13. Constance E. Padwick, *Temple Gairdner of Cairo* (London: SPCK, 1930), 142.

14. Merad, *Christian Hermit*, 25.

15. Virginia Cobb, "Methods for Work among Muslims" (paper given at the Teheran Conference, 1969).

16. Stephen Neill, *Christian Faith and Other Faiths* (Downers Grove, Ill.: InterVarsity Press, 1984), 89.

17. Vincent Donovan, *Christianity Rediscovered* (Maryknoll, N.Y.: Orbis Books, 1991).

Chapter 7

1. Mazhar Mallouhi et al., eds., *An Eastern Reading of the Gospel of Luke* (Beirut: Dar al Jil, 1998), and *Genesis: The Origin of the World and Humanity* (Beirut: Dar al Jil, 2001), and *A Sufi Reading of the Gospel of John* (Beirut: Dar al Jil, 2004), all in Arabic.

2. *An Eastern Reading of the Gospel of Luke* explains the "Son of God" terminology as follows:

One matter which is often interpreted incorrectly is the title of our Lord Jesus Christ as the "Son of God." It must be stated emphatically that the term "Son of God" has no physical connotation at all. There is no hint in the term that God took a wife, and that he gave birth to a son by her. God forbid! This idea is totally unacceptable. We bear witness that God is one and there is no God but God. He is spirit and has no body so can have no son in a physical sense. It is true that he was not born nor does he beget in a biological manner. So this term "son" is not to be understood in a literal sense. This should not be difficult to understand as in our Arabic language we use the term "son" in a non-literal sense for many things, e.g. son of the road, son of Baghdad, son of Morocco, son of the desert, son of break, son of Damascus. We know these terms do not mean a biological relationship. A person belongs to Baghdad or Syria, or has a characteristic, like the words used to describe a corrupt man, son of shame, or denoting a noble person, son of halal (ritual purity).

To understand this term "Son of God" another term used in Scripture will help us. Christ is also called the "Word of God." It is clear that this is not to be taken literally but figuratively. Our Lord Jesus Christ is not a book, or a letter of the alphabet. When he is referred to as "Word of God" it means he translates God to man. He is the means of communication and revelation between God and man. After our father Adam (peace be upon him) sinned in the garden, man's open relationship with God was broken. Our Lord Jesus Christ (the Word of God) was sent to re-establish the relationship between man and God.

We cannot separate a person and his word. If your friend Mustafa gives you his word he gives you himself. Mustafa's word is the expressed revelation of himself. We understand that the word is the expression of the hidden thought. Unless I put my thought into words you cannot understand it. It is mysterious and hidden. God is spirit so he is hidden and distant from us. In order for us to know what he is like and what we must be like, his hidden thought becomes revealed. Our Lord Jesus Christ is called the Word because he is the revealed thought of God. This is the same meaning as "son." My words are the offspring of my thought. So the Word, our Lord Jesus Christ (his peace be upon us), is the offspring of the thought of God. In this sense of being offspring he is called "son." He is the eternal word of God spoken into human existence so that we may clearly understand the nature of God and follow him in perfect submission. Remembering that God's Holy Word declares God is one, it speaks of the Word of God and Son of God as one and the same: "In the beginning was the Word, the word was with God, and the word was God. . . . The word was the true light and he was coming into the world. . . . He was not born of human stock but of God himself. . . . The word was made flesh and lived among us and we saw the glory that is his as the only son of the father" (The Noble Gospel, John 1:1–14).

Why did God decide this was necessary? In the following chapters we will see how since the beginning of human history man has failed to perfectly follow God. God sent his prophets to every generation but each time they were rejected and not understood and God's word was not perfectly obeyed. So finally God sent his own perfectly clear eternal Word to speak into human history. The Word of God came down to earth and took on humanity to perfectly reveal himself to man.

"For God so loved the world that he sent his only Son" (The Noble Gospel John 3:16). Ibn al Arabi echoes this loving giving of God in Bezels of Wisdom in his beautiful description of the great urge within the divine for the reality of his being, which is love, to be poured out into existence. The divine longing to be known is love, and he describes the release of this longing as a breathing which expresses and relieves the longing. This creative exhalation of the "Breath of the Merciful" ("Irrahmaan") takes us to the birth image through the root of the word rahima, meaning womb. For Ibn al Arabi love and mercy are not just an attitude, but the very principle by which all things were created and exist and by which all things in the divine mind are released into actuality, as objects of the divine witness and perception.

This concept of creation and birth is closely tied into the very nature of God the merciful. Dr. Muhammad Shahroor in "Al Kitab and the Quran" p. 254 also describes the same meanings for "ir-rahmaan." The word "irrahmaan" comes from "Rahm" and it means gentle, compassionate and merciful and family relationship. The Quran Al Karim added to the word another meaning, "to give birth." From this came the word "Rahmaan." Of course we know that God does not himself give birth physically but he brings into existence things that were not by his powerful word.

Ibn al Arabi unwittingly describes the nature of our Lord Jesus Christ in his description of the perfect man. He writes that it is the Perfect Man who perfectly combines within himself, in harmony, heaven and earth within the context of the realization of the oneness of being, who is at once the eye by which the divine subject sees himself and the perfectly polished mirror that perfectly reflects the divine light. Christians believe as the Noble Gospel states in Colossians 1:15, 18 that "Christ is the express image of the invisible God. For God was pleased to have all his fullness dwell in him." Our Lord Jesus Christ is at once the perfect man, "Son of Adam," born of a woman and the perfect "Son of God"; his origin is from God and he has no human father. Our Lord Jesus Christ is the Word of God, the living utterance of God, his complete expression. We are not able to separate the word (the expression of the thought) from the thought. God is One: his thought and his word, his power and his spirit.

The term "Son of God" is also used figuratively speaking of a special relationship. In our tradition the eldest son has a special place within the family. But in the case of the only child born to the parents being a one and only son, what a precious child this son is! So the term the "only Son of God" tells us of how special and precious our Lord Jesus Christ, God's own word, is to him. This special relationship of a son to his father is based on love, dependence and obedience. Through this expression God uses a term out of human experience to give us insight into the divine, of which we have no knowledge or experience. The father and son love each other mutually. The son depends upon the father and the father protects the son. The son is also obedient to the father and shows him honor. The son, in this case, perfectly inherits all the attributes of his father because he is his word. When God had completed the revelation of himself to man through his word, his word returned to God in heaven, but continues to be present through the Holy Spirit.

Our Lord Jesus Christ did not have a human father. His birth was by the power of the Holy Spirit. This is why he is called the "Son of God." In order to understand the Scriptures, the eternal living Word, our Lord Jesus Christ must open our minds through the Spirit of God.

3. *An Eastern Reading of the Gospel of Luke* explains the "Trinity" as follows:

Another much misunderstood word is the term "trinity." This word does not appear in the Gospel Sharif but was coined by a Tunisian theologian, Tertullian (AD 160–225), attempting to describe the nature and activity of God as described in the Holy Scriptures. And it was accepted by the church's leaders as an adequate expression of this truth. But this term has been the cause of much misunderstanding and is accused, by those who have not studied its true meaning, of referring to God as being three gods: God, Christ and Mary (Ask God's forgiveness). Since the scriptures plainly declare God is one and has no associate, nor did he take a wife and give birth to a son in a biological manner, the word trinity does not mean God is three gods. So what is its meaning?

The doctrine of the Trinity does not conflict with the Oneness of God. The trinity formula "Father, Son and Holy Spirit" is not a numerical term, but refers to the modes of the being of God.

1. It is a term referring to the One God, the originator of all things, who has the power to create, or the Father.
2. The very same God, and no other, has the power to speak forth his Word; spoken in the life of Our Lord Jesus Christ, or the Word of God/son of God (understood as above)
3. The very same and only God has the power to give his comfort and guidance or the comforter, or Holy Spirit.

God is One: His creative thought, and his spoken word, and his powerful spirit. This is what is meant by the term "trinity." He cannot be separated from his word/son and his spirit. When we contemplate the greatness of God and the difficulties of elucidating him with human terms we realize there are no adequate human terms by which to explain the mystery of God, or his activity."

4. Fouad Ajami, *The Dream Palace of the Arabs* (New York: Vintage Books, 1998), 42.

5. His son, Gibran Tueni, a former Minister of Parliament in Lebanon, was assassinated in December 2005 for being a public advocate for Lebanese self-rule—out from under Syria.

6. Reported in *Al Ahram*, 2 April 1989.

Chapter 8

1. Lecture delivered 28 April 2006 at the Tunisian Writers' Union by poet Dr. Muhammad Al-Ghazzi, Professor of Literature, University of Tunis.

2. From an interview with Mazhar Mallouhi by *Assahafa* newspaper in Tunis, April 20, 1992.

3. From an article by Bashir Jumkar in "Al Ittihad Alichtiraki" in Morocco, September 14, 1998.

About the Author

Paul-Gordon Chandler is a U.S. Episcopal priest serving in the Middle East. He grew up in Muslim West Africa, and has lived and worked extensively throughout the Islamic world with churches, Christian publishing, and relief and development agencies. He is the author of *God's Global Mosaic* and is married with two children. He can be reached via www.paulgordonchandler.com.

CPSIA information can be obtained
at www.ICGtesting.com
Printed in the USA
LVHW090237090320
649314LV00001B/23